The author of *The Case for Christ*, an investigative journalist with a legal background, probes with bulldog-like tenacity the evidence for the truth of biblical Christianity. Believers and agnostics alike will learn from this fast-paced book.

THE LATE BRUCE M. METZGER

Lee Strobel asks the questions a tough-minded skeptic would ask and provides convincing answers to all of them. His book is so good I read it out loud to my wife evenings after dinner. Every inquirer should have this book.

PHILLIP E. JOHNSON, bestselling author and law professor,
University of California at Berkeley

An utterly fascinating treatment of the subject. It is truly a unique book which I wholeheartedly recommend.

RAVI ZACHARIAS

Nobody knows how to sift truth from fiction like an experienced investigative reporter, or to argue a case like someone trained at Yale Law School. Lee Strobel brings both qualifications to this remarkable book. In addition to his own tremendous testimony as atheist-turned-Christian, the author marshals the irrefutable depositions of recognized "expert witnesses" to build his ironclad case for Jesus Christ. I agree that *The Case for Christ* sets a new standard among existing contemporary apologetics.

THE LATE D. JAMES KENNEDY

I have never met anyone who has worked harder to provide seekers and believers alike with the rational underpinnings of the Christian faith. This book will become a classic.

BILL HYBELS, Senior Pastor, Willow Creek Community Church

I was thrilled to be a part of *The Case for Christ*. It is one of the most readable books in Christian evidences on the market, and I believe that it will have a wide impact. Anyone who is interested in the historical basis for Christianity should read this book.

J. P. MORELAND, Distinguished Professor of Philosophy,
Talbot School of Theology, Biola University, LaMirada, California

Educated in law and journalism, Lee Strobel interviewed thirteen leading scholars and authorities, asking the tough questions about Jesus of Nazareth and the biblical record of his life. Lee concludes that it would actually require much more faith for an atheist to maintain atheism than it would to trust in Jesus. I believe Lee is right. *The Case for Christ* presents overwhelming historical evidence that Jesus is who he claimed to be.

LUIS PALAU

A convincing case, an exciting read.

PETER KREEFT, Philosophy Professor, Boston College

Lee Strobel's brilliant investigative, fact-filled journalism adroitly assembles the overwhelming evidence of the claims of Christ. This book is a must for every Christian's reference and library, and should be shared with others.

THE LATE DR. BILL BRIGHT

As few people in our generation, Lee Strobel understands the mind-set of modern skeptics. More than an apologetic, this masterful work answers underlying questions of persons examining the claims of Christ. It is as fascinating as it is convincing.

DR. ROBERT E. COLEMAN, Distinguished Senior Professor of Discipleship and Evangelism at Gordon-Conwell

Lee Strobel has written a book that will surely become one of the most read works in popular apologetics. Lee uses his background in law and journalism to narrate his discussion with over a dozen leading evangelical scholars. The former atheist knows how to ask the right questions. The evidence is indeed convincing in *The Case for Christ*.

DR. THOM S. RAINER, President and CEO of LifeWay Christian Resources

Lee Strobel's writings are always creative, captivating, and convincing. This time I watched some of his work firsthand as he crafted a book that is persuasive without being manipulative, stimulating without being heavy, and fascinating without being fluffy. I can enthusiastically encourage you to read this cutting-edge book.

GARY COLLINS, PhD, Distinguished Professor at Richmont Graduate University

THE CASE FOR
Christ

—

*A Journalist's Personal Investigation
of the Evidence for Jesus*

LEE
STROBEL

NEW YORK TIMES BESTSELLING AUTHOR

ZONDERVAN

The Case for Christ
Copyright © 1998, 2016 by Lee Strobel

Requests for information should be addressed to:
Zondervan, 3900 Sparks Dr. SE, Grand Rapids, Michigan 49546

ISBN 978-0-310-34586-2 (softcover)

ISBN 978-0-310-34616-6 (ebook)

Library of Congress Cataloging-in-Publication Data

Strobel, Lee, 1952–
     The case for Christ: a journalist's personal investigation of the evidence for
Jesus / Lee Strobel
        p. cm.
     Includes bibliographical references and index.
     ISBN 978-0-310-22646-8 (hardcover)
     1. Jesus Christ—Person and offices. 2. Apologetics. I. Title.
BT202.S82   1998
232.9'08—dc21   98-7642

Cover design: Faceout Studios
Cover photography: Shutterstock®
Interior design: Beth Shagene

First printing July 2016 / Printed in the United States of America

Contents

PART 3: **Researching the Resurrection**

Acknowledgments

I am extremely thankful for the insights and contributions that a variety of people have made to this book. In particular, I'm indebted to Bill Hybels, who allowed me to produce a series of presentations on this topic at Willow Creek Community Church; my wife, Leslie, who came up with the idea of translating that concept into a book; and my editor, John Sloan, whose creative input greatly enhanced the project.

Also, I'm grateful to Mark Mittelberg and Garry Poole for their ongoing encouragement and assistance; Chad Meister and Bob and Gretchen Passantino for their research and ideas; Russ Robinson for his legal perspective; my assistant Jodi Walle for her invaluable help; and my daughter, Alison, and son, Kyle, for their behind-the-scenes contributions.

Finally, I'd like to thank the scholars who allowed me to interview them for this book. Again and again I was impressed not only by their knowledge and wisdom but also by their humble and sincere faith—as well as their desire to help spiritual seekers investigate the outrageous claims of Jesus.

Reopening the Investigation of a Lifetime

In the parlance of prosecutors, the attempted murder case against James Dixon was "a dead-bang winner." Open and shut. Even a cursory examination of the evidence was enough to establish that Dixon shot police sergeant Richard Scanlon in the abdomen during a scuffle on Chicago's south side.

Piece by piece, item by item, witness by witness, the evidence tightened a noose around Dixon's neck. There were fingerprints and a weapon, eyewitnesses and a motive, a wounded cop and a defendant with a history of violence. Now the criminal justice system was poised to trip the trap door that would leave Dixon dangling by the weight of his own guilt.

The facts were simple. Sergeant Scanlon had rushed to West 108th Place after a neighbor called police to report a man with a gun. Scanlon arrived to find Dixon noisily arguing with his girlfriend through the front door of her house. Her father emerged when he saw Scanlon, figuring it was safe to come outside.

Suddenly a fight broke out between Dixon and the father. The sergeant quickly intervened in an attempt to break it up. A shot rang out; Scanlon staggered away, wounded in his midsection. Just then two other squad cars arrived, screeching to a halt, and officers ran over to restrain Dixon.

A .22-caliber gun belonging to Dixon—covered with his fingerprints and with one bullet having been fired—was found nearby, where he had apparently flung it after the shooting. The father had been unarmed; Scanlon's revolver remained in his holster. Powder burns on Scanlon's skin showed that he had been shot at extremely close range.

Fortunately, his wound wasn't life-threatening, although it was serious enough to earn him a medal for bravery, proudly pinned on his chest by the police superintendent himself. As for Dixon, when police ran his rap sheet, they found he had previously been convicted of shooting someone else. Apparently, he had a propensity for violence.

And there I sat almost a year later, taking notes in a nearly deserted Chicago courtroom while Dixon publicly admitted that, yes, he was guilty of shooting the fifteen-year police veteran. On top of all the other evidence, the confession clinched it. Criminal court judge Frank Machala ordered Dixon imprisoned, then rapped his gavel to signal that the case was closed. Justice had been served.

I slipped my notebook into the inside pocket of my sports coat and ambled downstairs toward the pressroom. At the most, I figured my editor would give me three paragraphs to tell the story in the next day's *Chicago Tribune*. Certainly, that's all it deserved. This wasn't much of a tale.

Or so I thought.

The Whisper of an Informant

I answered the phone in the pressroom and recognized the voice right away—it was an informant I had cultivated during the year I had been covering the criminal courts building. I could tell he had something hot for me, because the bigger the tip, the faster and softer he would talk—and he was whispering a mile a minute.

"Lee, do you know that Dixon case?" he asked.

"Yeah, sure," I replied. "Covered it two days ago. Pretty routine."

"Don't be so sure. The word is that a few weeks before the shooting, Sergeant Scanlon was at a party, showing off his pen gun."

"His what?"

"A pen gun. It's a .22-caliber pistol that's made to look like a fountain pen. They're illegal for anyone to carry, including cops."

When I told him I didn't see the relevance of this, his voice got even more animated. "Here's the thing: Dixon didn't shoot Scanlon. Scanlon was wounded when his own pen gun accidentally went off in his shirt pocket. He framed Dixon so he wouldn't get in trouble for carrying an unauthorized weapon. Don't you see? Dixon is innocent!"

"Impossible!" I exclaimed.

"Check out the evidence yourself," came his reply. "See where it really points."

I hung up the phone and dashed up the stairs to the prosecutor's office, pausing briefly to catch my breath before strolling inside. "You know the Dixon case?" I asked casually, not wanting to tip my hand too early. "If you don't mind, I'd like to go over the details once more."

Color drained from his face. "Uh, I can't talk about it," he stammered. "No comment."

It turned out that my informant had already passed along his suspicions to the prosecutor's office. Behind the scenes, a grand jury was being convened to reconsider the evidence. Amazingly, unexpectedly, the once airtight case against James Dixon was being reopened.

New Facts for a New Theory

At the same time, I started my own investigation, studying the crime scene, interviewing witnesses, talking with Dixon, and examining the physical evidence. As I thoroughly checked out the case, the strangest thing happened: all the new facts that I uncovered—and even the old evidence that had once pointed so convincingly toward Dixon's guilt—snugly fit the pen gun theory.

- Witnesses said that before Scanlon arrived on the scene, Dixon had been pounding his gun on the door of his girlfriend's house. The gun discharged in a downward direction; in the cement of the front porch there was a chip that was consistent with a bullet's impact. This would account for the bullet that was missing from Dixon's gun.

- Dixon said he didn't want to be caught with a gun, so he hid it in some grass across the street before police arrived. I found a witness who corroborated that. This explained why the gun had been found some distance from the shooting scene even though nobody had ever seen Dixon throw it.

- There were powder burns concentrated inside—but not above—the left pocket of Scanlon's shirt. The bullet hole was at the bottom of the pocket. Conclusion: A weapon had somehow discharged in the pocket's interior.

- Contrary to statements in the police report, the bullet's trajectory had been at a downward angle. Below Scanlon's shirt pocket was a bloody rip where the bullet had exited after going through some flesh.

- Dixon's rap sheet hadn't told the whole story about him. Although he had spent three years in prison for an earlier shooting, the appellate court had freed him after determining that he had been wrongly convicted. It turns out that police had concealed a key defense witness and that a prosecution witness had lied. So much for Dixon's record of violent tendencies.

An Innocent Man Is Freed

Finally I put the crucial question to Dixon: "If you were innocent, why in the world did you plead guilty?"

Dixon sighed. "It was a plea bargain," he said, referring to the practice in which prosecutors recommend a reduced sentence if a defendant pleads guilty and thus saves everybody the time and expense of a trial.

"They said if I pleaded guilty, they would sentence me to one year in prison. I'd already spent 362 days in jail waiting for my trial. All I had to do was admit I did it and I'd go home in a few days. But if I insisted on a trial and the jury found me guilty—well, they'd throw the book at me. They'd give me twenty years for shooting a cop. It wasn't worth the gamble. I wanted to go home . . ."

"And so," I said, "you admitted doing something that you didn't do."

Dixon nodded. "That's right."

In the end Dixon was exonerated, and he later won a lawsuit against the police department. Scanlon was stripped of his medal, was indicted by a grand jury, pleaded guilty to official misconduct, and was fired from the department.[1] As for me, my stories were splashed across the front page. Much more important, I had learned some big lessons as a young reporter.

One of the most obvious lessons was that evidence can be aligned to point in more than one direction. For example, there had easily been enough proof to convict Dixon of shooting the sergeant. But the key questions were these: Had the collection of evidence really been thorough? And which explanation best fit the totality of the facts? Once the pen gun theory was offered, it became clear that this scenario accounted for the full body of evidence in the most optimal way.

And there was another lesson. One reason the evidence originally looked so convincing to me was because it fit my preconceptions at the time. To me, Dixon was an obvious troublemaker, a failure, the unemployed product of a broken family. The cops were the good guys. Prosecutors didn't make mistakes.

Looking through those lenses, all the original evidence seemed to fall neatly into place. Where there had been inconsistencies or gaps, I naively glossed them over. When police told me the case was airtight, I took them at their word and didn't delve much further.

But when I changed those lenses—trading my biases for an attempt at objectivity—I saw the case in a whole new light. Finally I allowed the evidence to lead me to the truth, regardless of whether it fit my original presuppositions.

That was a long time ago. My biggest lessons were yet to come.

From Dixon to Jesus

The reason I've recounted this unusual case is because in a way my spiritual journey has been a lot like my experience with James Dixon.

For much of my life I was a skeptic. In fact, I considered myself an atheist. To me, there was far too much evidence that God was merely a product of wishful thinking, of ancient mythology, of primitive superstition. How could there be a loving God if he consigned people to hell just for not believing in him? How could miracles contravene the basic laws of nature? Didn't evolution satisfactorily explain how life originated? Doesn't scientific reasoning dispel belief in the supernatural?

As for Jesus, didn't you know that he never claimed to be God? He was a revolutionary, a sage, an iconoclastic Jew—but God? No, that thought never occurred to him! I could point you to plenty of university professors who said so—and certainly they could be trusted, couldn't they? Let's face it: even a cursory examination of the evidence demonstrates convincingly that Jesus had only been a human being just like you and me, although with unusual gifts of kindness and wisdom.

But that's all I had ever really given the evidence: a cursory look. I had read just enough philosophy and history to find support for my skepticism—a fact here, a scientific theory there, a pithy quote, a clever argument. Sure, I could see some gaps and inconsistencies, but I had a strong motivation to ignore them: a self-serving and immoral lifestyle that I would be compelled to abandon if I were ever to change my views and become a follower of Jesus.

As far as I was concerned, the case was closed. There was enough proof for me to rest easy with the conclusion that the divinity of Jesus was nothing more than the fanciful invention of superstitious people.

Or so I thought.

Answers for an Atheist

It wasn't a phone call from an informant that prompted me to reexamine the case for Christ. It was my wife.

Leslie stunned me in the autumn of 1979 by announcing that she had become a Christian. I rolled my eyes and braced for the worst, feeling like the victim of a bait-and-switch scam. I had married one Leslie—the fun Leslie, the carefree Leslie, the risk-taking Leslie—and now I feared she was going to turn into some sort of sexually repressed prude who would trade our upwardly mobile lifestyle for all-night prayer vigils and volunteer work in grimy soup kitchens.

Instead I was pleasantly surprised—even fascinated—by the fundamental changes in her character, her integrity, and her personal confidence. Eventually I wanted to get to the bottom of what was prompting these subtle but significant shifts in my wife's attitudes, so I launched an all-out investigation into the facts surrounding the case for Christianity.

Setting aside my self-interest and prejudices as best I could, I read books, interviewed experts, asked questions, analyzed history, explored archaeology, studied ancient literature, and for the first time in my life picked apart the Bible verse by verse.

I plunged into the case with more vigor than with any story I had ever pursued. I applied the training I had received at Yale Law School as well as my experience as legal affairs editor of the *Chicago Tribune*.

And over time the evidence of the world—of history, of science, of philosophy, of psychology—began to point toward the unthinkable.

It was like the James Dixon case revisited.

Judging for Yourself

Maybe you too have been basing your spiritual outlook on the evidence you've observed around you or gleaned long ago from books, college professors, family members, or friends. But is your conclusion really the best possible explanation for the evidence? If you were to dig deeper—to confront your preconceptions and systematically seek out proof—what would you find?

That's what this book is about. In effect, I'm going to retrace and expand upon the spiritual journey I took for nearly two years. I'll take you along as I interview thirteen leading scholars and authorities who have impeccable academic credentials.

I have crisscrossed the country—from Minnesota to Georgia, from Virginia to California—to elicit their expert opinions, to challenge them with the objections I had when I was a skeptic, to force them to defend their positions with solid data and cogent arguments, and to test them with the very questions that you might ask if given the opportunity.

In this quest for truth, I've used my experience as a legal affairs journalist to look at numerous categories of proof—eyewitness evidence, documentary evidence, corroborating evidence, rebuttal evidence, scientific evidence, psychological evidence, circumstantial evidence, and, yes, even fingerprint evidence (that sounds intriguing, doesn't it?).

These are the same classifications that you'd encounter in a courtroom. And maybe taking a legal perspective is the best way to envision this process—with you in the role of a juror.

If you were selected for a jury in a real trial, you would be asked to affirm up front that you haven't formed any preconceptions about the case. You would be required to vow that you would be open-minded and fair, drawing your conclusions based on the weight of the facts and not on your whims or prejudices. You would be urged to thoughtfully consider the credibility of the witnesses, carefully sift the testimony, and rigorously subject the evidence to your common sense and logic. I'm asking you to do the same thing while reading this book.

Ultimately it's the responsibility of jurors to reach a verdict. That doesn't mean they have one-hundred-percent certainty, because we can't have absolute proof about virtually anything in life. In a trial, jurors are asked to weigh the evidence and come to the best possible conclusion. In other words, harkening back to the James Dixon case, which scenario fits the facts most snugly?

That's your task. I hope you take it seriously, because there may be more than just idle curiosity hanging in the balance. If Jesus is to be believed—and I realize that may be a big if for you at this point—then nothing is more important than how you respond to him.

But who was he really? Who did he claim to be? And is there any credible evidence to back up his assertions? That's what we'll seek to determine as we board a flight for Denver to conduct our first interview.

PART 1

Examining the Record

CHAPTER 1

The Eyewitness Evidence

Can the Biographies of Jesus Be Trusted?

When I first met shy and soft-spoken Leo Carter, he was a seventeen-year-old veteran of Chicago's grittiest neighborhood. His testimony had put three killers in prison. And he was still carrying a .38-caliber slug in his skull—a grisly reminder of a horrific saga that began when he witnessed Elijah Baptist gun down a local grocer.

Leo and a friend, Leslie Scott, were playing basketball when they saw Elijah, then a sixteen-year-old delinquent with thirty arrests on his rap sheet, slay Sam Blue outside his grocery store.

Leo had known the grocer since childhood. "When we didn't have any food, he'd give us some," Leo explained to me in a quiet voice. "So when I went to the hospital and they said he was dead, I knew I'd have to testify about what I saw."

Eyewitness testimony is powerful. One of the most dramatic moments in a trial is when a witness describes in detail the crime that he or she saw and then points confidently toward the defendant as being the perpetrator. Elijah Baptist knew that the only way to avoid prison would be to somehow prevent Leo Carter and Leslie Scott from doing just that.

So Elijah and two of his pals went hunting. Soon they tracked down Leo and Leslie, who were walking down the street with Leo's brother Henry, and they dragged all three at gunpoint to a darkened loading dock nearby.

"I like you," Elijah's cousin said to Leo, "but I've got to do this."

With that, he pressed a pistol to the bridge of Leo's nose and yanked the trigger.

The gun roared; the bullet penetrated at a slight angle, blinding Leo in his right eye and embedding in his head. When he crumbled to the ground, another shot was fired, this bullet lodging two inches from his spine.

As Leo watched from his sprawled position, pretending he was dead, he saw his sobbing brother and friend ruthlessly executed at close range. When Elijah and his gang fled, Leo crawled to safety.

Somehow, against all odds, Leo Carter lived. The bullet, too precarious to be removed, remained in his skull. Despite searing headaches that strong medication couldn't dull, he became the sole eyewitness against Elijah Baptist at his trial for killing grocer Sam Blue. The jurors believed Leo, and Elijah was sentenced to eighty years in prison.

Again Leo was the only eyewitness to testify against Elijah and his two companions in the slayings of his brother and his friend. And once more his word was good enough to land the trio in prison for the rest of their lives.

Leo Carter is one of my heroes. He made sure justice was served, even though he paid a monumental price for it. When I think of eyewitness testimony, even to this day—all these years later—his face still appears in my mind.[1]

Testimony from Distant Time

Yes, eyewitness testimony can be compelling and convincing. When a witness has had ample opportunity to observe a crime, when there's no bias or ulterior motives, when the witness is truthful and fair, the climactic act of pointing out a defendant in a courtroom can be enough to doom that person to prison or worse.

And eyewitness testimony is just as crucial in investigating historical matters—even the issue of whether Jesus Christ is the unique Son of God.

But what eyewitness accounts do we possess? Do we have the testimony of anyone who personally interacted with Jesus, who listened to his teachings, who saw his miracles, who witnessed his death, and who perhaps even encountered him after his alleged resurrection? Do we have any records from first-century "journalists" who interviewed eyewitnesses, asked tough questions, and faithfully recorded what they scrupulously determined to be true? Equally important, how well would these accounts withstand the scrutiny of skeptics?

I knew that just as Leo Carter's testimony clinched the convictions of three brutal murderers, eyewitness accounts from the mists of distant time could help resolve the most important spiritual issue of all. To get solid answers, I arranged to interview the nationally renowned scholar who literally wrote the book on the topic: Dr. Craig Blomberg, author of *The Historical Reliability of the Gospels*.

I knew Blomberg was smart; in fact, even his appearance fit the stereotype. Tall (six feet two) and lanky, with short, wavy brown hair unceremoniously combed forward, a fuzzy beard, and thick, rimless glasses, he looked like the type who would have been valedictorian of his high school (he was), a National Merit Scholar (he was), and a *magna cum laude* graduate from a prestigious seminary (he was, from Trinity Evangelical Divinity School).

But I wanted someone who was more than just intelligent and educated. I was searching for an expert who wouldn't gloss over nuances or blithely dismiss challenges to the records of Christianity. I wanted someone with integrity, someone who has grappled with the most potent critiques of the faith and who speaks authoritatively but without the kind of sweeping statements that conceal rather than deal with critical issues.

I was told Blomberg was exactly what I was looking for, and I flew to Denver wondering if he could measure up. Admittedly, I had a few doubts, especially when my research yielded one profoundly disturbing fact that he would probably have preferred had remained hidden: Blomberg still holds out hope that his beloved childhood heroes, the Chicago Cubs, will win the World Series in his lifetime.

Frankly, that was enough to make me a bit suspicious of his discernment.

THE FIRST INTERVIEW:
Craig L. Blomberg, PhD

Craig Blomberg is widely considered to be one of the country's foremost authorities on the biographies of Jesus, which are called the four gospels. He received his doctorate in New Testament from Aberdeen University in Scotland, later serving as a senior research fellow at Tyndale House at Cambridge University in England, where he was part of an elite group of international scholars that produced a series of acclaimed works on Jesus. For the last dozen years he has been a professor of New Testament at the highly respected Denver Seminary.

In addition to *The Historical Reliability of the Gospels*, Blomberg's books include *The Historical Reliability of John's Gospel, Jesus and the Gospels, Interpreting the Parables, Can We Still Believe the Bible?*, and commentaries on the Gospel of Matthew and 1 Corinthians. He also helped edit volume six of *Gospel Perspectives*, which deals at length with the miracles of Jesus, and he coauthored *Introduction to Biblical Interpretation* and *A Handbook of New Testament Exegesis*. He contributed chapters on the historicity of the gospels to the award-winning book *Jesus Under Fire*. His memberships include the Society for the Study of the New Testament, Society of Biblical Literature, and the Institute for Biblical Research.

As I expected, his office had more than its share of scholarly volumes stacked on the shelves (he was even wearing a tie emblazoned with drawings of books).

However, I quickly noted that his office walls were dominated not by dusty tomes from ancient historians but by artwork from his young daughters. Their whimsical and colorful depictions of llamas, houses, and flowers weren't haphazardly pinned up as a casual afterthought; they had obviously been treated as prizes—painstakingly matted, carefully framed, and personally autographed by Elizabeth and Rachel themselves. Clearly, I thought to myself, this man has a heart as well as a brain.

Blomberg speaks with the precision of a mathematician (yes, he taught mathematics too, earlier in his career), carefully measuring each word out of an apparent reluctance to tread even one nuance beyond where the evidence warrants. Exactly what I was looking for.

As he settled into a high-back chair, cup of coffee in hand, I too sipped some coffee to ward off the Colorado chill. Since I sensed Blomberg was a get-to-the-point kind of guy, I decided to start my interview by cutting to the core of the issue.*

Eyewitnesses to History

"Tell me this," I said with an edge of challenge in my voice, "is it really possible to be an intelligent, critically thinking person and still believe that the four gospels were written by the people whose names have been attached to them?"

Blomberg set his cup of coffee on the edge of his desk and looked intently at me. "The answer is yes," he said with conviction.

He sat back and continued. "It's important to acknowledge that strictly speaking, the gospels are anonymous. But the uniform testimony of the early church was that Matthew, also known as Levi, the tax collector and one of the twelve disciples, was the author of the first gospel in the New Testament; that John Mark, a companion of Peter, was the author of the gospel we call Mark; and that Luke, known as Paul's 'beloved physician,' wrote both the gospel of Luke and the Acts of the Apostles."

"How uniform was the belief that they were the authors?" I asked.

"There are no known competitors for these three gospels," he said. "Apparently, it was just not in dispute."

Even so, I wanted to test the issue further. "Excuse my skepticism," I said, "but would anyone have had a motivation to lie by claiming these people wrote these gospels, when they really didn't?"

Blomberg shook his head. "Probably not. Remember, these were unlikely characters," he said, a grin breaking on his face. "Mark and Luke weren't even among the twelve disciples. Matthew was, but as a former hated tax collector, he would have been the most infamous character next to Judas Iscariot, who betrayed Jesus!

"Contrast this with what happened when the fanciful apocryphal gospels were written much later. People chose the names of well-known

---

*All interviews edited for conciseness, clarity, and content.

and exemplary figures to be their fictitious authors—Philip, Peter, Mary, James. Those names carried a lot more weight than the names of Matthew, Mark, and Luke. So to answer your question, there would not have been any reason to attribute authorship to these three less-respected people if it weren't true."

That sounded logical, but it was obvious that he was conveniently leaving out one of the gospel writers. "What about John?" I asked. "He was extremely prominent; in fact, he wasn't just one of the twelve disciples, but one of Jesus' inner three, along with James and Peter."

"Yes, he's the one exception," Blomberg conceded with a nod. "And interestingly, John is the only gospel about which there is some question about authorship."

"What exactly is in dispute?"

"The name of the author isn't in doubt—it's certainly John," Blomberg replied. "The question is whether it was John the apostle or a different John.

"You see, the testimony of a Christian writer named Papias, dated about AD 125, refers to John the apostle and John the elder, and it's not clear from the context whether he's talking about one person from two perspectives or two different people. But granted that exception, the rest of the early testimony is unanimous that it was John the apostle—the son of Zebedee—who wrote the gospel."

"And," I said in an effort to pin him down further, "you're convinced that he did?"

"Yes, I believe the substantial majority of the material goes back to the apostle," he replied. "However, if you read the gospel closely, you can see some indication that its concluding verses may have been finalized by an editor. Personally, I have no problem believing that somebody closely associated with John may have functioned in that role, putting the last verses into shape and potentially creating the stylistic uniformity of the entire document.

"But in any event," he stressed, "the gospel is obviously based on eyewitness material, as are the other three gospels."

Delving into Specifics

While I appreciated Blomberg's comments so far, I wasn't ready to move on yet. The issue of who wrote the gospels is tremendously important, and I wanted specific details—names, dates, quotations. I finished off my coffee and put the cup on his desk. Pen poised, I prepared to dig deeper.

"Let's go back to Mark, Matthew, and Luke," I said. "What specific evidence do you have that they are the authors of the gospels?"

Blomberg leaned forward. "Again, the oldest and probably most significant testimony comes from Papias, who in about AD 125 specifically affirmed that Mark had carefully and accurately recorded Peter's eyewitness observations. In fact, he said Mark 'made no mistake' and did not include 'any false statement.' And Papias said Matthew had preserved the teachings of Jesus as well.

"Then Irenaeus, writing about AD 180, confirmed the traditional authorship. In fact, here—," he said, reaching for a book. He flipped it open and read Irenaeus' words.

Matthew published his own Gospel among the Hebrews in their own tongue, when Peter and Paul were preaching the Gospel in Rome and founding the church there. After their departure, Mark, the disciple and interpreter of Peter, himself handed down to us in writing the substance of Peter's preaching. Luke, the follower of Paul, set down in a book the Gospel preached by his teacher. Then John, the disciple of the Lord, who also leaned on his breast, himself produced his Gospel while he was living at Ephesus in Asia.[2]

I looked up from the notes I was taking. "OK, let me clarify this," I said. "If we can have confidence that the gospels were written by the disciples Matthew and John, by Mark, the companion of the disciple Peter, and by Luke, the historian, companion of Paul, and sort of a first-century journalist, we can be assured that the events they record are based on either direct or indirect eyewitness testimony."

As I was speaking, Blomberg was mentally sifting my words. When I finished, he nodded.

"Exactly," he said crisply.

Ancient versus Modern Biographies

There were still some troubling aspects of the gospels that I needed to clarify. In particular, I wanted to better understand the kind of literary genre they represented.

"When I go to the bookstore and look in the biography section, I don't see the same kind of writing that I see in the gospels," I said. "When somebody writes a biography these days, they thoroughly delve into the person's life. But look at Mark—he doesn't talk about the birth of Jesus or really anything through Jesus' early adult years. Instead he focuses on a three-year period and spends half his gospel on the events leading up to and culminating in Jesus' last week. How do you explain that?"

Blomberg held up a couple of fingers. "There are two reasons," he replied. "One is literary and the other is theological.

"The literary reason is that basically, this is how people wrote biographies in the ancient world. They did not have the sense, as we do today, that it was important to give equal proportion to all periods of an individual's life or that it was necessary to tell the story in strictly chronological order or even to quote people verbatim, as long as the essence of what they said was preserved. Ancient Greek and Hebrew didn't even have a symbol for quotation marks.

"The only purpose for which they thought history was worth recording was because there were some lessons to be learned from the characters described. Therefore the biographer wanted to dwell at length on those portions of the person's life that were exemplary, that were illustrative, that could help other people, that gave meaning to a period of history."

"And what's the theological reason?" I asked.

"It flows out of the point I just made. Christians believe that as wonderful as Jesus' life and teachings and miracles were, they were meaningless if it were not historically factual that Christ died and was raised from the dead and that this provided atonement, or forgiveness, of the sins of humanity.

"So Mark in particular, as the writer of probably the earliest gospel, devotes roughly half his narrative to the events leading up to and including one week's period of time and culminating in Christ's death and resurrection.

"Given the significance of the crucifixion," he concluded, "this makes perfect sense in ancient literature."

The Mystery of Q

In addition to the four gospels, scholars often refer to what they call Q, which stands for the German word *Quelle*, or "source."[3] Because of similarities in language and content, it has traditionally been assumed that Matthew and Luke drew upon Mark's earlier gospel in writing their own. In addition, scholars have said that Matthew and Luke also incorporated some material from this mysterious Q, material that is absent from Mark.

"What exactly is Q?" I asked Blomberg.

"It's nothing more than a hypothesis," he replied, again leaning back comfortably in his chair. "With few exceptions, it's just sayings or teachings of Jesus, which once may have formed an independent, separate document.

"You see, it was a common literary genre to collect the sayings of respected teachers, sort of as we compile the top music of a singer and put it into a 'best of' album. Q may have been something like that. At least that's the theory."

But if Q existed before Matthew and Luke, it would constitute early material about Jesus. Perhaps, I thought, it can shed some fresh light on what Jesus was really like.

"Let me ask this," I said. "If you isolate just the material from Q, what kind of picture of Jesus do you get?"

Blomberg stroked his beard and stared at the ceiling for a moment as he pondered the question. "Well, you have to keep in mind that Q was a collection of sayings, and therefore it didn't have the narrative material that would have given us a more fully orbed picture of Jesus," he replied, speaking slowly as he chose each word with care.

"Even so, you find Jesus making some very strong claims—for instance, that he was wisdom personified and that he was the one by whom God will judge all humanity, whether they confess him or disavow him. A significant scholarly book has argued recently that if you isolate all the Q sayings, one actually gets the same kind of picture of Jesus—of someone who made audacious claims about himself—as you find in the gospels more generally."

I wanted to push him further on this point. "Would he be seen as a miracle worker?" I inquired.

"Again," he replied, "you have to remember that you wouldn't get many miracle stories per se, because they're normally found in the narrative, and Q is primarily a list of sayings."

He stopped to reach over to his desk, pick up a leather-bound Bible, and rustle through its well-worn pages.

"But, for example, Luke 7:18–23 and Matthew 11:2–6 say that John the Baptist sent his messengers to ask Jesus if he really was the Christ, the Messiah they were waiting for. Jesus replied in essence, 'Tell him to consider my miracles. Tell him what you've seen: the blind see, the deaf hear, the lame walk, the poor have good news preached to them.'

"So even in Q," he concluded, "there is clearly an awareness of Jesus' ministry of miracles."

Blomberg's mention of Matthew brought to mind another question concerning how the gospels were put together. "Why," I asked, "would Matthew—purported to be an eyewitness to Jesus—incorporate part of a gospel written by Mark, whom everybody agrees was not an eyewitness? If Matthew's gospel was really written by an eyewitness, you would think he would have relied on his own observations."

Blomberg smiled. "It only makes sense if Mark was indeed basing his account on the recollections of the eyewitness Peter," he said. "As you've said yourself, Peter was among the inner circle of Jesus and was privy to seeing and hearing things that other disciples didn't. So it would make sense for Matthew, even though he was an eyewitness, to rely on Peter's version of events as transmitted through Mark."

Yes, I thought to myself, that did make some sense. In fact, an analogy began to form in my mind from my years as a newspaper reporter. I recalled being part of a crowd of journalists that once cornered the famous Chicago political patriarch, the late Mayor Richard J. Daley, to pepper him with questions about a scandal that was brewing in the police department. He made some remarks before escaping to his limousine.

Even though I was an eyewitness to what had taken place, I immediately went to a radio reporter who had been closer to Daley, and asked him to play back his tape of what Daley had just said. This way, I could make sure I had his words correctly written down.

That, I mused, was apparently what Matthew did with Mark—although Matthew had his own recollections as a disciple, his quest for accuracy prompted him to rely on some material that came directly from Peter in Jesus' inner circle.

The Unique Perspective of John

Feeling satisfied with Blomberg's initial answers concerning the first three gospels—called the Synoptics, which means "to view at the same time," because of their similar outline and interrelationship[4]—next I turned my attention to John's gospel. Anyone who reads all four gospels will immediately recognize that there are obvious differences between the Synoptics and the gospel of John, and I wanted to know whether this means there are irreconcilable contradictions between them.

"Could you clarify the differences between the Synoptic Gospels and John's gospel?" I asked Blomberg.

His eyebrows shot up. "*Huge* question!" he exclaimed. "I hope to write a whole book on the topic."

After I assured him I was only after the essentials of the issue, not an exhaustive discussion, he settled back into his chair.

"Well, it's true that John is more different than similar to the Synoptics," he began. "Only a handful of the major stories that appear in the other three gospels reappear in John, although that changes noticeably when one comes to Jesus' last week. From that point forward the parallels are much closer.

"There also seems to be a very different linguistic style. In John, Jesus uses different terminology, he speaks in long sermons, and there seems to be a higher Christology—that is, more direct and more blatant claims that Jesus is one with the Father; God himself; the Way, the Truth, and the Life; the Resurrection and the Life."

"What accounts for the differences?" I asked.

"For many years the assumption was that John knew everything

Matthew, Mark, and Luke wrote, and he saw no need to repeat it, so he consciously chose to supplement them. More recently it has been assumed that John is largely independent of the other three gospels, which could account for not only the different choices of material but also the different perspectives on Jesus."

Jesus' Most Audacious Claim

"There are some theological distinctives to John," I observed.

"No question, but do they deserve to be called contradictions? I think the answer is no, and here's why: for almost every major theme or distinctive in John, you can find parallels in Matthew, Mark, and Luke, even if they're not as plentiful."

That was a bold assertion. I promptly decided to put it to the test by raising perhaps the most significant issue of all concerning the differences between the Synoptics and John's gospel.

"John makes very explicit claims of Jesus being God, which some attribute to the fact that he wrote later than the others and began embellishing things," I said. "Can you find this theme of deity in the Synoptics?"

"Yes, I can," he said. "It's more implicit, but you find it there. Think of the story of Jesus walking on the water, found in Matthew 14:22–33 and Mark 6:45–52. Most English translations hide the Greek by quoting Jesus as saying, 'Take courage! It is I.' Actually, the Greek literally says, 'Fear not, I am.' Those last two words are identical to what Jesus said in John 8:58, when he took upon himself the divine name 'I AM,' which is the way God revealed himself to Moses in the burning bush in Exodus 3:14. So Jesus is revealing himself as the one who has the same divine power over nature as Yahweh, the God of the Old Testament."

I nodded. "That's one example," I said. "Do you have any others?"

"Yes, I could go on along these lines," Blomberg said. "For instance, Jesus' most common title for himself in the first three gospels is 'Son of Man,' and—"

I raised my hand to stop him. "Hold on," I said. Reaching into my briefcase, I pulled out a book and leafed through it until I located the quote I was looking for. "Karen Armstrong, the former nun who wrote the bestseller *A History of God*, said it seems that the term 'Son of Man' 'simply stressed the weakness and mortality of the human condition,' so by using it, Jesus was merely emphasizing that 'he was a frail human being who would one day suffer and die.'[5] If that's true," I said, "that doesn't sound like much of a claim to deity."

Blomberg's expression turned sour. "Look," he said firmly, "contrary to popular belief, 'Son of Man' does not primarily refer to Jesus' humanity. Instead, it's a direct allusion to Daniel 7:13–14."

With that, he opened the Old Testament and read those words of the prophet Daniel.

> In my vision at night I looked, and there before me was one like a son of man, coming with the clouds of heaven. He approached the Ancient of Days and was led into his presence. He was given authority, glory and sovereign power; all peoples, nations and men of every language worshiped him. His dominion is an everlasting dominion that will not pass away, and his kingdom is one that will never be destroyed.

Blomberg shut the Bible. "So look at what Jesus is doing by applying the term 'Son of Man' to himself," he continued. "This is someone who approaches God himself in his heavenly throne room and is given universal authority and dominion. That makes 'Son of Man' a title of great exaltation, not of mere humanity."

Later I came upon a comment by another scholar whom I would soon interview for this book, William Lane Craig, who has made a similar observation.

> "Son of Man" is often thought to indicate the humanity of Jesus, just as the reflex expression "Son of God" indicates his divinity. In fact, just the opposite is true. The Son of Man was a divine figure in the Old Testament book of Daniel who would come at the end of the world to judge mankind and rule forever. Thus, the claim to be the Son of Man would be in effect a claim to divinity.[6]

Continued Blomberg: "In addition, Jesus claims to forgive sins in the Synoptics, and that's something only God can do. Jesus accepts prayer and worship. Jesus says, 'Whoever acknowledges me, I will acknowledge before my Father in heaven.' Final judgment is based on one's reaction to—whom? This mere human being? No, that would be a very arrogant claim. Final judgment is based on one's reaction to Jesus *as God.*

"As you can see, there's all sorts of material in the Synoptics about the deity of Christ that then merely becomes more explicit in John's gospel."

The Gospels' Theological Agenda

In authoring the last gospel, John did have the advantage of being able to mull over theological issues for a longer period of time. So I asked Blomberg, "Doesn't the fact that John was writing with more of a theological bent mean that his historical material may have been tainted and therefore less reliable?"

"I don't believe John is more theological," Blomberg stressed. "He just has a different cluster of theological emphases. Matthew, Mark, and Luke each have very distinctive theological angles that they want to highlight: Luke, the theologian of the poor and of social concern; Matthew, the theologian trying to understand the relationship of Christianity and Judaism; Mark, who shows Jesus as the suffering servant. You can make a long list of the distinctive theologies of Matthew, Mark, and Luke."

I interrupted because I was afraid Blomberg was missing my broader point. "OK, but don't those theological motivations cast doubt on their ability and willingness to accurately report what happened?" I asked. "Isn't it likely that their theological agenda would prompt them to color and twist the history they recorded?"

"It certainly means that, as with any ideological document, we have to consider that as a possibility," he admitted. "There are people with axes to grind who distort history to serve their ideological ends, but unfortunately people have concluded that always happens, which is a mistake.

"In the ancient world the idea of writing dispassionate, objective history merely to chronicle events, with no ideological purpose, was unheard of. Nobody wrote history if there wasn't a reason to learn from it."

I smiled. "I suppose you could say that makes everything suspect," I suggested.

"Yes, at one level it does," he replied. "But if we can reconstruct reasonably accurate history from all kinds of other ancient sources, we ought to be able to do that from the gospels, even though they too are ideological."

Blomberg thought for a moment, searching his mind for an appropriate analogy to drive home his point. Finally he said, "Here's a modern parallel, from the experience of the Jewish community, that might clarify what I mean.

"Some people, usually for anti-Semitic purposes, deny or downplay the horrors of the Holocaust. But it has been the Jewish scholars who've created museums, written books, preserved artifacts, and documented eyewitness testimony concerning the Holocaust.

"Now, they have a very ideological purpose—namely, to ensure that such an atrocity never occurs again—but they have also been the most faithful and objective in their reporting of historical truth.

"Christianity was likewise based on certain historical claims that God uniquely entered into space and time in the person of Jesus of Nazareth, so the very ideology that Christians were trying to promote required as careful historical work as possible."

He let his analogy sink in. Turning to face me more directly, he asked, "Do you see my point?"

I nodded to indicate that I did.

Hot News from History

It's one thing to say that the gospels are rooted in direct or indirect eyewitness testimony; it's another to claim that this information was reliably preserved until it was finally written down years later. This, I knew, was a major point of contention, and I wanted to challenge Blomberg with this issue as forthrightly as I could.

Again I picked up Armstrong's popular book *A History of God*. "Listen to something else she wrote," I said.

> We know very little about Jesus. The first full-length account of his life was St. Mark's gospel, which was not written until about the year 70, some forty years after his death. By that time, historical

facts had been overlaid with mythical elements which expressed the meaning Jesus had acquired for his followers. It is this meaning that St. Mark primarily conveys rather than a reliable straightforward portrayal.[7]

Tossing the book back into my open briefcase, I turned to Blomberg and continued. "Some scholars say the gospels were written so far after the events that legend developed and distorted what was finally written down, turning Jesus from merely a wise teacher into the mythological Son of God. Is that a reasonable hypothesis, or is there good evidence that the gospels were recorded earlier than that, before legend could totally corrupt what was ultimately recorded?"

Blomberg's eyes narrowed, and his voice took on an adamant tone. "There are two separate issues here, and it's important to keep them separate," he said. "I do think there's good evidence for suggesting early dates for the writing of the gospels. But even if there wasn't, Armstrong's argument doesn't work anyway."

"Why not?" I asked.

"The standard scholarly dating, even in very liberal circles, is Mark in the 70s, Matthew and Luke in the 80s, John in the 90s. But listen: that's still within the lifetimes of various eyewitnesses of the life of Jesus, including hostile eyewitnesses who would have served as a corrective if false teachings about Jesus were going around.

"Consequently, these late dates for the gospels really aren't all that late. In fact, we can make a comparison that's very instructive.

"The two earliest biographies of Alexander the Great were written by Arrian and Plutarch more than four hundred years after Alexander's death in 323 BC, yet historians consider them to be generally trustworthy. Yes, legendary material about Alexander did develop over time, but it was only in the centuries after these two writers.

"In other words, the first five hundred years kept Alexander's story pretty much intact; legendary material began to emerge over the next five hundred years. So whether the gospels were written sixty years or thirty years after the life of Jesus, the amount of time is negligible by comparison. It's almost a nonissue."

I could see what Blomberg was saying. At the same time, I had some reservations about it. To me, it seemed intuitively obvious that the shorter the gap between an event and when it was recorded in writing, the less likely those writings would fall victim to legend or faulty memories.

"Let me concede your point for the moment, but let's get back to the dating of the gospels," I said. "You indicated that you believe they were written sooner than the dates you mentioned."

"Yes, sooner," he said. "And we can support that by looking at the book of Acts, which was written by Luke. Acts ends apparently unfinished—Paul is a central figure of the book, and he's under house arrest in Rome. With that, the book abruptly halts. What happens to Paul? We don't find out from Acts, probably because the book was written before Paul was put to death."

Blomberg was getting more wound up as he went. "That means Acts cannot be dated any later than AD 62. Having established that, we can then move backward from there. Since Acts is the second of a two-part work, we know the first part—the Gospel of Luke—must have been written earlier than that. And since Luke incorporates parts of the gospel of Mark, that means Mark is even earlier.

"If you allow maybe a year for each of those, you end up with Mark written no later than about AD 60, maybe even the late 50s. If Jesus was put to death in AD 30 or 33, we're talking about a maximum gap of thirty years or so."

He sat back in his chair with an air of triumph. "Historically speaking, especially compared with Alexander the Great," he said, "that's like a news flash!"

Indeed, that was impressive, closing the gap between the events of Jesus' life and the writing of the gospels to the point where it was negligible by historical standards. However, I still wanted to push the issue. My goal was to turn the clock back as far as I could to get to the very earliest information about Jesus.

Going Back to the Beginning

I stood and strolled over to the bookcase. "Let's see if we can go back even further," I said, turning toward Blomberg. "How early can we date the fundamental beliefs in Jesus' atonement, his resurrection, and his unique association with God?"

"It's important to remember that the books of the New Testament are not in chronological order," he began. "The gospels were written after almost all the letters of Paul, whose writing ministry probably began in the late 40s. Most of his major letters appeared during the 50s. To find the earliest information, one goes to Paul's epistles and then asks, 'Are there signs that even earlier sources were used in writing them?'"

"And," I prompted, "what do we find?"

"We find that Paul incorporated some creeds, confessions of faith, or hymns from the earliest Christian church. These go way back to the dawning of the church soon after the resurrection.

"The most famous creeds include Philippians 2:6–11, which talks about Jesus being 'in very nature God,' and Colossians 1:15–20, which describes him as being 'the image of the invisible God,' who created all things and through whom all things are reconciled with God 'by making peace through his blood, shed on the cross.'

"Those are certainly significant in explaining what the earliest Christians were convinced about Jesus. But perhaps the most important creed in terms of the historical Jesus is 1 Corinthians 15, where Paul uses technical language to indicate he was passing along this oral tradition in relatively fixed form."

Blomberg located the passage in his Bible and read it to me.

For what I received I passed on to you as of first importance: that Christ died for our sins according to the Scriptures, that he was buried, that he was raised on the third day according to the Scriptures, and that he appeared to Cephas, and then to the Twelve. After that, he appeared to more than five hundred of the brothers and sisters at the same time, most of whom are still living, though some have fallen asleep. Then he appeared to James, then to all the apostles.[8]

"And here's the point," Blomberg said. "If the crucifixion was as early as AD 30, Paul's conversion was about 32. Immediately Paul was ushered into Damascus, where he met with a Christian named Ananias and some other disciples. His first meeting with the apostles in Jerusalem would have been about AD 35. At some point along there,

Paul was given this creed, which had already been formulated and was being used in the early church.

"Now, here you have the key facts about Jesus' death for our sins, plus a detailed list of those to whom he appeared in resurrected form—all dating back to within two to five years of the events themselves!

"That's not later mythology from forty or more years down the road, as Armstrong suggested. A good case can be made for saying that Christian belief in the resurrection, though not yet written down, can be dated to within two years of that very event.

"This is enormously significant," he said, his voice rising a bit in emphasis. "Now you're not comparing thirty to sixty years with the five hundred years that's generally acceptable for other data—you're talking about two!"

I couldn't deny the importance of that evidence. It certainly seemed to take the wind out of the charge that the resurrection—which is cited by Christians as the crowning confirmation of Jesus' divinity—was merely a mythological concept that developed over long periods of time as legends corrupted the eyewitness accounts of Christ's life. For me, this struck especially close to home—as a skeptic, that was one of my biggest objections to Christianity.

I leaned against the bookcase. We had covered a lot of material, and Blomberg's climactic assertion seemed like a good place to pause.

A Short Recess

It was getting late in the afternoon. We had been talking for quite a while without a break. However, I didn't want to end our conversation without putting the eyewitness accounts to the same kind of tests to which a lawyer or journalist would subject them. I needed to know: Would they stand up under that scrutiny, or would they be exposed as questionable at best or unreliable at worst?

The necessary groundwork having been laid, I invited Blomberg to stand and stretch his legs before we sat back down to resume our discussion.

Deliberations
Questions for Reflection or Group Study

1. How have your opinions been influenced by someone's eyewitness account of an event? What are some factors you routinely use to evaluate whether someone's story is honest and accurate? How do you think the gospels would stand up to that kind of scrutiny?

2. Do you believe that the gospels can have a theological agenda while at the same time being trustworthy in what they report? Why or why not? Do you find Blomberg's Holocaust analogy helpful in thinking through this issue?

3. How and why does Blomberg's description of the early information about Jesus affect your opinion about the reliability of the gospels?

For Further Evidence
More Resources on This Topic

Barnett, Paul. *Is the New Testament Reliable?* Second edition. Downers Grove, IL: InterVarsity Academic, 2005.

Bauckham, Richard. *Jesus and the Eyewitnesses.* Grand Rapids: Eerdmans, 2008.

Blomberg, Craig L. *Can We Still Believe the Bible?* Grand Rapids: Brazos Press, 2014.

——————. *The Historical Reliability of the Gospels.* Second edition. Downers Grove, IL: InterVarsity Academic. 2007.

——————. *The Historical Reliability of John's Gospel.* Downers Grove, IL: InterVarsity Press, 2001.

Bruce, F. F. *The New Testament Documents: Are They Reliable?* Grand Rapids: Eerdmans, 1960.

Cowan, Stephen B., and Terry L. Wilder. *In Defense of the Bible.* Nashville, TN: Broadman & Holman, 2013.

Eddy, Paul Rhodes, and Gregory A. Boyd. *The Jesus Legend: A Case for the Historical Reliability of the Synoptic Jesus Tradition.* Grand Rapids: Baker Academic, 2007.

Keener, Craig S. *The Historical Jesus of the Gospels*. Reprint edition. Grand Rapids: Eerdmans, 2012.

Roberts, Mark D. *Can We Trust the Gospels?* Wheaton, IL: Crossway, 2007.

Stein, Robert H. "Criteria for the Gospels' Authenticity." In *Contending With Christianity's Critics*, Paul Copan and William Lane Craig, eds., 88–103. Nashville, TN: B&H Academic, 2009.

CHAPTER 2

Testing the
Eyewitness Evidence

*Do the Biographies of Jesus
Stand Up to Scrutiny?*

Sixteen-year-old Michael McCullough's words were so faint that jurors couldn't hear them above the soft puffing sound of the mechanical respirator that was keeping him alive. A lip-reader had to hunch over Michael's bed, discern what he was saying, and repeat his testimony to the makeshift courtroom.

Paralyzed from the neck down by a bullet that severed his spinal cord, Michael was too frail to be transported to the courthouse for the trial of the two youths accused of attacking him. Instead the judge, jury, defendants, lawyers, reporters, and spectators crowded into Michael's hospital room, which was declared a temporary branch of Cook County Circuit Court.

Under questioning by prosecutors, Michael recalled how he left his apartment at a Chicago housing project with two dollars in his pocket. He said he was accosted in a stairway by the two defendants, who intentionally shot him in the face as they tried to steal his money. His story was backed up by two other youths who had watched in horror as the assault took place.

The defendants never denied the shooting; instead they claimed that the gun accidentally discharged while they were waving it around. Defense attorneys knew that the only way they could get their clients off with a reduced sentence was if they could succeed in undermining the testimony that the shooting was a vicious and premeditated act of violence.

They did their best to cast doubt on the eyewitness accounts. They questioned the witnesses' ability to view what happened, but they failed to make any inroads. They tried to exploit inconsistencies in the stories, but the accounts harmonized on the central points. They demanded more corroboration, but clearly no more was needed.

They raised hints about character, but the victim and witnesses were law-abiding youths with no criminal record. They hoped to show a bias against the defendants, but they couldn't find one. They questioned whether one witness, a nine-year-old boy named Keith, was old enough to understand what it meant to tell the truth under oath, but it was obvious to everyone that he did.

With defense attorneys unable to shake the credibility of the victim and the prosecution witnesses, the two defendants were convicted of attempted murder and sentenced to fifty years in the penitentiary. Eighteen days later Michael died.[1]

Defense attorneys have a challenging job: to raise questions, to generate doubts, to probe the soft and vulnerable spots of a witness's story. They do this by subjecting the testimony to a variety of tests. The idea is that honest and accurate testimony will withstand scrutiny, while false, exaggerated, or misleading testimony will be exposed.

In Michael's case justice prevailed because the jurors could tell that the witnesses and victim were sincerely and precisely recounting what they had experienced.

Now let's return to our investigation of the historical evidence concerning Jesus. The time had come to subject Dr. Blomberg's testimony to tests that would either reveal its weaknesses or underscore its strength. Many of these would be the same tests that had been used by defense attorneys in Michael's case so many years earlier.

"There are eight different tests I'd like to ask you about," I said to Blomberg as we sat down after our fifteen-minute break.

Blomberg picked up a fresh cup of steaming black coffee and leaned back. I wasn't sure, but it seemed he was looking forward to the challenge.

"Go ahead," he said.

1. The Intention Test

This test seeks to determine whether it was the stated or implied intention of the writers to accurately preserve history. "Were these first-century writers even interested in recording what actually happened?" I asked.

Blomberg nodded. "Yes, they were," he said. "You can see that at the beginning of the gospel of Luke, which reads very much like prefaces to other generally trusted historical and biographical works of antiquity."

Picking up his Bible, Blomberg read the opening of Luke's gospel.

> Many have undertaken to draw up an account of the things that have been fulfilled among us, just as they were handed down to us by those who from the first were eyewitnesses and servants of the word. With this in mind, since I myself have carefully investigated everything from the beginning, I too decided to write an orderly account for you, most excellent Theophilus, so that you may know the certainty of the things you have been taught.[2]

"As you can see," Blomberg continued, "Luke is clearly saying he intended to write accurately about the things he investigated and found to be well-supported by witnesses."

"What about the other gospels?" I asked. "They don't start with similar declarations; does that mean their writers didn't have the same intentions?"

"It's true that Mark and Matthew don't have this kind of explicit statement," came Blomberg's reply. "However, they are close to Luke in terms of genre, and it seems reasonable that Luke's historical intent would closely mirror theirs."

"And John?" I asked.

"The only other statement of purpose in the gospels comes in John 20:31: 'These are written that you may believe that Jesus is the Messiah, the Son of God, and that by believing you may have life in his name.'"

"That," I objected, "sounds more like a theological statement than a historical one."

"I'll grant you that," Blomberg replied. "But if you're going to be convinced enough to believe, the theology has to flow from accurate history. Besides, there's an important piece of implicit evidence that can't be overlooked. Consider the way the gospels are written—in a sober and responsible fashion, with accurate incidental details, with obvious care and exactitude. You don't find the outlandish flourishes and blatant mythologizing that you see in a lot of other ancient writings.

"What does all that add up to?" he asked. Then he answered his own question: "It seems quite apparent that the goal of the gospel writers was to attempt to record what had actually occurred."

Answering Objections

However, is that what really happened? There's a competing and contradictory scenario that has been promoted by some critics.

They have said that early Christians were convinced Jesus was going to be returning during their lifetime to consummate history, so they didn't think it was necessary to preserve any historical records about his life or teachings. After all, why bother if he's going to come and end the world at any moment?

"So," I said, "years later when it became obvious that Jesus wasn't coming back right away, they found they didn't have any accurate historical material to draw on in writing the gospels. Nothing had been captured for historical purposes. Isn't that what really happened?"

"There are certainly sects and groups, including religious ones throughout history, for which that argument works, but not with early Christianity," Blomberg replied.

"Why not?" I challenged him. "What was so different about Christianity?"

"First, I think the premise is a bit overstated. The truth is that the majority of Jesus' teachings presuppose a significant span of time before the end of the world," he said. "But second, even if some of Jesus' followers did think he might come back fairly quickly, remember that Christianity was born out of Judaism.

"For eight centuries the Jews lived with the tension between the repeated pronouncements of prophets that the Day of the Lord was at hand and the continuing history of Israel. And still the followers of these prophets recorded, valued, and preserved the words of the prophets. Given that Jesus' followers looked upon him as being even greater than a prophet, it seems very reasonable that they would have done the same thing."

While that did seem reasonable, some scholars have also raised a second objection that I wanted to pose to Blomberg. "They say that early Christians frequently believed that the physically departed Jesus was speaking through them with messages, or 'prophecies,' for their church," I said. "Since these prophecies were considered as authoritative as Jesus' own words when he was alive on earth, the early Christians didn't distinguish between these newer sayings and the original words of the historical Jesus. As a result, the gospels blend these two types of material, so we don't really know what goes back to the historical Jesus and what doesn't. That's a troubling charge to a lot of people. How do you respond to that?"

"That argument has less historical support than the previous one," he said with a smile. "In fact, within the New Testament itself there is evidence that disproves this hypothesis.

"There are occasions when early Christian prophecy is referred to, but it's always distinguished from what the Lord has said. For example, in 1 Corinthians 7 Paul clearly distinguishes when he has a word from the Lord and when he is quoting the historical Jesus. In the book of Revelation one can clearly distinguish the handful of times in which Jesus directly speaks to this prophet—traditionally assumed to be John the apostle—and when John is recounting his own inspired visions.

"And in 1 Corinthians 14, when Paul is discussing the criteria for true prophecy, he talks about the responsibility of the local church to test the prophets. Drawing on his Jewish background, we know that the criteria for true prophecy would have included whether the prediction comes true and whether these new statements cohere with previously revealed words of the Lord.

"But the strongest argument is what we never find in the gospels. After Jesus' ascension there were a number of controversies that threatened the early church—should believers be circumcised, how should speaking in tongues be regulated, how to keep Jew and Gentile united, what are the appropriate roles for women in ministry, whether believers could divorce non-Christian spouses.

"These issues could have been conveniently resolved if the early Christians had simply read back into the gospels what Jesus had told them from the world beyond. But this never happened. The continuance of these controversies demonstrates that Christians were interested in distinguishing between what happened during Jesus' lifetime and what was debated later in the churches."

2. The Ability Test

Even if the writers intended to reliably record history, were they able to do so? How can we be sure that the material about Jesus' life and teachings was well preserved for thirty years before it was finally written down in the gospels?

I asked Blomberg, "Won't you concede that faulty memories, wishful thinking, and the development of legend would have irreparably contaminated the Jesus tradition prior to the writing of the gospels?"

He started his answer by establishing the context. "We have to remember that we're in a foreign land in a distant time and place and in a culture that has not yet invented computers or even the printing press," he replied. "Books—or actually, scrolls of papyrus—were relatively rare. Therefore education, learning, worship, teaching in religious communities—all this was done by word of mouth.

"Rabbis became famous for having the entire Old Testament committed to memory. So it would have been well within the capability of Jesus' disciples to have committed much more to memory than appears in all four gospels put together—and to have passed it along accurately."

"Wait a second," I interjected. "Frankly, that kind of memorization seems incredible. How is that possible?"

"Yes, it is difficult for us to imagine today," he conceded, "but this was an oral culture, in which there was great emphasis placed on memorization. And remember that eighty to ninety percent of Jesus' words were originally in poetic form. This doesn't mean stuff that rhymes, but it has a meter, balanced lines, parallelism, and so forth—and this would have created a great memory help.

"The other thing that needs to be said is that the definition of memorization was more flexible back then. In studies of cultures with oral traditions, there was freedom to vary how much of the story was told on any given occasion—what was included, what was left out, what was paraphrased, what was explained, and so forth.

"One study suggested that in the ancient Middle East, anywhere from ten to forty percent of any given retelling of sacred tradition could vary from one occasion to the next. However, there were always fixed points that were unalterable, and the community had the right to intervene and correct the storyteller if he erred on those important aspects of the story.

"It's an interesting"—he paused, searching his mind for the right word—"*coincidence* that ten to forty percent is pretty consistently the amount of variation among the Synoptics on any given passage."

Blomberg was hinting at something; I wanted him to be more explicit. "Spell it out for me," I said. "What precisely are you saying?"

"I'm saying that it's likely that a lot of the similarities and differences among the Synoptics can be explained by assuming that the disciples and other early Christians had committed to memory a lot of what Jesus said and did, but they felt free to recount this information in various forms, always preserving the significance of Jesus' original teachings and deeds."

Still, I had some question about the ability of these early Christians to accurately preserve this oral tradition. I had too many memories of childhood party games in which words got garbled within a matter of minutes.

Playing Telephone

You've probably played the game of telephone yourself: one child whispers something into another child's ear—for instance, "You're my best friend"—and this gets whispered to others around a big circle until at the end it comes out grossly distorted—perhaps, "You're a brutish fiend."

"Let's be candid," I said to Blomberg. "Isn't this a good analogy for what probably happened to the oral tradition about Jesus?"

Blomberg wasn't buying that explanation. "No, not really," he said. "Here's why: When you're carefully memorizing something and taking care not to pass it along until you're sure you've got it right, you're doing something very different from playing the game of telephone.

"In telephone half the fun is that the person may not have got it right or even heard it right the first time, and they cannot ask the person to repeat it. Then you immediately pass it along, also in whispered tones that make it more likely the next person will goof something up even more. So yes, by the time it has circulated through a room of thirty people, the results can be hilarious."

"Then why," I asked, "isn't that a good analogy for passing along ancient oral tradition?"

Blomberg sipped his coffee before answering. "If you really wanted to develop that analogy in light of the checks and balances of the first-century community, you'd have to say that every third person, out loud in a very clear voice, would have to ask the first person, 'Do I still have it right?' and change it if he didn't.

"The community would constantly be monitoring what was said and intervening to make corrections along the way. That would preserve the integrity of the message," he said. "And the result would be very different from that of a childish game of telephone."

3. The Character Test

This test looks at whether it was in the character of these writers to be truthful. Was there any evidence of dishonesty or immorality that might taint their ability or willingness to transmit history accurately?

Blomberg shook his head. "We simply do not have any reasonable evidence to suggest they were anything but people of great integrity," he said.

"We see them reporting the words and actions of a man who called them to as exacting a level of integrity as any religion has ever known," he said. "In addition, they were willing to live out their beliefs despite persecution, deprivation, and suffering, which shows great character."[3]

"In terms of honesty, in terms of truthfulness, in terms of virtue and morality, these people had a track record that should be envied."

4. The Consistency Test

Here's a test that skeptics often charge the gospels with failing. After all, aren't they hopelessly contradictory with each other? Aren't there irreconcilable discrepancies among the various gospel accounts? And if there are, how can anyone trust anything they say?

Blomberg acknowledged that there are numerous points at which the gospels appear to disagree. "These range all the way from very minor variations in wording to the most famous apparent contradictions," he said.

"My own conviction is, once you allow for the elements I've talked about earlier—of paraphrase, of abridgment, of explanatory additions, of selection, of omission—the gospels are extremely consistent with each other by ancient standards, which are the only standards by which it's fair to judge them."

"Ironically," I pointed out, "if the gospels had been identical to each other, word for word, this would have raised charges that the authors had conspired among themselves to coordinate their stories in advance, and that would have cast doubt on them."

"That's right," Blomberg agreed. "If the gospels were too consistent, that in itself would invalidate them as independent witnesses. People would then say we really only have one testimony that everybody else is just parroting."

My mind flashed to the words of Simon Greenleaf of Harvard Law School, one of history's most important legal figures and the author of an influential treatise on evidence. After studying the consistency among the four gospel writers, he offered this evaluation: "There is enough of a discrepancy to show that there could have been no previous concert among them; and at the same time such substantial agreement as to show that they all were independent narrators of the same great transaction."[4]

From the perspective of a classical historian, German scholar Hans Stier has concurred that agreement over basic data and divergence of details suggest credibility, because fabricated accounts tend to be fully consistent and harmonized. "Every historian," he wrote, "is especially skeptical at that moment when an extraordinary happening is only reported in accounts which are completely free of contradictions."[5]

While that's true, I didn't want to ignore the difficulties that are raised by the ostensible discrepancies among the gospels. I decided to probe the issue further by pressing Blomberg on some apparent clear-cut contradictions that skeptics frequently seize upon as examples of why the gospels are unreliable.

Coping with Contradictions

I began with a well-known story of a healing. "In Matthew it says a centurion himself came to ask Jesus to heal his servant," I pointed out. "However, Luke says the centurion sent the elders to do this. Now, that's an obvious contradiction, isn't it?"

"No, I don't think so," Blomberg replied. "Think about it this way: in our world today, we may hear a news report that says, 'The president today announced that . . .' when in fact the speech was written by a speechwriter and delivered by the press secretary—and with a little luck, the president might have glanced at it somewhere in between. Yet nobody accuses that broadcast of being in error.

"In a similar way, in the ancient world it was perfectly understood and accepted that actions were often attributed to people when in fact they occurred through their subordinates or emissaries—in this case through the elders of the Jewish people."

"So you're saying that Matthew and Luke can both be right at the same time?"

"That's exactly what I'm saying," he replied.

That seemed plausible, so I posed a second example. "What about Mark and Luke saying that Jesus sent the demons into the swine at Gerasa, while Matthew says it was in Gadara. People look at that and say this is an obvious contradiction that cannot be reconciled—it's two different places. Case closed."

"Well, don't shut the case yet," Blomberg chuckled. "Here's one possible solution: one was a town; the other was a province."

That seemed a little too glib for me. He appeared to be skimming over the real difficulties that are raised by this issue.

"It gets more complicated than that," I said. "Gerasa, the town, wasn't anywhere near the Sea of Galilee, yet that's where the demons, after going into the swine, supposedly took the herd over the cliff to their deaths."

"OK, good point," he said. "But there have been ruins of a town that have been excavated at exactly the right point on the eastern shore of the Sea of Galilee. The English form of the town's name often gets pronounced 'Khersa,' but as a Hebrew word translated or transliterated into Greek, it could have come out sounding something very much like 'Gerasa.' So it may very well have been in Khersa—whose spelling in Greek was rendered as Gerasa—in the province of Gadara."

"Well done," I conceded with a smile. "I'll surrender on that one. But here's a problem that's not so easy: What about the discrepancies between the genealogies of Jesus in Matthew and Luke? Skeptics often point to them as being hopelessly in conflict."

"This is another case of multiple options," he said.

"Such as?"

"The two most common have been that Matthew reflects Joseph's lineage, because most of his opening chapter is told from Joseph's perspective, and Joseph, as the adoptive father, would have been the legal ancestor through whom Jesus' royal lineage would have been traced. These are themes that are important for Matthew.

"Luke, then, would have traced the genealogy through Mary's lineage. And since both are from the ancestry of David, once you get that far back the lines converge.

"A second option is that both genealogies reflect Joseph's lineage in order to create the necessary legalities. But one is Joseph's human lineage—the gospel of Luke—and the other is Joseph's legal lineage, with the two diverging at the points where somebody in the line did not have a direct offspring. They had to raise up legal heirs through various Old Testament practices.

"The problem is made greater because some names are omitted, which was perfectly acceptable by standards of the ancient world. And there are textual variants—names, being translated from one language into another, often took on different spellings and were then easily confused for the name of a different individual."

Blomberg had made his point: There are at least some rational explanations. Even if they might not be airtight, at least they provide a reasonable harmonization of the gospel accounts.

Not wanting our conversation to degenerate into a stump-the-scholar game, I decided to move on. In the meantime Blomberg and I agreed that the best overall approach would be to study each issue individually to see whether there's a rational way to resolve the apparent conflict among the gospels. Certainly there's no shortage of authoritative books that thoroughly examine, sometimes in excruciating detail, how these differences might be reconciled.[6]

"And," said Blomberg, "there are occasions when we may need to hold judgment in abeyance and simply say that since we've made sense out of the vast majority of the texts and determined them to be trustworthy, we can then give them the benefit of the doubt when we're not sure on some of the other details."

5. The Bias Test

This test analyzes whether the gospel writers had any biases that would have colored their work. Did they have any vested interest in skewing the material they were reporting on?

"We can't underestimate the fact that these people loved Jesus," I pointed out. "They were not neutral observers; they were his devoted followers. Wouldn't that make it likely that they would change things to make him look good?"

"Well, I'll concede this much," Blomberg replied, "it creates the potential for this to happen. But on the other hand, people can so honor and respect someone that it prompts them to record his life with great integrity. That's the way they would show their love for him. And I think that's what happened here.

"Besides, these disciples had nothing to gain except criticism, ostracism, and martyrdom. They certainly had nothing to win financially. If anything, this would have provided pressure to keep quiet, to deny Jesus, to downplay him, even to forget they ever met him—yet because of their integrity, they proclaimed what they saw, even when it meant suffering and death."

6. The Cover-up Test

When people testify about events they saw, they will often try to protect themselves or others by conveniently forgetting to mention details that are embarrassing or hard to explain. As a result, this raises uncertainty about the veracity of their entire testimony.

So I asked Blomberg, "Did the gospel writers include any material that might be embarrassing, or did they cover it up to make themselves look good? Did they report anything that would be uncomfortable or difficult for them to explain?"

"There's actually quite a bit along those lines," he said. "There's a large body of Jesus' teaching called the hard sayings of Jesus. Some of it is very ethically demanding. If I were inventing a religion to suit my fancy, I probably wouldn't tell myself to be as perfect as my heavenly Father is perfect, or define adultery to include lust in my heart."

"But," I protested, "there are demanding statements in other religions as well."

"Yes, that's true, which is why the more persuasive kind of hard sayings are those that could be embarrassing for what the church wanted to teach about Jesus."

That response seemed vague. "Give me some examples," I said.

Blomberg thought for a moment, then said, "For instance, Mark 6:5 says that Jesus could do few miracles in Nazareth because the people there had little faith, which seems to limit Jesus' power. Jesus said in Mark 13:32 that he didn't know the day or the hour of his return, which seems to limit his omniscience.

"Now, ultimately theology hasn't had a problem with these statements, because Paul himself, in Philippians 2:5–8, talks about God in Christ voluntarily and consciously limiting the independent exercise of his divine attributes.

"But if I felt free to play fast and loose with gospel history, it would be much more convenient to just leave out that material altogether, and then I wouldn't have to go through the hassle of explaining it.

"Jesus' baptism is another example. You can explain why Jesus, who was without sin, allowed himself to be baptized, but why not make things easier by leaving it out altogether? On the cross Jesus cried out,

'My God, my God, why hast thou forsaken me?' It would have been in the self-interest of the writers to omit that because it raises too many questions."

"Certainly," I added, "there's plenty of embarrassing material about the disciples."

"Absolutely," Blomberg said. "Mark's perspective of Peter is pretty consistently unflattering. And he's the ringleader! The disciples repeatedly misunderstand Jesus. James and John want the places at Jesus' right and left hand, and he has to teach them hard lessons about servant leadership instead. They look like a bunch of self-serving, self-seeking, dull-witted people a lot of the time.

"Now, we already know that the gospel writers were selective; John's gospel ends by saying, somewhat hyperbolically, that the whole world couldn't contain all the information that could have been written about Jesus. So had they left some of this out, that in and of itself wouldn't necessarily have been seen as falsifying the story.

"But here's the point: If they didn't feel free to leave out stuff when it would have been convenient and helpful to do so, is it really plausible to believe that they outright added and fabricated material with no historical basis?"

Blomberg let the question hang for a while before concluding with confidence, "I'd say not."

7. The Corroboration Test

I introduced this next test by asking Blomberg, "When the gospels mention people, places, and events, do they check out to be correct in cases in which they can be independently verified?" Often such corroboration is invaluable in assessing whether a writer has a commitment to accuracy.

"Yes, they do, and the longer people explore this, the more the details get confirmed," Blomberg replied. "Within the last hundred years archaeology has repeatedly unearthed discoveries that have confirmed specific references in the gospels, particularly the gospel of John—ironically, the one that's supposedly so suspect!

"Now, yes, there are still some unresolved issues, and there have been times when archaeology has created new problems, but those are a tiny minority compared with the number of examples of corroboration.

"In addition, we can learn through non-Christian sources a lot of facts about Jesus that corroborate key teachings and events in his life. And when you stop to think that ancient historians for the most part dealt only with political rulers, emperors, kings, military battles, official religious people, and major philosophical movements, it's remarkable how much we can learn about Jesus and his followers even though they fit none of those categories at the time these historians were writing."

That was a concise and helpful answer. However, while I had no reason to doubt Blomberg's assessment, I decided it would be worthwhile to do some further research along these lines. I picked up my pen and jotted a reminder to myself in the margin of my notes: *Get expert opinions from archaeologist and historian.*

8. The Adverse Witness Test

This test asks the question, Were others present who would have contradicted or corrected the gospels if they had been distorted or false? In other words, do we see examples of contemporaries of Jesus complaining that the gospel accounts were just plain wrong?

"Many people had reasons for wanting to discredit this movement and would have done so if they could have simply told history better," Blomberg said.

"Yet look at what his opponents did say. In later Jewish writings Jesus is called a sorcerer who led Israel astray—which acknowledges that he really did work marvelous wonders, although the writers dispute the source of his power.

"This would have been a perfect opportunity to say something like, 'The Christians will tell you he worked miracles, but we're here to tell you he didn't.' Yet that's the one thing we never see his opponents saying. Instead they implicitly acknowledge that what the gospels wrote—that Jesus performed miracles—is true."

I asked, "Could this Christian movement have taken root right there in Jerusalem—in the very area where Jesus had done much of his ministry, had been crucified, buried, and resurrected—if people who knew him were aware that the disciples were exaggerating or distorting the things that he did?"

"I don't believe so," Blomberg replied. "We have a picture of what was initially a very vulnerable and fragile movement that was being subjected to persecution. If critics could have attacked it on the basis that it was full of falsehoods or distortions, they would have.

"But," he emphasized in conclusion, "that's exactly what we don't see."

A Faith Buttressed by Facts

I'll admit I was impressed by Blomberg. Informed and articulate, scholarly and convincing, he had constructed a strong case for the reliability of the gospels. His evidence for their traditional authorship, his analysis of the extremely early date of fundamental beliefs about Jesus, his well-reasoned defense of the accuracy of the oral tradition, his thoughtful examination of apparent discrepancies—all of his testimony had established a solid foundation for me to build on.

Yet there was still a long way to go in determining whether Jesus is the unique Son of God. In fact, after talking with Blomberg, my next assignment became clear: Figure out whether these gospels, shown by Blomberg to be so trustworthy, have been reliably handed down to us over the centuries. How can we be sure that the texts we're reading today bear any resemblance to what was originally written in the first century? What's more, how do we know that the gospels are telling us the full story about Jesus?

I looked at my watch. If traffic was light, I'd make my plane back to Chicago. As I gathered my notes and unplugged my recording equipment, I happened to glance once more at the children's paintings on Blomberg's wall—and suddenly for a moment I thought of him not as a scholar, not as an author, not as a professor, but as a father who sits on the edge of his daughters' beds at night and speaks quietly to them about what's really important in life.

What does he tell them, I wondered, about the Bible, about God, about this Jesus who makes such outrageous claims about himself?

I couldn't resist one last line of questions. "What about your own faith?" I asked. "How has all your research affected your beliefs?"

I barely got the words out of my mouth before he replied. "It has strengthened them, no question. I know from my own research that there's very strong evidence for the trustworthiness of the gospel accounts."

He was quiet for a moment, then continued. "You know, it's ironic: The Bible considers it praiseworthy to have a faith that does not require evidence. Remember how Jesus replied to doubting Thomas: 'You believe because you see; blessed are those who have not seen and yet believe.' And I know evidence can never compel or coerce faith. We cannot supplant the role of the Holy Spirit, which is often a concern of Christians when they hear discussions of this kind.

"But I'll tell you this: There are plenty of stories of scholars in the New Testament field who have not been Christians, yet through their study of these very issues have come to faith in Christ. And there have been countless more scholars, already believers, whose faith has been made stronger, more solid, more grounded, because of the evidence—and that's the category I fall into."

As for me, I had originally been in the first category—no, not a scholar but a skeptic, an iconoclast, a hard-nosed reporter on a quest for the truth about this Jesus who said he was the Way and the Truth and the Life.

I clicked my briefcase closed and stood to thank Blomberg. I would fly back to Chicago satisfied that once again my spiritual quest was off to a good start.

Deliberations
Questions for Reflection or Group Study

1. Overall, how have Blomberg's responses to these eight evidential tests affected your confidence in the reliability of the gospels? Why?

2. Which of these eight tests do you consider the most persuasive and why?

3. When people you trust give slightly different details of the same event, do you automatically doubt their credibility, or do you see if there's a reasonable way to reconcile their accounts? How convincing did you find Blomberg's analysis of the apparent contradictions among the gospels?

For Further Evidence
More Resources on This Topic

Archer, Gleason L. *New International Encyclopedia of Bible Difficulties*. Grand Rapids: Zondervan, 2001.

Beilby, James K., and Paul Rhodes Eddy, eds. *The Historical Jesus: Five Views*. Downers Grove, IL: InterVarsity Academic, 2009.

Köstenberger, Andreas J., Darrell L. Bock, and Josh Chatraw. *Truth in a Culture of Doubt: Engaging Skeptical Challenges to the Bible*. Nashville, TN: B&H Academic, 2014.

Komoszewski, J. Ed, M. James Sawyer, and Daniel B. Wallace. *Reinventing Jesus*. Grand Rapids: Kregel, 2006.

Marshall, I. Howard. *I Believe in the Historical Jesus*. Grand Rapids: Eerdmans, 1977.

Morrow, Jonathan. *Questioning the Bible*. Chicago: Moody, 2014.

Strobel, Lee. *The Case for the Real Jesus*. Grand Rapids: Zondervan, 2007.

Wallace, J. Warner. *Cold-Case Christianity*. Colorado Springs, CO: David C. Cook, 2013.

CHAPTER 3

The Documentary Evidence

Were Jesus' Biographies Reliably Preserved for Us?

As a reporter at the *Chicago Tribune*, I was a "document rat"—I spent countless hours rummaging through court files and sniffing for tidbits of news. It was painstaking and time consuming, but the rewards were worth it. I managed to scoop the competition with front-page stories on a regular basis.

For example, I once stumbled upon some top-secret grand jury transcripts that had inadvertently been put in a public file. My subsequent articles exposed massive bid-rigging behind some of Chicago's biggest public works projects, including the construction of major expressways.

But the most eye-popping cache of documents I ever uncovered came in a landmark case in which Ford Motor Company was charged with reckless homicide for the fiery deaths of three teenagers in a subcompact Pinto. It was the first time a U.S. manufacturer had been criminally charged for allegedly marketing a dangerous product.

When I checked the court file in tiny Winamac, Indiana, I found scores of confidential Ford memos revealing that the automaker knew in advance that the Pinto could explode when struck from behind at about twenty miles an hour. The documents indicated that the automaker decided against improving the car's safety to save a few dollars per vehicle and to increase its luggage space.

A Ford lawyer, who happened to be strolling through the courthouse, spotted me making photocopies of the documents. Frantically he rushed into court to get a judicial order sealing the file from the public's view.

But it was too late. My story, headlined "Ford Ignored Pinto Fire Peril, Secret Memos Show," was bannered in the *Tribune* and then flashed throughout the country.[1]

Authenticating the Documents

Obtaining secret corporate memos is one thing; verifying their authenticity is another. Before a journalist can publish his or her contents or a prosecutor can admit the documents as evidence in a trial, steps must be taken to make sure they're genuine.

Concerning the so-called Pinto papers, could the Ford letterheads on which they were written be counterfeits? Could the signatures be forgeries? How could I know for sure? And since the memos had obviously been photocopied numerous times, how could I be confident that their contents hadn't been tampered with? In other words, how could I be certain that each copied document was identical to the original memo, which I didn't possess?

What's more, how could I be positive that these memos told the whole story? After all, they represented just a small fraction of the internal correspondence at Ford. What if there were other memos, still hidden from the public's view, that would shed a whole different light on the matter if they were revealed?

These are significant questions, and they're equally relevant in examining the New Testament. When I hold a Bible in my hands, essentially I'm holding copies of ancient historical records. The original manuscripts of the biographies of Jesus—Matthew, Mark, Luke, and John—and all the other books of the Old and New Testaments have long ago crumbled into dust. So how can I be sure that these modern-day versions—the end product of countless copying throughout the ages—bear any resemblance to what the authors originally wrote?

In addition, how can I tell if these four biographies are telling the whole story? What if there were other biographies of Jesus that have been censored because the early church didn't like the image of Jesus they portrayed? How could I have confidence that church politics haven't squelched biographies of Jesus that were every bit as accurate as the four that were finally included in the New Testament, and that

would shed important new light on the words and deeds of this controversial carpenter from Nazareth?

These two issues—whether Jesus' biographies were reliably preserved
for us and whether equally accurate biographies have been suppressed
by the church—merited careful consideration. I knew that there was
one scholar universally recognized as a leading authority on these matters. I flew to Newark and drove a rental car to Princeton to visit him
on short notice.

THE SECOND INTERVIEW:
Bruce M. Metzger, PhD

I found eighty-four-year-old Bruce Metzger on a Saturday afternoon
at his usual hangout, the library at Princeton Theological Seminary,
where, he said with a smile, "I like to dust off the books."

Actually, he wrote some of the best of them, especially when the
topic is the text of the New Testament. In all, he authored or edited
fifty books, including *The New Testament: Its Background, Growth, and
Content*; *The Text of the New Testament*; *The Canon of the New Testament*;
Manuscripts of the Greek Bible; *Textual Commentary on the Greek New
Testament*; *Introduction to the Apocrypha*; and *The Oxford Companion to
the Bible*. Several have been translated into German, Chinese, Japanese,
Korean, Malagasy, and other languages. He also was coeditor of *The New
Oxford Annotated Bible with the Apocrypha* and general editor of more
than twenty-five volumes in the series *New Testament Tools and Studies*.

Metzger's education included a master's degree from Princeton
Theological Seminary and both a master's degree and a doctorate from
Princeton University. He was awarded honorary doctorates by five colleges and universities, including St. Andrews University in Scotland,
the University of Munster in Germany, and Potchefstroom University
in South Africa.

In 1969 he served as resident scholar at Tyndale House, Cambridge,
England. He was a visiting fellow at Clare Hall, University of Cambridge,
in 1974, and at Wolfson College, Oxford, in 1979. At the time of the
interview, he was professor emeritus at Princeton Theological Seminary
after a forty-six-year career teaching the New Testament.[2]

Metzger was chairman of the New Revised Standard Version Bible Committee, a corresponding fellow of the British Academy, and served on the Kuratorium of the Vetus Latina Institute at the Monastery of Beuron, Germany. He was president of the Society of Biblical Literature, the International Society for New Testament Studies, and the North American Patristic Society.

If you scan the footnotes of any authoritative book on the text of the New Testament, the odds are you're going to see Metzger cited time after time. His books are mandatory reading in universities and seminaries around the world. He is held in the highest regard by scholars from across a wide range of theological beliefs.

In many ways Metzger, born in 1914, was a throwback to an earlier generation. Alighting from a gray Buick he called "my gas buggy," he was wearing a dark gray suit and blue paisley tie, which is about as casual as he got during his visits to the library, even on a weekend. His white hair was neatly combed; his eyes, bright and alert, were framed by rimless glasses. He walked slower than he used to, but he had no difficulty methodically climbing the stairway to the second floor, where he conducted his research in an obscure and austere office.

And he hadn't lost his sense of humor. He showed me a tin canister he inherited as chairman of the Revised Standard Version Bible Committee. He opened the lid to reveal the ashes of an RSV Bible that had been torched in a 1952 bonfire during a protest by a fundamentalist preacher.

"It seems he didn't like it when the committee changed 'fellows' of the King James Version to 'comrades' in Hebrews 1:9," Metzger explained with a chuckle. "He accused them of being communists!"

Though Metzger's speech was hesitant at times and he was prone to replying in quaint phrases like "Quite so," he continued to remain on the cutting edge of New Testament scholarship. When I asked for some statistics, he didn't rely on the numbers in his 1992 book on the New Testament; he had conducted fresh research to get up-to-date figures. His quick mind had no problem recalling details of people and places, and he was fully conversant with all the current debates among New Testament experts.

His office, about the size of a jail cell, was windowless and painted institutional gray. It had two wooden chairs; he insisted I take the more comfortable one. That was part of his charm. He was thoroughly kind, surprisingly modest and self-effacing, with a gentle spirit that made me want to someday grow old with the same mellow kind of grace.

We got acquainted with each other for a while, and then I turned to the first issue I wanted to address: How can we be sure the biographies of Jesus were handed down to us in a reliable way?

Copies of Copies of Copies

"I'll be honest with you," I said to Metzger. "When I first found out that there are no surviving originals of the New Testament, I was really skeptical. I thought, If all we have are copies of copies of copies, how can I have any confidence that the New Testament we have today bears any resemblance whatsoever to what was originally written? How do you respond to that?"

"This isn't an issue that's unique to the Bible; it's a question we can ask of other documents that have come down to us from antiquity," he replied. "But what the New Testament has in its favor, especially when compared with other ancient writings, is the unprecedented multiplicity of copies that have survived."

"Why is that important?" I asked.

"Well, the more often you have copies that agree with each other, especially if they emerge from different geographical areas, the more you can cross-check them to figure out what the original document was like. The only way they'd agree would be where they went back genealogically in a family tree that represents the descent of the manuscripts."

"OK," I said, "I can see that having a lot of copies from various places can help. But what about the age of the documents? Certainly that's important as well, isn't it?"

"Quite so," he replied. "And this is something else that favors the New Testament. We have copies commencing within a couple of generations from the writing of the originals, whereas in the case of other ancient texts, maybe five, eight, or ten centuries elapsed between the original and the earliest surviving copy.

"In addition to Greek manuscripts, we also have translations of the gospels into other languages at a relatively early time—into Latin, Syriac, and Coptic. And beyond that, we have what may be called secondary translations made a little later, like Armenian and Gothic. And a lot of others—Georgian, Ethiopic, a great variety."

"How does that help?"

"Because even if we had no Greek manuscripts today, by piecing together the information from these translations from a relatively early date, we could actually reproduce the contents of the New Testament. In addition to that, even if we lost all the Greek manuscripts and the early translations, we could still reproduce the contents of the New Testament from the multiplicity of quotations in commentaries, sermons, letters, and so forth of the early church fathers."

While that seemed impressive, it was difficult to judge this evidence in isolation. I needed some context to better appreciate the uniqueness of the New Testament. How, I wondered, did it compare with other well-known works of antiquity?

A Mountain of Manuscripts

"When you talk about a great multiplicity of manuscripts," I said, "how does that contrast with other ancient books that are routinely accepted by scholars as being reliable? For instance, tell me about the writing of authors from about the time of Jesus."

Having anticipated the question, Metzger referred to some handwritten notes he had brought along.

"Consider Tacitus, the Roman historian who wrote his *Annals of Imperial Rome* in about AD 116," he began. "His first six books exist today in only one manuscript, and it was copied about AD 850. Books eleven through sixteen are in another manuscript dating from the eleventh century. Books seven through ten are lost. So there is a long gap between the time that Tacitus sought his information and wrote it down and the only existing copies.

"With regard to the first-century historian Josephus, we have nine Greek manuscripts of his work *The Jewish War*, and these copies were written in the tenth, eleventh, and twelfth centuries. There is a Latin translation from the fourth century and medieval Russian materials from the eleventh or twelfth century."

Those numbers were surprising. There is but the thinnest thread of manuscripts connecting these ancient works to the modern world. "By comparison," I asked, "how many New Testament Greek manuscripts are in existence today?"

Metzger's eyes got wide. "More than five thousand have been cataloged," he said with enthusiasm, his voice going up an octave.[3]

That was a mountain of manuscripts compared to the anthills of Tacitus and Josephus! "Is that unusual in the ancient world? What would the runner-up be?" I asked.

"The quantity of New Testament material is almost embarrassing in comparison with other works of antiquity," he said. "Next to the New Testament, the greatest amount of manuscript testimony is of Homer's *Iliad*, which was the bible of the ancient Greeks. There are fewer than 650 Greek manuscripts of it today. Some are quite fragmentary. They come down to us from the second and third century AD and following. When you consider that Homer composed his epic about 800 BC, you can see there's a very lengthy gap."

"Very lengthy" was an understatement; it was a thousand years! There was in fact no comparison: The manuscript evidence for the New Testament was overwhelming when juxtaposed against other revered writings of antiquity—works that modern scholars have absolutely no reluctance treating as authentic.

My curiosity about the New Testament manuscripts having been piqued, I asked Metzger to describe some of them for me.

"The earliest are fragments of papyrus, which was a writing material made from the papyrus plant that grew in the marshes of the Nile Delta in Egypt," he said. "There are now ninety-nine fragmentary pieces of papyrus that contain one or more passages or books of the New Testament.

"The most significant to come to light are the Chester Beatty Biblical Papyri, discovered about 1930. Of these, Beatty Biblical Papyrus number one contains portions of the four gospels and the book of Acts, and it dates from the third century. Papyrus number two contains large portions of eight letters of Paul, plus portions of Hebrews, dating to about the year 200. Papyrus number three has a sizable section of the book of Revelation, dating from the third century.

"Another group of important papyrus manuscripts was purchased by a Swiss bibliophile, M. Martin Bodmer. The earliest of these, dating from about 200, contains about two-thirds of the gospel of John. Another papyrus, containing portions of the gospels of Luke and John, dates from the third century."

At this point the gap between the writing of the biographies of Jesus and the earliest manuscripts was extremely small. But what is the oldest manuscript we possess? How close in time, I wondered, can we get to the original writings, which experts call "autographs"?

The Scrap That Changed History

"Of the entire New Testament," I said, "what is the earliest portion that we possess today?"

Metzger didn't have to ponder the answer. "That would be a fragment of the gospel of John containing material from chapter eighteen. It has five verses—three on one side, two on the other—and it measures about two and a half by three and a half inches," he said.

"How was it discovered?"

"It was purchased in Egypt as early as 1920, but it sat unnoticed for years among similar fragments of papyri. Then in 1934 C. H. Roberts of Saint John's College, Oxford, was sorting through the papyri at the John Rylands Library in Manchester, England. He immediately recognized this as preserving a portion of John's gospel. He was able to date it from the style of the script."

"And what was his conclusion?" I asked. "How far back does it go?"

"He concluded it originated between AD 100 to 150. Lots of other prominent paleographers, like Sir Frederic Kenyon, Sir Harold Bell, Adolf Deissmann, W. H. P. Hatch, Ulrich Wilcken, and others, have agreed with his assessment. Deissmann was convinced that it goes back at least to the reign of Emperor Hadrian, which was AD 117–138, or even Emperor Trajan, which was AD 98–117."

That was a stunning discovery. The reason: Skeptical German theologians in the last century argued strenuously that the fourth gospel was not even composed until at least the year 160—too distant from the events of Jesus' life to be of much historical use. They were able to influence generations of scholars, who scoffed at this gospel's reliability.

"This certainly blows that opinion out of the water," I commented.

"Yes, it does," he said. "Here we have, at a very early date, a fragment of a copy of John all the way over in a community along the Nile River in Egypt, far from Ephesus in Asia Minor, where the gospel was probably originally composed."

This finding has literally rewritten popular views of history, pushing the composition of John's gospel much closer to the days when Jesus walked the earth. I made a mental note to check with an archaeologist about whether any other findings have bolstered the confidence we can have in the fourth gospel.

A Wealth of Evidence

While papyrus manuscripts represent the earliest copies of the New Testament, there are also ancient copies written on parchment, which was made from the skins of cattle, sheep, goats, and antelope.

"We have what are called uncial manuscripts, which are written in all-capital Greek letters," Metzger explained. "Today we have 306 of these, several dating back as early as the third century. The most important are *Codex Sinaiticus*, which is the only complete New Testament in uncial letters, and *Codex Vaticanus*, which is not quite complete. Both date to about AD 350.

"A new style of writing, more cursive in nature, emerged in roughly AD 800. It's called minuscule, and we have 2,856 of these manuscripts. Then there are also lectionaries, which contain New Testament Scripture in the sequence it was to be read in the early churches at appropriate times during the year. A total of 2,403 of these have been cataloged. That puts the grand total of Greek manuscripts at 5,664."

In addition to the Greek documents, he said, there are thousands of other ancient New Testament manuscripts in other languages. There are 8,000 to 10,000 Latin Vulgate manuscripts, plus a total of 8,000 in Ethiopic, Slavic, and Armenian. In all, there are about 24,000 manuscripts in existence.

"What's your opinion, then?" I asked, wanting to confirm clearly what I thought I was hearing him say. "In terms of the multiplicity of manuscripts and the time gap between the originals and our first copies, how does the New Testament stack up against other well-known works of antiquity?"

"Extremely well," he replied. "We can have great confidence in the fidelity with which this material has come down to us, especially compared with any other ancient literary work."

That conclusion is shared by distinguished scholars throughout the world. Said the late F. F. Bruce, eminent professor at the University of Manchester, England, and author of *The New Testament Documents: Are They Reliable?*: "There is no body of ancient literature in the world which enjoys such a wealth of good textual attestation as the New Testament."[4]

Metzger had already mentioned the name of Sir Frederic Kenyon, former director of the British Museum and author of *The Palaeography of Greek Papyri*. Kenyon has said that "in no other case is the interval of time between the composition of the book and the date of the earliest manuscripts so short as in that of the New Testament."[5]

His conclusion: "The last foundation for any doubt that the Scriptures have come down to us substantially as they were written has now been removed."[6]

However, what about discrepancies among the various manuscripts? In the days before lightning-fast photocopying machines, manuscripts were laboriously hand-copied by scribes, letter by letter, word by word, line by line, in a process that was ripe for errors. Now I wanted to zero in on whether these copying mistakes have rendered our modern Bibles hopelessly riddled with inaccuracies.

Examining the Errors

"With the similarities in the way Greek letters are written and with the primitive conditions under which the scribes worked, it would seem inevitable that copying errors would creep into the text," I said.

"Quite so," Metzger conceded.

"And in fact, aren't there literally tens of thousands of variations among the ancient manuscripts that we have?"

"Quite so."

"Doesn't that therefore mean we can't trust them?" I asked, sounding more accusatory than inquisitive.

"No sir, it does not," Metzger replied firmly. "First let me say this: Eyeglasses weren't invented until 1373 in Venice, and I'm sure that astigmatism existed among the ancient scribes. That was compounded by the fact that it was difficult under any circumstances to read faded manuscripts on which some of the ink had flaked away. And there were other hazards—inattentiveness on the part of scribes, for example. So yes, although for the most part scribes were scrupulously careful, errors did creep in.

"But," he was quick to add, "there are factors counteracting that. For example, sometimes the scribe's memory would play tricks on him. Between the time it took for him to look at the text and then to write down the words, the order of words might get shifted. He may write down the right words but in the wrong sequence. This is nothing to be alarmed at, because Greek, unlike English, is an inflected language."

"Meaning . . . ," I prompted him.

"Meaning it makes a whale of a difference in English if you say, 'Dog bites man' or 'Man bites dog'—sequence matters in English. But in Greek it doesn't. One word functions as the subject of the sentence regardless of where it stands in the sequence; consequently, the meaning of the sentence isn't distorted if the words are out of what we consider to be the right order. So yes, some variations among manuscripts exist, but generally they're inconsequential variations like that. Differences in spelling would be another example."[7]

I keyed in on the most important issue. "How many doctrines of the church are in jeopardy because of variants?"

"I don't know of any doctrine that is in jeopardy," he responded confidently.

"None?"

"None," he repeated. "Now, the Jehovah's Witnesses come to our door and say, 'Your Bible is wrong in the King James Version of 1 John 5:7–8, where it talks about 'the Father, the Word, and the Holy Ghost: and these three are one.' They'll say, 'That's not in the earliest manuscripts.'

"And that's true enough. I think that these words are found in only about seven or eight copies, all from the fifteenth or sixteenth century. I acknowledge that is not part of what the author of 1 John was inspired to write.

"But that does not dislodge the firmly witnessed testimony of the Bible to the doctrine of the Trinity. At the baptism of Jesus, the Father speaks, his beloved Son is baptized, and the Holy Spirit descends on him. At the ending of 2 Corinthians Paul says, 'May the grace of the Lord Jesus Christ, and the love of God, and the fellowship of the Holy Spirit be with you all.' There are many places where the Trinity is represented."

"So the variations, when they occur, tend to be minor rather than substantive?"

"Yes, yes, that's correct, and scholars work very carefully to try to resolve them by getting back to the original meaning. The more significant variations do not overthrow any doctrine of the church. Any good Bible will have notes that will alert the reader to variant readings of any consequence. But again, these are rare."

However, even if it's true that the transmission of the New Testament through history has been unprecedented in its reliability, how do we know that we have the whole picture?

What about allegations that church councils squelched equally legitimate documents because they didn't like the picture of Jesus they portrayed? How do we know that the twenty-seven books of the New Testament represent the best and most reliable information? Why is it that our Bibles contain Matthew, Mark, Luke, and John, but many other ancient gospels—the Gospel of Philip, the Gospel of the Egyptians, the Gospel of Truth, the Gospel of the Nativity of Mary—were excluded?

It was time to turn to the question of the "canon," a term that comes from a Greek word meaning "rule," "norm," or "standard" and that describes the books that have become accepted as official in the church and included in the New Testament.[8] Metzger is considered a leading authority in that field.

"A High Degree of Unanimity"

"How did the early church leaders determine which books would be considered authoritative and which would be discarded?" I asked. "What criteria did they use in determining which documents would be included in the New Testament?"

"Basically, the early church had three criteria," he said. "First, the books must have apostolic authority—that is, they must have been written either by apostles themselves, who were eyewitnesses to what they wrote about, or by followers of apostles. So in the case of Mark and Luke, while they weren't among the twelve disciples, early tradition has it that Mark was a helper of Peter, and Luke was an associate of Paul.

"Second, there was the criterion of conformity to what was called the rule of faith. That is, was the document congruent with the basic Christian tradition that the church recognized as normative? And third, there was the criterion of whether a document had had continuous acceptance and usage by the church at large."

"They merely applied those criteria and let the chips fall where they may?" I asked.

"Well, it wouldn't be accurate to say that these criteria were simply applied in a mechanical fashion," he replied. "There were certainly different opinions about which criterion should be given the most weight.

"But what's remarkable is that even though the fringes of the canon remained unsettled for a while, there was actually a high degree of unanimity concerning the greater part of the New Testament within the first two centuries. And this was true among very diverse congregations scattered over a wide area."

"So," I said, "the four gospels we have in the New Testament today met those criteria, while others didn't?"

"Yes," he said. "It was, if I may put it this way, an example of 'survival of the fittest.' In talking about the canon, Arthur Darby Nock used to tell his students at Harvard, 'The most traveled roads in Europe are the best roads; that's why they're so heavily traveled.' That's a good analogy. British commentator William Barclay said it this way: 'It is the simple truth to say that the New Testament books became canonical because no one could stop them doing so.'

"We can be confident that no other ancient books can compare with the New Testament in terms of importance for Christian history or doctrine. When one studies the early history of the canon, one walks away convinced that the New Testament contains the best sources for the history of Jesus. Those who discerned the limits of the canon had a clear and balanced perspective of the gospel of Christ.

"Just read these other documents for yourself. They're written later than the four gospels, in the second, third, fourth, fifth, even sixth century, long after Jesus, and they're generally quite banal. They carry names like the Gospel of Peter and the Gospel of Mary that are unrelated to their real authorship. On the other hand, the four gospels in the New Testament were readily accepted with remarkable unanimity as being authentic in the story they told."

Yet I knew that some liberal scholars, most notably members of the well-publicized Jesus Seminar, believe the Gospel of Thomas ought to be elevated to equal status with the four traditional gospels. Did this mysterious gospel fall victim to political wars within the church, eventually being excluded because of its unpopular doctrines? I decided I'd better probe Metzger on this point.

The "Secret Words" of Jesus

"Dr. Metzger, the Gospel of Thomas, which was among the Nag Hammadi documents found in Egypt in 1945, claims it contains 'the secret words which the living Jesus spoke and Didymus Judas Thomas wrote down.' Why was it excluded by the church?"

Metzger was thoroughly acquainted with the work. "The Gospel of Thomas came to light in a fifth-century copy in Coptic, which I've translated into English," he said. "It contains 114 sayings attributed to Jesus but no narrative of what he did, and seems to have been written in Greek in Syria about AD 140.[9] In some cases I think this gospel correctly reports what Jesus said, with slight modifications."

This was certainly an intriguing statement. "Please elaborate," I said.

"For instance, in the Gospel of Thomas Jesus says, 'A city built on a high hill cannot be hidden.' Here the adjective *high* is added, but the rest reads like Matthew's gospel. Or Jesus says, 'Render to Caesar the things that are Caesar's, render to God the things that are God's, render to me the things that are mine.' In this case the later phrase has been added.

"However, there are some things in Thomas that are totally alien to the canonical gospels. Jesus says, 'Split wood; I am there. Lift up a stone, and you will find me there.' That's pantheism, the idea that Jesus is coterminous with the substance of this world. That's contrary to anything in the canonical gospels.

"The Gospel of Thomas ends with a note saying, 'Let Mary go away from us, because women are not worthy of life.' Jesus is quoted as saying, 'Lo, I shall lead her in order to make her a male, so that she too may become a living spirit, resembling you males. For every woman who makes herself male will enter into the kingdom of heaven.'"

Metzger's eyebrows shot up as if he were surprised at what he had just uttered. "Now, this is *not* the Jesus we know from the four canonical gospels!" he said emphatically.

I asked, "What about the charge that Thomas was purposefully excluded by church councils in some sort of conspiracy to silence it?"

"That's just not historically accurate," came Metzger's response. "What the synods and councils did in the fifth century and following was to ratify what already had been accepted by high and low Christians alike. It is not right to say that the Gospel of Thomas was excluded by some fiat on the part of a council; the right way to put it is, the Gospel of Thomas excluded itself! It did not harmonize with other testimony about Jesus that early Christians accepted as trustworthy."

"So you would disagree with anyone who would try to elevate Thomas to the same status as that of the four gospels?" I asked.

"Yes, I would very much disagree. I think the early church exercised a judicious act in discarding it. To take it up now, it seems to me, would be to accept something that's less valid than the other gospels," he replied. "Now, don't get me wrong. I think the Gospel of Thomas is an interesting document, but it's mixed up with pantheistic and anti-feminist statements that certainly deserve to be given the left foot of fellowship, if you know what I mean.

"You have to understand that the canon was not the result of a series of contests involving church politics. The canon is rather the separation that came about because of the intuitive insight of Christian believers. They could hear the voice of the Good Shepherd in the gospel of John; they could hear it only in a muffled and distorted way in the Gospel of Thomas, mixed in with a lot of other things.

"When the pronouncement was made about the canon, it merely ratified what the general sensitivity of the church had already determined. You see, the canon is a list of authoritative books more than it is an authoritative list of books. These documents didn't derive their authority from being selected; each one was authoritative before anyone gathered them together. The early church merely listened and sensed that these were authoritative accounts.

"For somebody now to say that the canon emerged only after councils and synods made these pronouncements would be like saying, 'Let's get several academies of musicians to make a pronouncement that the music of Bach and Beethoven is wonderful.' I would say, 'Thank you for nothing! We knew that before the pronouncement was made.' We know it because of sensitivity to what is good music and what is not. The same with the canon."

Even so, I pointed out that some New Testament books, notably James, Hebrews, and Revelation, were more slowly accepted into the canon than others. "Should we therefore be suspicious of them?" I asked.

"To my mind, that just shows how careful the early church was," he replied. "They weren't 'gung ho,' sweeping in every last document that happened to have anything about Jesus in it. This shows deliberation and careful analysis.

"Of course, even today parts of the Syrian church refuse to accept the book of Revelation, yet the people belonging to that church are Christian believers. From my point of view, I accept the book of Revelation as a wonderful part of the Scriptures."

He shook his head. "I think they impoverish themselves by not accepting it."

The "Unrivaled" New Testament

Metzger had been persuasive. No serious doubts lingered concerning whether the New Testament's text had been reliably preserved for us through the centuries. One of Metzger's distinguished predecessors at Princeton Theological Seminary, Benjamin Warfield, who held four doctorates and taught systematic theology until his death in 1921, put it this way:

> If we compare the present state of the New Testament text with that of any other ancient writing, we must . . . declare it to be marvelously correct. Such has been the care with which the New Testament has been copied—a care which has doubtless grown out of true reverence for its holy words. . . . The New Testament [is] unrivaled among ancient writings in the purity of its text as actually transmitted and kept in use.[10]

In terms of which documents were accepted into the New Testament, generally there has never been any serious dispute about the authoritative nature of twenty of the New Testament's twenty-seven books—from Matthew through Philemon, plus 1 Peter and 1 John. This, of course, includes the four gospels that represent Jesus' biographies.[11] The remaining seven books, though questioned for a time by some early church leaders, "were finally and fully recognized by the church generally," according to Geisler and Nix.[12]

As for the "pseudepigrapha," the proliferation of gospels, epistles, and apocalypses in the first few centuries after Jesus—including the Gospels of Nicodemus, Barnabas, Bartholomew, Andrew, the Epistle of Paul to the Laodiceans, the Apocalypse of Stephen, and others—they are "fanciful and heretical . . . neither genuine nor valuable as a whole," and "virtually no orthodox Father, canon or council" considered them to be authoritative or deserving of inclusion in the New Testament.[13]

In fact, I accepted Metzger's challenge by reading many of them myself. Compared with the careful, sober, precise, eyewitness quality of Matthew, Mark, Luke, and John, these works truly deserve the description they received from Eusebius, the early church historian: "Totally absurd and impious."[14] They were too far removed from Jesus' ministry to contribute anything meaningful to my investigation, having been written as late as the fifth and sixth centuries, and their often mythical qualities disqualify them from being historically credible.

With all that established, the time had arrived for my investigation to advance to its next phase. I was curious: How much evidence is there for this miracle-working first-century carpenter *outside* the gospels? Do ancient historians confirm or contradict the New Testament's claims about his life, teachings, and miracles? I knew this required a trip to Ohio to visit one of the country's leading scholars in that field.

As we stood, I thanked Dr. Metzger for his time and expertise. He smiled warmly and offered to walk me downstairs. I didn't want to consume any more of his Saturday afternoon, but my curiosity wouldn't let me leave Princeton without satisfying myself about one remaining issue.

"All these decades of scholarship, of study, of writing textbooks, of delving into the minutiae of the New Testament text—what has all this done to your personal faith?" I asked.

"Oh," he said, sounding happy to discuss the topic, "it has increased the basis of my personal faith to see the firmness with which these materials have come down to us, with a multiplicity of copies, some of which are very, very ancient."

"So," I started to say, "scholarship has not diluted your faith—"

He jumped in before I could finish my sentence. "On the contrary," he stressed, "it has built it. I've asked questions all my life, I've dug into the text, I've studied this thoroughly, and today I know with confidence that my trust in Jesus has been well placed."

He paused while his eyes surveyed my face. Then he added, for emphasis, "*Very* well placed."

Deliberations
Questions for Reflection or Group Study

1. Having read the interview with Dr. Metzger, how would you rate the reliability of the process by which the New Testament was transmitted to us? What are some reasons you find this process trustworthy or not?

2. Scan a copy of the New Testament and examine some of the notes in the margins that talk about variant readings. What are some examples you find? How does the presence of these notations affect your understanding of the passages?

3. Do the criteria for determining whether a document should be included in the New Testament seem reasonable? Why or why not? Are there other criteria you believe should be added? What disadvantages do modern scholars have in second-guessing the early church's decisions concerning whether a document should be included in the Bible?

For Further Evidence
More Resources on This Topic

Bruce, F. F. *The Canon of Scripture.* Downers Grove, IL: InterVarsity Press, 1996.

Evans, Craig, and Emanuel Tov, eds. *Exploring the Origins of the Bible.* Grand Rapids: Baker Academic, 2008.

Evans, Craig A. *Fabricating Jesus: How Modern Scholars Distort the Gospels.* Downers Grove, IL: InterVarsity Press, 2008.

Geisler, Norman L., and William E. Nix. *From God to Us.* New edition. Chicago: Moody Press, 2012.

Jones, Timothy Paul. *Misquoting Truth.* Annotated Edition. Downers Grove, IL: InterVarsity Press, 2007.

Kruger, Michael J. *Canon Revisited.* Wheaton, IL: Crossway, 2012.

————. *The Question of Canon.* Downers Grove, IL: IVP Academic, 2013.

Lightfoot, Neil R. *How We Got the Bible*. Third edition. Grand Rapids: Baker, 2010.

Metzger, Bruce M., and Bart D. Ehrman. *The Text of the New Testament: Its Transmission, Corruption, and Restoration*. Fourth edition. New York and Oxford: Oxford University Press, 2005.

Metzger, Bruce M. *The Canon of the New Testament*. Reprint edition. Oxford: Oxford University Press, 1997.

Patzia, Arthur G. *The Making of the New Testament*. Downers Grove, IL: InterVarsity Press, 1995.

Perrin, Nicholas. *Lost in Transmission?* Nashville, TN: Nelson, 2007.

Porter, Stanley E. *How We Got the New Testament*. Grand Rapids: Baker Academic, 2013.

Wallace, Daniel B. *Revisiting the Corruption of the New Testament*. Grand Rapids: Kregel Academic and Professional, 2011.

Wegner, Paul D. *The Journey from Texts to Translations*. Grand Rapids: Baker, 1999.

CHAPTER 4

The Corroborating Evidence

*Is There Credible Evidence for Jesus
outside His Biographies?*

Harry Aleman turned and stabbed his finger at me. "*You*," he sputtered, spitting out the word with disgust. "Why do you keep writing those things about me?" Then he spun around and disappeared down a back stairwell to escape the reporters who were pursuing him through the courthouse.

Actually, it was hard to be a crime reporter in Chicago during the 1970s and *not* write about Harry Aleman. He was, after all, the quintessential crime syndicate hit man. And Chicagoans, in a perverse way, love to read about the mob.

Prosecutors desperately wanted to put Aleman in prison for one of the cold-blooded executions they suspected he had committed on behalf of his syndicate bosses. The problem, of course, was the difficulty of finding anyone willing to testify against a mobster of Aleman's frightening reputation.

Then came their big break. One of Aleman's former cronies, Louis Almeida, was arrested on his way to murder a labor official in Pennsylvania. Convicted of weapons charges and sentenced to a decade in prison, Almeida agreed to testify against Aleman in the unsolved slaying of a Teamsters Union shop steward in Chicago—if prosecutors would agree to show leniency toward Almeida.

This meant Almeida had a motive to cooperate, which would undoubtedly tarnish his credibility to some degree. Prosecutors realized they would need to bolster his testimony to ensure a conviction, so they went searching for someone to corroborate Almeida's account.

Webster's dictionary defines *corroborate* this way: "To make more certain; confirm: He corroborated my account of the accident."[1] Corroborative evidence supports other testimony; it affirms or backs up the essential elements of an eyewitness account. It can be a public record, a photograph, or additional testimony from a second or third person. It can verify a person's entire testimony or just key parts of it.

In effect, corroborative evidence acts like the support wires that keep a tall antenna straight and unwavering. The more corroborative evidence, the stronger and more secure the case.

But where would prosecutors find corroboration of Almeida's story? It came from a surprising source: a quiet, law-abiding citizen named Bobby Lowe told investigators he had been walking his dog when he saw Aleman murder the union steward. Despite Aleman's bone-chilling notoriety, Lowe agreed to back up Almeida's story by testifying against the mobster.

The Power of Corroboration

At Aleman's trial Lowe and Almeida mesmerized jurors with their stories. Almeida's account of driving the getaway car dovetailed with Lowe's straightforward description of seeing Aleman murder his victim on a public sidewalk the evening of September 27, 1972.

Prosecutors thought they had woven an airtight case against the feared hit man, yet throughout the trial they sensed something was amiss. Their skepticism first surfaced when Aleman decided against having a jury trial, opting instead to have a judge hear his case.

At the end of the trial the prosecutors' worst suspicions were realized: despite compelling testimony by Lowe and Almeida, the judge ended up declaring Aleman innocent and letting him go free.

What had happened? Remember, this took place in Cook County, Illinois, where corruption so often lurks. Years later it was revealed that the judge had been slipped ten thousand dollars in return for the acquittal. When an FBI informant disclosed the bribe, the then-retired judge committed suicide—and prosecutors refiled the murder charge against Aleman.

By the time the second trial was held, the law had been changed so that prosecutors could demand that a jury hear the case. That's what they did—and finally, a full twenty-five years after the murder, Aleman was found guilty and sentenced to prison, where he later died.[2]

In spite of the delays, the Aleman saga shows how significant corroborative evidence can be. And the same is true in dealing with historical issues. We've already heard, through Dr. Craig Blomberg's testimony, that in the gospels there is excellent eyewitness evidence for the life, teachings, death, and resurrection of Jesus. But is there any other evidence to corroborate that? Are there writings outside the gospels that affirm or support any of the essentials about Jesus or early Christianity?

In other words, is there any additional documentation that can help seal the case for Christ, as Bobby Lowe's testimony sealed the case against Harry Aleman? The answer, according to our next witness, is yes—and the amount and quality of that evidence may very well surprise you.

THE THIRD INTERVIEW:
Edwin M. Yamauchi, PhD

As I entered the imposing brick building that houses the office of Edwin Yamauchi at Miami University in picturesque Oxford, Ohio, I walked underneath a stone arch bearing this inscription: "Ye shall know the truth, and the truth will make you free." As one of the country's leading experts in ancient history, Yamauchi has been on a quest for historical truth for much of his life.

Born in Hawaii in 1937, the son of immigrants from Okinawa, Yamauchi started from humble beginnings. His father died just before the Japanese attack on Pearl Harbor, leaving his mother to earn a meager living as a maid for wealthy families. While lacking formal education herself, she encouraged her son to read and study, giving him beautifully illustrated books that instilled in him a lifelong love of learning.

Certainly his academic accomplishments have been impressive. After earning a bachelor's degree in Hebrew and Hellenistics, Yamauchi received master's and doctoral degrees in Mediterranean studies from Brandeis University.

He has been awarded eight fellowships, from the Rutgers Research Council, National Endowment for the Humanities, the American Philosophical Society, and others. He has studied twenty-two languages, including Arabic, Chinese, Egyptian, Russian, Syriac, Ugaritic, and even Comanche.

He has delivered seventy-one papers before learned societies; lectured at more than one hundred seminaries, universities, and colleges, including Yale, Princeton, and Cornell; served as chairman and then president of the Institute for Biblical Research and president of the Conference on Faith and History; and published eighty articles in thirty-seven scholarly journals.

In 1968 he participated in the first excavations of the Herodian temple in Jerusalem, revealing evidence of the temple's destruction in AD 70. Archaeology has also been the theme of several of his books, including *The Stones and the Scriptures*; *The Scriptures and Archaeology*; and *The World of the First Christians*.

Though born into a Buddhist background, Yamauchi has been following Jesus ever since 1952, the year I was born. I was especially curious to see whether his long-term commitment to Christ would color his assessment of the historical evidence. In other words, would he scrupulously stick to the facts, or be tempted to draw conclusions that went beyond where the evidence warranted?

I found Yamauchi to have a gentle and unassuming demeanor. Although generally soft-spoken, he's intensely focused. He provides thorough and detailed answers to questions, often pausing to supplement his verbal response by offering photocopies of scholarly articles he has written on the topic. A good scholar knows you can never have too much data.

Inside his book-cluttered office, in the heart of a heavily wooded campus ablaze in autumn colors, we sat down to talk about the topic that still brings a glint to his eyes, even after so many years of research and teaching.

Affirming the Gospels

Because of my interview with Blomberg, I didn't want to suggest that we needed to go beyond the gospels in order to find reliable evidence concerning Jesus. So I started by asking Yamauchi this question: "As a historian, could you give me your assessment of the historical reliability of the gospels themselves?"

"On the whole, the gospels are excellent sources," he replied. "As a matter of fact, they're the most trustworthy, complete, and reliable sources for Jesus. The incidental sources really don't add much detailed information; however, they are valuable as corroborative evidence."

"OK, that's what I want to discuss—the corroborative evidence," I said. "Let's be honest: some people scoff at how much there really is. For example, in 1979 Charles Templeton wrote a novel called *Act of God*, in which a fictional archaeologist made a statement that reflects the beliefs of a lot of people."

I pulled out the book and read the relevant paragraph.

The [Christian] church bases its claims mostly on the teachings of an obscure young Jew with messianic pretentions who, let's face it, didn't make much of an impression in his lifetime. There isn't a single word about him in secular history. Not a word. No mention of him by the Romans. Not so much as a reference by Josephus.[3]

"Now," I said a little pointedly, "that doesn't sound as if there's much corroboration of the life of Jesus outside the Bible."

Yamauchi smiled and shook his head. "Templeton's archaeologist is simply mistaken," he replied in a dismissive tone, "because we do have very, very important references to Jesus in Josephus and Tacitus.

"The gospels themselves say that many who heard him—even members of his own family—did not believe in Jesus during his lifetime, yet he made such an impression that today Jesus is remembered everywhere, whereas Herod the Great, Pontius Pilate, and other ancient rulers are not as widely known. So he certainly did make an impression on those who believed in him."

He paused, then added, "He did not, of course, among those who did not believe in him."

Testimony by a Traitor

Templeton and Yamauchi had both mentioned Josephus, a first-century historian who's well known among scholars but whose name is unfamiliar to most people today. "Give me some background about him," I said, "and tell me how his testimony provides corroboration concerning Jesus."

"Yes, of course," Yamauchi answered as he crossed his legs and settled deeper into his chair. "Josephus was a very important Jewish historian of the first century. He was born in AD 37, and he wrote most of his four works toward the end of the first century.

"In his autobiography he defended his behavior in the Jewish-Roman War, which took place from AD 66 to 74. You see, he had surrendered to the Roman general Vespasian during the siege of Jotapata, even though many of his colleagues committed suicide rather than give up."

The professor chuckled and said, "Josephus decided it wasn't God's will for him to commit suicide. He then became a defender of the Romans."

Josephus sounded like a colorful character; I wanted more details about him so I could better understand his motivations and prejudices. "Paint me a portrait of him," I said.

"He was a priest, a Pharisee, and he was somewhat egotistical. His most ambitious work was called *The Antiquities*, which was a history of the Jewish people from Creation until his time. He probably completed it in about AD 93.

"As you can imagine from his collaboration with the hated Romans, Josephus was extremely disliked by his fellow Jews. But he became very popular among Christians, because in his writings he refers to James, the brother of Jesus, and to Jesus himself."

Here was our first example of corroboration for Jesus outside the gospels. "Tell me about those references," I said.

Replied Yamauchi, "In *The Antiquities* he describes how a high priest named Ananias took advantage of the death of the Roman governor Festus—who is also mentioned in the New Testament—in order to have James killed."

He leaned over to his bookshelf, pulled out a thick volume, and flipped to a page whose location he seemed to know by heart. "Ah, here it is," he said. "'He convened a meeting of the Sanhedrin and brought before them a man named James, the brother of Jesus, who was called the Christ, and certain others. He accused them of having transgressed the law and delivered them up to be stoned.'[4]

"I know of no scholar," Yamauchi asserted confidently, "who has successfully disputed this passage. L. H. Feldman noted that if this had been a later Christian addition to the text, it would have likely been more laudatory of James. So here you have a reference to the brother of Jesus—who had apparently been converted by the appearance of the risen Christ, if you compare John 7:5 and 1 Corinthians 15:7—and corroboration of the fact that some people considered Jesus to be the Christ, which means 'the Anointed One' or 'Messiah.'"

"There Lived Jesus . . ."

I knew that Josephus had written an even lengthier section about Jesus, which is called the *Testimonium Flavianum*. I knew too that this passage was among the most hotly disputed in ancient literature because on its surface it appears to provide sweeping corroboration of Jesus' life, miracles, death, and resurrection. But is it authentic? Or has it been doctored through the years by people favorable to Jesus?

I asked Yamauchi for his opinion, and it was instantly clear I had tapped into an area of high interest for him. He uncrossed his legs and sat up straight in his chair. "This is a fascinating passage," he said with enthusiasm, leaning forward, book in hand. "But yes, it is controversial." With that he read it to me.

> About this time there lived Jesus, a wise man, if indeed one ought to call him a man. For he was one who wrought surprising feats and was a teacher of such people as accept the truth gladly. He won over many Jews and many of the Greeks. He was the Christ. When Pilate, upon hearing him accused by men of the highest standing among us, had condemned him to be crucified, those who had in the first place come to love him did not give up their affection for him. On the third day he appeared to them restored to life, for the

prophets of God had prophesied these and countless other marvelous things about him. And the tribe of Christians, so called after him, has still to this day not disappeared.[5]

The wealth of corroboration for Jesus was readily evident. "You agreed this was controversial—what have scholars concluded about this passage?" I asked.

"Scholarship has gone through three trends about it," he said. "For obvious reasons, the early Christians thought it was a wonderful and thoroughly authentic attestation of Jesus and his resurrection. They loved it. Then the entire passage was questioned by at least some scholars during the Enlightenment.

"But today there's a remarkable consensus among both Jewish and Christian scholars that the passage as a whole is authentic, although there may be some interpolations."

I raised an eyebrow. "Interpolations—would you define what you mean by that?"

"That means early Christian copyists inserted some phrases that a Jewish writer like Josephus would not have written," Yamauchi said.

He pointed to a sentence in the book. "For instance, the first line says, 'About this time there lived Jesus, a wise man.' That phrase is not normally used of Jesus by Christians, so it seems authentic for Josephus. But the next phrase says, 'if indeed one ought to call him a man.' This implies Jesus was more than human, which appears to be an interpolation."

I nodded to let him know I was following him so far.

"It goes on to say, 'For he was one who wrought surprising feats and was a teacher of such people as accept the truth gladly. He won over many Jews and many of the Greeks.' That seems to be quite in accord with the vocabulary Josephus uses elsewhere, and it's generally considered authentic.

"But then there's this unambiguous statement, 'He was the Christ.' That seems to be an interpolation—"

"Because," I interrupted, "Josephus says in his reference to James that Jesus was '*called* the Christ.'"

"That's right," said Yamauchi. "It's unlikely Josephus would have flatly said Jesus was the Messiah here, when elsewhere he merely said he was *considered* to be the Messiah by his followers.

"The next part of the passage—which talks about Jesus' trial and crucifixion and the fact that his followers still loved him—is unexceptional and considered genuine. Then there's this phrase: 'On the third day he appeared to them restored to life.'

"Again, this is a clear declaration of belief in the resurrection, and thus it's unlikely that Josephus wrote it. So these three elements seem to have been interpolations."

"What's the bottom line?" I asked.

"That the passage in Josephus probably was originally written about Jesus, although without those three points I mentioned. But even so, Josephus corroborates important information about Jesus: that he was the martyred leader of the church in Jerusalem and that he was a wise teacher who had established a wide and lasting following, despite the fact that he had been crucified under Pilate at the instigation of some of the Jewish leaders."

The Importance of Josephus

While these references did offer some important independent verification about Jesus, I wondered why a historian like Josephus wouldn't have said more about such an important figure of the first century. I knew that some skeptics, like Boston University philosopher Michael Martin, have made this same critique.

So I asked for Yamauchi's reaction to this statement by Martin, who doesn't believe Jesus ever lived: "If Jesus did exist, one would have expected Josephus . . . to have said more about him. . . . It is unexpected that Josephus mentioned him . . . in passing while mentioning other Messianic figures and John the Baptist in greater detail."[6]

Yamauchi's response seemed uncharacteristically strong. "From time to time some people have tried to deny the existence of Jesus, but this is really a lost cause," he said with a tone of exasperation. "There is overwhelming evidence that Jesus did exist, and these hypothetical questions are really very vacuous and fallacious.

"But I'd answer by saying this: Josephus was interested in political matters and the struggle against Rome, so for him John the Baptist was more important because he seemed to pose a greater political threat than did Jesus."

I jumped in. "Hold on a second. Aren't there some scholars who have portrayed Jesus as a Zealot or at least sympathetic to the Zealots?" I asked, referring to a first-century revolutionary group that opposed Rome politically.

Yamauchi dismissed the objection with a wave of his hand. "That is a position the gospels themselves do not support," he replied, "because remember, Jesus didn't even object to paying taxes to the Romans. Therefore, because Jesus and his followers didn't pose an immediate political threat, it's certainly understandable that Josephus isn't more interested in this sect—even though in hindsight it turned out to be very important indeed."

"So in your assessment, how significant are these two references by Josephus?"

"Highly significant," Yamauchi replied, "especially since his accounts of the Jewish War have proved to be very accurate; for example, they've been corroborated through archaeological excavations at Masada as well as by historians like Tacitus. He's considered to be a pretty reliable historian, and his mentioning of Jesus is considered extremely important."

"A Most Mischievous Superstition"

Yamauchi had just mentioned the most important Roman historian of the first century, and I wanted to discuss what Tacitus had to say about Jesus and Christianity. "Could you spell out what he corroborates?" I asked.

Yamauchi nodded. "Tacitus recorded what is probably the most important reference to Jesus outside the New Testament," he said. "In AD 115 he explicitly states that Nero persecuted the Christians as scapegoats to divert suspicion away from himself for the great fire that had devastated Rome in AD 64."

Yamauchi stood and walked over to a shelf, scanning it for a certain book. "Ah yes, here it is," he said, withdrawing a thick volume and leafing through it until he found the right passage, which he then read to me.

Nero fastened the guilt and inflicted the most exquisite tortures on a class hated for their abominations, called Christians by the populace. Christus, from whom the name had its origin, suffered the extreme penalty during the reign of Tiberius at the hands of one of our procurators, Pontius Pilatus, and a most mischievous superstition, thus checked for the moment, again broke out not only in Judaea, the first source of the evil, but even in Rome. . . . Accordingly, an arrest was first made of all who pleaded guilty: then, upon their information, an immense multitude was convicted, not so much of the crime of firing the city, as of hatred against mankind.[7]

I was already familiar with that passage, and I was wondering how Yamauchi would respond to an observation by a leading scholar named J. N. D. Anderson. "He speculates that when Tacitus says this 'mischievous superstition' was 'checked for the moment' but later 'again broke out,' he was unconsciously bearing testimony to the belief of early Christians that Jesus had been crucified but then rose from the grave," I said. "Do you agree with him?"

Yamauchi thought for a moment. "This has certainly been the interpretation of some scholars," he replied, seeming to duck my request for his opinion. But then he made a crucial point: "Regardless of whether the passage had this specifically in mind, it does provide us with a very remarkable fact, which is this: Crucifixion was the most abhorrent fate that anyone could undergo, and the fact that there was a movement based on a crucified man has to be explained.

"How can you explain the spread of a religion based on the worship of a man who had suffered the most ignominious death possible? Of course, the Christian answer is that he was resurrected. Others have to come up with some alternative theory if they don't believe that. But none of the alternative views, to my mind, are very persuasive."

I asked him to characterize the weight of Tacitus's writings concerning Jesus.

"This is an important testimony by an unsympathetic witness to the success and spread of Christianity, based on a historical figure—Jesus—who was crucified under Pontius Pilate," he said. "And it's significant that Tacitus reported that an 'immense multitude' held so strongly to their beliefs that they were willing to die rather than recant."

Chanting "As If to a God"

I knew that another Roman, called Pliny the Younger, had also referred to Christianity in his writings. "He corroborated some important matters, too, didn't he?" I asked.

"That's right. He was the nephew of Pliny the Elder, the famous encyclopedist who died in the eruption of Vesuvius in AD 79. Pliny the Younger became governor of Bithynia in northwestern Turkey. Much of his correspondence with his friend, Emperor Trajan, has been preserved to the present time."

Yamauchi pulled out a photocopy of a book page, saying, "In book 10 of these letters he specifically refers to the Christians he has arrested."

I have asked them if they are Christians, and if they admit it, I repeat the question a second and third time, with a warning of the punishment awaiting them. If they persist, I order them to be led away for execution; for, whatever the nature of their admission, I am convinced that their stubbornness and unshakable obstinacy ought not to go unpunished . . . .

They also declared that the sum total of their guilt or error amounted to no more than this: they had met regularly before dawn on a fixed day to chant verses alternately amongst themselves in honor of Christ as if to a god, and also to bind themselves by oath, not for any criminal purpose, but to abstain from theft, robbery, and adultery. . . .

This made me decide it was all the more necessary to extract the truth by torture from two slave-women, whom they called deaconesses. I found nothing but a degenerate sort of cult carried to extravagant lengths.[8]

"How important is this reference?" I asked.

"Very important. It was probably written about AD 111, and it attests to the rapid spread of Christianity, both in the city and in the rural area, among every class of persons, slave women as well as Roman citizens, since he also says that he sends Christians who are Roman citizens to Rome for trial.

"And it talks about the worship of Jesus as God, that Christians maintained high ethical standards, and that they were not easily swayed from their beliefs."

The Day the Earth Went Dark

To me, one of the most problematic references in the New Testament is where the gospel writers claim that the earth went dark during part of the time that Jesus hung on the cross. Wasn't this merely a literary device to stress the significance of the crucifixion, and not a reference to an actual historical occurrence? After all, if darkness had fallen over the earth, wouldn't there be at least some mention of this extraordinary event outside the Bible?

However, Dr. Gary Habermas has written about a historian named Thallus who in AD 52 wrote a history of the eastern Mediterranean world since the Trojan War. Although Thallus's work has been lost, it was quoted by Julius Africanus in about AD 221—and it made reference to the darkness that the gospels had written about![9]

"Could this," I asked, "be independent corroboration of this biblical claim?"

Explained Yamauchi, "In this passage Julius Africanus says, 'Thallus, in the third book of his histories, explains away the darkness as an eclipse of the sun—unreasonably, as it seems to me.'

"So Thallus apparently was saying yes, there had been darkness at the time of the crucifixion, and he speculated it had been caused by an eclipse. Africanus then argues that it couldn't have been an eclipse, given when the crucifixion occurred."

Yamauchi reached over to his desk to retrieve a piece of paper. "Let me quote what scholar Paul Maier said about the darkness in a footnote in his 1968 book *Pontius Pilate*," he said, reading these words:

This phenomenon, evidently, was visible in Rome, Athens, and other Mediterranean cities. According to Tertullian . . . it was a "cosmic" or "world event." Phlegon, a Greek author from Caria writing a chronology soon after 137 AD, reported that in the fourth year of the 202nd Olympiad (i.e., 33 AD) there was "the greatest eclipse of the sun" and that "it became night in the sixth hour of the day [i.e., noon] so that stars even appeared in the heavens. There was a great earthquake in Bithynia, and many things were overturned in Nicaea."[10]

Yamauchi concluded, "So there is, as Paul Maier points out, non-biblical attestation of the darkness that occurred at the time of Jesus' crucifixion. Apparently, some found the need to try to give it a natural explanation by saying it was an eclipse."

A Portrait of Pilate

Yamauchi's mentioning of Pilate reminded me of how some critics have questioned the accuracy of the gospels because of the way they portray this Roman leader. While the New Testament paints him as being vacillating and willing to yield to the pressures of a Jewish mob by executing Jesus, other historical accounts picture him as being obstinate and inflexible.

"Doesn't this represent a contradiction between the Bible and secular historians?" I asked.

"No, it really doesn't," said Yamauchi. "Maier's study of Pilate shows that his protector or patron was Sejanus and that Sejanus fell from power in AD 31 because he was plotting against the emperor."

I was puzzled. "What does that have to do with anything?" I asked.

"Well, this loss would have made Pilate's position very weak in AD 33, which is most likely when Jesus was crucified," the professor responded. "So it would certainly be understandable that Pilate would have been reluctant to offend the Jews at that time and to get into further trouble with the emperor. That means the biblical description is most likely correct."[11]

Other Jewish Accounts

Having talked primarily about Roman corroboration of Jesus, I wanted to turn a corner at this point and discuss whether any other Jewish accounts besides that of Josephus verify anything about Jesus. I asked Yamauchi about references to Jesus in the Talmud, an important Jewish work finished about AD 500 that incorporates the Mishnah, compiled about AD 200.

"Jews, as a whole, did not go into great detail about heretics," he replied. "There are a few passages in the Talmud that mention Jesus, calling him a false messiah who practiced magic and who was justly condemned to death. They also repeat the rumor that Jesus was born of a Roman soldier and Mary, suggesting there was something unusual about his birth."

"So," I said, "in a negative way these Jewish references do corroborate some things about Jesus."

"Yes, that's right," he said. "Professor M. Wilcox put it this way in an article that appeared in a scholarly reference work:"

> The Jewish traditional literature, although it mentions Jesus only quite sparingly (and must in any case be used with caution), supports the gospel claim that he was a healer and miracle-worker, even though it ascribes these activities to sorcery. In addition, it preserves the recollection that he was a teacher, and that he had disciples (five of them), and that at least in the earlier Rabbinic period not all of the sages had finally made up their minds that he was a "heretic" or a "deceiver."[12]

Evidence apart from the Bible

Although we were finding quite a few references to Jesus outside the gospels, I was wondering why there were not even more of them. While I knew that few historical documents from the first century have survived, I asked, "Overall, shouldn't we have expected to find more about Jesus in ancient writings outside the Bible?"

"When people begin religious movements, it's often not until many generations later that people record things about them," Yamauchi said. "But the fact is that we have better historical documentation for Jesus than for the founder of any other ancient religion."

That caught me off guard. "Really?" I said. "Can you elaborate on that?"

"For example, although the Gathas of Zoroaster, about 1000 BC, are believed to be authentic, most of the Zoroastrian scriptures were not put into writing until after the third century AD. The most popular Parsi biography of Zoroaster was written in AD 1278.

"The scriptures of Buddha, who lived in the sixth century BC, were not put into writing until after the Christian era, and the first biography of Buddha was written in the first century AD. Although we have the sayings of Muhammad, who lived from AD 570 to 632, in the Qur'an, his biography was not written until 767—more than a full century after his death.

"So the situation with Jesus is unique—and quite impressive in terms of how much we can learn about him aside from the New Testament."

I wanted to pick up on that theme and summarize what we had gleaned about Jesus so far from nonbiblical sources. "Let's pretend we didn't have any of the New Testament or other Christian writings," I said. "Even without them, what would we be able to conclude about Jesus from ancient non-Christian sources, such as Josephus, the Talmud, Tacitus, Pliny the Younger, and others?"

Yamauchi smiled. "We would still have a considerable amount of important historical evidence; in fact, it would provide a kind of outline for the life of Jesus," he said.

Then he went on, raising a finger to emphasize each point. "We would know that first, Jesus was a Jewish teacher; second, many people believed that he performed healings and exorcisms; third, some people believed he was the Messiah; fourth, he was rejected by the Jewish leaders; fifth, he was crucified under Pontius Pilate in the reign of Tiberius; sixth, despite this shameful death, his followers, who believed that he was still alive, spread beyond Palestine so that there were multitudes of them in Rome by AD 64; and seventh, all kinds of people from the cities and countryside—men and women, slave and free—worshiped him as God."

This was indeed an impressive amount of independent corroboration. And not only can the contours of Jesus' life be reconstructed apart from the Bible, but there's even more that can be gleaned about him from material so old that it actually predates the gospels themselves.

Corroborating Early Details

The apostle Paul never met Jesus prior to Jesus' death, but he said he did encounter the resurrected Christ and later consulted with some of the eyewitnesses to make sure he was preaching the same message they were. Because he began writing his New Testament letters years before the gospels were written down, they contain extremely early reports concerning Jesus—so early that nobody can make a credible claim that they had been seriously distorted by legendary development.

"Luke Timothy Johnson, the scholar from Emory University, contends that Paul's letters represent 'valuable external verification' of the 'antiquity and ubiquity' of the traditions about Jesus,"[13] I said to Yamauchi. "Do you agree with him?"

We had been talking for quite a while. Yamauchi stood briefly to stretch his legs before settling back down. "There's no question that Paul's writings are the earliest in the New Testament," he said, "and that they do make some very significant references to the life of Jesus."

"Can you spell them out?" I asked.

"Well, he refers to the fact that Jesus was a descendant of David, that he was the Messiah, that he was betrayed, that he was tried, crucified for our sins, and buried, and that he rose again on the third day and was seen by many people—including James, the brother of Jesus who hadn't believed in him prior to his crucifixion.

"It's also interesting that Paul doesn't mention some of the things that are highly significant in the gospels—for instance, Jesus' parables and miracles—but he focuses on Jesus' atoning death and resurrection. Those, for Paul, were the most important things about Jesus—and indeed they transformed Paul from being a persecutor of Christians into becoming history's foremost Christian missionary, who was willing to go through all sorts of hardships and deprivation because of his faith.

"Paul also corroborates some important aspects of the character of Jesus—his humility, his obedience, his love for sinners, and so forth. He calls Christians to have the mind of Christ in the second chapter of Philippians. This is a famous passage in which Paul is probably quoting from an early Christian hymn about the emptying of Christ, who was equal to God yet took the form of a man, of a slave, and suffered the extreme penalty, the crucifixion. So Paul's letters are an important witness to the deity of Christ—he calls Jesus 'the Son of God' and 'the image of God.'"

I interrupted by saying, "The fact that Paul, who came from a monotheistic Jewish background, worshiped Jesus as God is extremely significant, isn't it?"

"Yes," he said, "and it undermines a popular theory that the deity of Christ was later imported into Christianity by Gentile beliefs. It's just not so. Even Paul at this very early date was worshiping Jesus as God.

"I have to say that all this corroboration by Paul is of the utmost importance. And we have other early letters by the eyewitnesses James and Peter, too. James, for instance, has recollections of Jesus' Sermon on the Mount."

Truly Raised from the Dead

We also have volumes of writings by the "apostolic fathers," who were the earliest Christian writers after the New Testament. They authored the Epistle of Clement of Rome, the Epistles of Ignatius, the Epistle of Polycarp, the Epistle of Barnabas, and others. In many places these writings attest to the basic facts about Jesus, particularly his teachings, his crucifixion, his resurrection, and his divine nature.

"Which of these writings do you consider most significant?" I asked.

Yamauchi pondered the question. While he didn't name the one he thought was most significant, he did cite the seven letters of Ignatius as being among the most important of the writings of the apostolic fathers. Ignatius, the bishop of Antioch in Syria, was martyred during the reign of Trajan before AD 117.

"What is significant about Ignatius," said Yamauchi, "is that he emphasized both the deity of Jesus and the humanity of Jesus, as against the Docetic heresy, which denied that Jesus was really human. He also stressed the historical underpinnings of Christianity; he wrote in one letter, on his way to being executed, that Jesus was truly persecuted under Pilate, was truly crucified, was truly raised from the dead, and that those who believe in him would be raised, too."[14]

Put all this together—Josephus, the Roman historians and officials, the Jewish writings, the letters of Paul and the apostolic fathers—and you've got persuasive evidence that corroborates all the essentials found in the biographies of Jesus. Even if you were to throw away every last copy of the gospels, you'd still have a picture of Jesus that's extremely compelling—in fact, it's a portrait of the unique Son of God.

I stood and thanked Yamauchi for sharing his time and expertise. "I know there's a lot more we could talk about, since entire books have been written on this topic," I said. "But before we end, I'd like to ask you one last question. A personal one, if that's all right."

The professor rose to his feet. "Yes, that's fine," he said.

I glanced around his modest office, which was filled to the brim with books and manuscripts, records and journals, computer disks and papers, all products of a lifetime of scholarly research into a world of long ago.

"You've spent forty years studying ancient history and archaeology," I said. "What has been the result in your own spiritual life? Have your studies bolstered or weakened your faith in Jesus Christ?"

He looked down at the floor momentarily, then raised his eyes and looked squarely into mine. He said in a firm but sincere voice, "There's no question—my studies have greatly strengthened and enriched my spiritual life. They have given me a better understanding of the culture and historical context of the events.

"This doesn't mean that I don't recognize that there are some issues that still remain; within this lifetime we will not have full knowledge. But these issues don't even begin to undermine my faith in the essential trustworthiness of the gospels and the rest of the New Testament.

"I think the alternative explanations, which try to account for the spread of Christianity through sociological or psychological reasons, are very weak." He shook his head. "Very weak."

Then he added, "For me, the historical evidence has reinforced my commitment to Jesus Christ as the Son of God who loves us and died for us and was raised from the dead. It's that simple."

Truth That Sets Us Free

As I emerged from Yamauchi's building into a sea of college students scurrying from place to place in order to make their next class, I reflected on how satisfying my drive to tiny Oxford, Ohio, had been. I came seeking corroboration for Jesus, and I walked away with a rich reservoir of material affirming every major aspect of his life, miracles, deity, and victory over death.

I knew that our brief conversation had only scratched the surface. Under my arm I was carrying *The Verdict of History*, which I had reread in preparation for my interview.[15] In it, historian Gary Habermas details a total of thirty-nine ancient sources documenting the life of Jesus, from which he enumerates more than one hundred reported facts concerning Jesus' life, teachings, crucifixion, and resurrection.[16]

What's more, twenty-four of the sources cited by Habermas, including seven secular sources and several of the earliest creeds of the church, specifically concern the divine nature of Jesus. "These creeds reveal that the church did not simply teach Jesus' deity a generation later, as is so often repeated in contemporary theology, because this doctrine is definitely present in the earliest church," Habermas writes. His conclusion: "The best explanation for these creeds is that they properly represent Jesus' own teachings."[17]

That is stunning corroboration for the most important assertion by the most influential individual who has ever lived.

I zipped up my coat as I headed for my car. Glancing back one more time, I saw the October sun illuminating the stone inscription I had first noticed when I walked onto the campus of this thoroughly secular university: "Ye shall know the truth, and the truth will make you free."

Deliberations
Questions for Reflection or Group Study

1. Is there an incident in your life in which you doubted someone's story until he or she offered some corroborating evidence? How was that experience similar to learning about the kind of corroborative evidence that Yamauchi presented?

2. What do you consider to be the most persuasive corroboration that Yamauchi talked about? Why?

3. Ancient sources say that early Christians clung to their beliefs rather than disavow them in the face of torture. Why do you think they had such strongly held conviction?

For Further Evidence
More Resources on This Topic

Bruce, F. F. *Jesus and Christian Origins Outside the New Testament.* Grand Rapids: Eerdmans, 1974.

France, R. T. *The Evidence for Jesus.* Vancouver, Canada: Regent College Publishing, 2006.

Habermas, Gary. *The Historical Jesus: Ancient Evidence for the Life of Christ.* Joplin, MO: College Press, 1996.

McDowell, Josh, and Bill Wilson. *He Walked Among Us.* Nashville: Thomas Nelson, 1994.

Schäfer, Peter. *Jesus in the Talmud.* Princeton, NJ: Princeton University Press, 2009.

Van Voorst, Robert E. *Jesus Outside the New Testament.* Grand Rapids: Eerdmans, 2000.

Yamauchi, Edwin M. "Jesus Outside the New Testament: What Is the Evidence?" In *Jesus Under Fire*, Michael J. Wilkins and J. P. Moreland, eds., 207–230. Grand Rapids: Zondervan, 1995.

CHAPTER 5

The Scientific Evidence

Does Archaeology Confirm or Contradict Jesus' Biographies?

There was something surreal about my lunch with Dr. Jeffrey Mac-Donald. There he was, casually munching on a tuna fish sandwich and potato chips in a conference room of a North Carolina courthouse, making upbeat comments and generally enjoying himself. In a nearby room a dozen jurors were taking a break after hearing gruesome evidence that MacDonald had brutally murdered his wife and two young daughters.

As we were finishing our meal, I couldn't restrain myself from asking MacDonald the obvious questions. "How can you act as if nothing is wrong?" I said, my voice mixed with astonishment and indignation. "Aren't you the slightest bit concerned that those jurors are going to find you guilty?"

MacDonald casually waved his half-eaten sandwich in the general direction of the jury room. "Them?" he chortled. "They'll never convict me!"

Then, apparently realizing how cynical those words sounded, he quickly added, "I'm innocent, you know."

That was the last time I ever heard him laugh. Within days the former Green Beret and emergency room physician was found guilty of stabbing to death his wife, Colette, and his daughters, Kimberly, age five, and Kristen, age two. He was promptly sentenced to life in prison and carted off in handcuffs.

MacDonald, whose story was masterfully recounted by Joe McGinniss in the bestseller and TV movie *Fatal Vision*, was cocky enough to think that his alibi would help him get away with murder.

He had told investigators that he was asleep on the couch when drug-crazed hippies awakened him in the middle of the night. He said he fought them off, getting stabbed and knocked unconscious in the process. When he awakened, he found his family slaughtered.

Detectives were skeptical from the start. The living room showed few signs of a life-and-death struggle. MacDonald's wounds were superficial. Though he had poor eyesight, he was somehow able to provide detailed descriptions of his attackers even though he had not been wearing his glasses.

However, skepticism alone doesn't win convictions; that requires hard evidence. In MacDonald's case detectives relied on scientific proof to untangle his web of lies and convict him of the slayings.

There's a wide variety of scientific evidence that's commonly used in trials, ranging from DNA typing to forensic anthropology to toxicology. In MacDonald's case it was serology (blood evidence) and trace evidence that dispatched him to the penitentiary.

In an extraordinary—and for prosecutors, fortuitous—coincidence, each member of MacDonald's family had a different blood type. By analyzing where bloodstains were found, investigators were able to reconstruct the sequence of events that deadly evening—and it directly contradicted MacDonald's version of what happened.

Scientific study of tiny blue pajama threads, which were found scattered in various locations, also refuted his alibi. And microscopic analysis demonstrated that holes in his pajamas could not have been made, as he claimed, by an ice pick wielded by the home invaders. In short, it was FBI technicians in white lab coats who were really behind MacDonald's conviction.[1]

Scientific evidence can also make important contributions to the question of whether the New Testament accounts of Jesus are accurate. While serology and toxicology aren't able to shed any light on the issue, another category of scientific proof—the discipline of archaeology— has great bearing on the reliability of the gospels.

Sometimes called the study of durable rubbish, archaeology involves the uncovering of artifacts, architecture, art, coins, monuments, documents, and other remains of ancient cultures. Experts study these relics to learn what life was like in the days when Jesus walked the dusty roads of ancient Palestine.

Hundreds of archaeological findings from the first century have been unearthed, and I was curious: Did they undermine or undergird the eyewitness stories about Jesus? At the same time, my curiosity was tempered by skepticism. I have heard too many Christians make exorbitant claims that archaeology can prove a lot more than it really can. I wasn't interested in more of the same.

So I went on a quest for a recognized authority who has personally dug among the ruins of the Middle East, who has an encyclopedic knowledge of ancient findings, and who possesses enough scientific restraint to acknowledge the limits of archaeology while at the same time explaining how it can illuminate life in the first century.

THE FOURTH INTERVIEW:
John McRay, PhD

When scholars and students study archaeology, many turn to John McRay's thorough and dispassionate 432-page textbook *Archaeology and the New Testament*. When the Arts and Entertainment Television Network wanted to ensure the accuracy of its *"Mysteries of the Bible"* program, they called McRay as well. And when *National Geographic* needed a scientist who could explain the intricacies of the biblical world, again the phone rang in McRay's office at well-respected Wheaton College in suburban Chicago.

Having studied at Hebrew University, the École Biblique et Archéologique Française in Jerusalem, Vanderbilt University Divinity School, and the University of Chicago (where he earned his doctorate in 1967), McRay was a professor of New Testament and archaeology at Wheaton for more than fifteen years. His articles have appeared in seventeen encyclopedias and dictionaries, his research has been featured in the *Bulletin of the Near East Archaeology Society* and other academic journals, and he has presented twenty-nine scholarly papers at professional societies.

McRay is also a former research associate and trustee of the W. F. Albright Institute of Archaeological Research in Jerusalem; a former trustee of the American Schools of Oriental Research; a trustee of the Near East Archaeological Society; and a member of the editorial boards of *Archaeology in the Biblical World* and the *Bulletin for Biblical Research*, which is published by the Institute for Biblical Research.

As much as McRay enjoys writing and teaching about the ancient world, he relishes opportunities to personally explore archaeological digs. He supervised excavating teams at Caesarea, Sepphoris, and Herodium, all in Israel, over an eight-year period. He has studied Roman archaeological sites in England and Wales, analyzed digs in Greece, and retraced much of the apostle Paul's journeys.

At age sixty-six, McRay's hair is turning silvery and his glasses have become thicker, but he still exudes an air of adventure. Over the desk in his office—and in fact also over his bed at home—is a detailed horizontal photograph of Jerusalem. "I live in the shadow of it," he remarked, a sense of longing in his voice, as he pointed out specific locations of excavations and significant findings.

His office features the kind of cozy couch you'd find on the front porch of a country home. I settled into it while McRay, casually dressed in an open-necked shirt and a sports jacket that looked comfortably worn, leaned back in his desk chair.

Seeking to test whether he would overstate the influence of archaeology, I decided to open our interview by asking him what it *can't* tell us about the reliability of the New Testament. After all, as McRay notes in his textbook, even if archaeology can establish that the cities of Medina and Mecca existed in western Arabia during the sixth and seventh centuries, that doesn't prove that Muhammad lived there or that the Qur'an is true.

"Archaeology has made some important contributions," he began, speaking in a drawl he picked up as a child in southeastern Oklahoma, "but it certainly can't prove whether the New Testament is the Word of God. If we dig in Israel and find ancient sites that are consistent with where the Bible said we'd find them, that shows that its history and geography are accurate. However, it doesn't confirm that what Jesus Christ said is right. Spiritual truths cannot be proved or disproved by archaeological discoveries."

As an analogy, he offered the story of Heinrich Schliemann, who searched for Troy in an effort to prove the historical accuracy of Homer's *Iliad*. "He did find Troy," McRay observed with a gentle smile, "but that didn't prove the *Iliad* was true. It was merely accurate in a particular geographical reference."

Once we had set some boundaries for what archaeology can't establish, I was anxious to begin exploring what it can tell us about the New Testament. I decided to launch into this topic by making an observation that grew out of my experience as an investigative journalist with a legal background.

Digging for the Truth

In trying to determine if a witness is being truthful, journalists and lawyers will test all the elements of his or her testimony that can be tested. If this investigation reveals that the person was wrong in those details, this casts considerable doubt on the veracity of his or her entire story. However, if the minutiae check out, this is some indication—not conclusive proof but some evidence—that maybe the witness is being reliable in his or her overall account.

For instance, if a man were telling about a trip he took from St. Louis to Chicago, and he mentioned that he had stopped in Springfield, Illinois, to see the movie *Titanic* at the Odeon Theater and that he had eaten a large Clark bar he bought at the concession counter, investigators could determine whether such a theater exists in Springfield as well as if it was showing this particular film and selling this specific brand and size of candy bar at the time he said he was there. If their findings contradict what the person claimed, this seriously tarnishes his trustworthiness. If the details check out, this doesn't prove that his entire story is true, but it does enhance his reputation for being accurate.

In a sense, this is what archaeology accomplishes. The premise is that if an ancient historian's incidental details check out to be accurate time after time, this increases our confidence in other material that the historian wrote but that cannot be as readily cross-checked.

So I asked McRay for his professional opinion. "Does archaeology affirm or undermine the New Testament when it checks out the details in those accounts?"

McRay was quick to answer. "Oh, there's no question that the credibility of the New Testament is enhanced," he said, "just as the credibility of any ancient document is enhanced when you excavate and find that the author was accurate in talking about a particular place or event."

As an example, he brought up his own digs in Caesarea on the coast of Israel, where he and others excavated the harbor of Herod the Great.

"For a long time people questioned the validity of a statement by Josephus, the first-century historian, that this harbor was as large as the one at Piraeus, which is a major harbor of Athens. People thought Josephus was wrong, because when you see the stones above the surface of the water in the contemporary harbor, it's not very big.

"But when we began to do underwater excavation, we found that the harbor extended far out into the water underground, that it had fallen down, and that its total dimensions were indeed comparable to the harbor at Piraeus. So it turns out Josephus was right after all. This was one more bit of evidence that Josephus knew what he was talking about."

So what about the New Testament writers? Did they really know what they were talking about? I wanted to put that issue to the test in my next line of questioning.

Luke's Accuracy As a Historian

The physician and historian Luke authored both the gospel bearing his name and the book of Acts, which together constitute about one-quarter of the entire New Testament. Consequently, a critical issue is whether Luke was a historian who could be trusted to get things right. "When archaeologists check out the details of what he wrote," I said, "do they find that he was careful or sloppy?"

"The general consensus of both liberal and conservative scholars is that Luke is very accurate as a historian," McRay replied. "He's erudite, he's eloquent, his Greek approaches classical quality, he writes as an educated man, and archaeological discoveries are showing over and over again that Luke is accurate in what he has to say."

In fact, he added, there have been several instances, similar to the story about the harbor, in which scholars initially thought Luke was wrong in a particular reference, only to have later discoveries confirm that he was correct in what he wrote.

For instance, in Luke 3:1 he refers to Lysanias being the tetrarch of Abilene in about AD 27. For years scholars pointed to this as evidence that Luke didn't know what he was talking about, since everybody knew that Lysanias was not a tetrarch but rather the ruler of Chalcis half a century earlier. If Luke can't get that basic fact right, they suggested, nothing he has written can be trusted.

That's when archaeology stepped in. "An inscription was later found from the time of Tiberius, from AD 14 to 37, which names Lysanias as tetrarch in Abila near Damascus—just as Luke had written," McRay explained. "It turned out there had been two government officials named Lysanias! Once more, Luke was shown to be exactly right."

Another example is Luke's reference in Acts 17:6 to "politarchs," which is translated as "city officials" by the NIV, in the city of Thessalonica. "For a long time people thought Luke was mistaken, because no evidence of the term 'politarchs' had been found in any ancient Roman documents," McRay said.

"However, an inscription on a first-century arch was later found that begins, 'In the time of the politarchs . . .' You can go to the British Museum and see it for yourself. And then, lo and behold, archaeologists have found more than thirty-five inscriptions that mention politarchs, several of these in Thessalonica from the same period Luke was referring to. Once again, the critics were wrong and Luke was shown to be right."

An objection popped into my mind. "Yes, but in his gospel Luke says that Jesus was walking *into* Jericho when he healed the blind man Bartimaeus, while Mark says he was coming *out* of Jericho.[2] Isn't this a clear-cut contradiction that casts doubt on the reliability of the New Testament?"

McRay wasn't stung by the directness of my question. "Not at all," came his response. "It only appears to be a contradiction because you're thinking in contemporary terms, in which cities are built and stay put. But that wasn't necessarily the case long ago.

"Jericho was in at least four different locations as much as a quarter of a mile apart in ancient times. The city was destroyed and resettled near another water supply or a new road or nearer a mountain or whatever. The point is, you can be coming out of one site where Jericho existed and be going into another one, like moving from one part of suburban Chicago to another part of suburban Chicago."

"What you're saying is that both Luke and Mark could be right?" I asked.

"That's correct. Jesus could have been going out of one area of Jericho and into another at the same time."

Again archaeology had answered another challenge to Luke. And given the large portion of the New Testament written by him, it's extremely significant that Luke has been established to be a scrupulously accurate historian, even in the smallest details. One prominent archaeologist carefully examined Luke's references to thirty-two countries, fifty-four cities, and nine islands, finding not a single mistake.[3]

Here's the bottom line: "If Luke was so painstakingly accurate in his historical reporting," said one book on the topic, "on what logical basis may we assume he was credulous or inaccurate in his reporting of matters that were far more important, not only to him but to others as well?"[4]

Matters, for example, like the resurrection of Jesus, the most influential evidence of his deity, which Luke says was firmly established by "many convincing proofs" (Acts 1:3).

The Reliability of John and Mark

Archaeology may support the credibility of Luke, but he isn't the only author of the New Testament. I wondered what scientists would have to say about John, whose gospel was sometimes considered suspect because he talked about locations that couldn't be verified. Some scholars charged that since he failed to get these basic details straight, John must not have been close to the events of Jesus' life.

That conclusion, however, has been turned upside down in recent years. "There have been several discoveries that have shown John to be very accurate," McRay pointed out. "For example, John 5:1–15 records how Jesus healed an invalid by the Pool of Bethesda. John provides the detail that the pool had five porticoes. For a long time people cited this as an example of John being inaccurate, because no such place had been found.

"But more recently the Pool of Bethesda has been excavated—it lies maybe forty feet below ground—and sure enough, there were five porticoes, which means colonnaded porches or walkways, exactly as John had described. And you have other discoveries—the Pool of Siloam from John 9:7, Jacob's Well from John 4:12, the probable location of the Stone Pavement near the Jaffa Gate where Jesus appeared before Pilate in John 19:13, even Pilate's own identity—all of which have lent historical credibility to John's gospel."

"So this challenges the allegation that the gospel of John was written so long after Jesus that it can't possibly be accurate," I said.

"Most definitely," he replied.

In fact, McRay reiterated what Dr. Bruce Metzger had told me about archaeologists finding a fragment of a copy of John 18 that leading papyrologists have dated to about AD 125. By demonstrating that copies of John existed this early and as far away as Egypt, archaeology has effectively dismantled speculation that John had been composed well into the second century, too long after Jesus' life to be reliable.

Other scholars have attacked the gospel of Mark, generally considered the first account of Jesus' life to be written. Atheist Michael Martin accuses Mark of being ignorant about Palestinian geography, which he says demonstrates that he could not have lived in the region at the time of Jesus. Specifically he cites Mark 7:31: "Then Jesus left the vicinity of Tyre and went through Sidon, down to the Sea of Galilee and into the region of the Decapolis."

"It has been pointed out," said Martin, "that given these directions Jesus would have been traveling directly *away* from the Sea of Galilee."[5]

When I posed Martin's critique to McRay, he furrowed his brow and then went into a flurry of activity, pulling a Greek version of Mark off his shelf, grabbing reference books, and unfolding large maps of ancient Palestine.

"What these critics seem to be assuming is that Jesus is getting in his car and zipping around on an interstate, but he obviously wasn't," he said.

Reading the text in the original language, taking into account the mountainous terrain and probable roads of the region, and considering the loose way "Decapolis" was used to refer to a confederation of ten cities that varied from time to time, McRay traced a logical route on the map that corresponded precisely with Mark's description.

"When everything is put into the appropriate context," he concluded, "there's no problem with Mark's account."

Again archaeological insights had helped explain what appeared at first to be a sticking point in the New Testament. I asked McRay a broad question about that: Had he ever encountered an archaeological finding that blatantly contravened a New Testament reference?

He shook his head. "Archaeology has not produced anything that is unequivocally a contradiction to the Bible," he replied with confidence. "On the contrary, as we've seen, there have been many opinions of skeptical scholars that have become codified into 'fact' over the years but that archaeology has shown to be wrong."

Still, there were some matters I needed to resolve. I pulled out my notes and got ready to challenge McRay with three long-standing riddles that I thought archaeology might have some trouble explaining.

PUZZLE 1: The Census

The birth narratives of Jesus claim that Mary and Joseph were required by a census to return to Joseph's hometown of Bethlehem. "Let me be blunt: this seems absurd on the face of it," I said. "How could the government possibly force all its citizens to return to their birthplace? Is there any archaeological evidence whatsoever that this kind of census ever took place?"

McRay calmly pulled out a copy of his book. "Actually, the discovery of ancient census forms has shed quite a bit of light on this practice," he said as he leafed through the pages. Finding the reference he was searching for, he quoted from an official governmental order dated AD 104.

> Gaius Vibius Maximus, Prefect of Egypt [says]: Seeing that the time has come for the house to house census, it is necessary to compel all those who for any cause whatsoever are residing out of their provinces to *return to their own homes*, that they may both carry out the regular order of the census and may also attend diligently to the cultivation of their allotments.[6]

"As you can see," he said as he closed the book, "that practice is confirmed by this document, even though this particular manner of counting people might seem odd to you. And another papyrus, this one from AD 48, indicates that the entire family was involved in the census."

What's more, scholars have pointed out that to avoid inflaming the population, Romans were known to sometimes let a census be taken on the basis of local customs. In the Jewish culture, this would mean that Mary and Joseph would need to register in their *ancestral* home.[7]

This, however, did not entirely dispose of the issue. Luke said the census that brought Joseph and Mary to Bethlehem was conducted when Quirinius was governing Syria and during the reign of Herod the Great.

"That poses a significant problem," I pointed out, "because Herod died in 4 BC, and Quirinius didn't begin ruling Syria until AD 6, conducting the census soon after that. There's a big gap there; how can you deal with such a major discrepancy in the dates?"

McRay knew I was raising an issue that scholars have wrestled with for years. He responded by telling me about a recent report by an archaeologist that he had found very small writings, or "micrographic" letters, on coins that showed Quirinius was a ruler in Syria and Cilicia from 11 BC until after Herod's death. This would mean there were two different officials named Quirinius, and the census would have taken place under an earlier one during the reign of Herod.

This sounded a bit speculative to me, but rather than bog down the conversation, I decided to mentally file this issue away for later analysis.

As it turned out, the archaeologist referenced by McRay died shortly after McRay and I spoke. He had never written any peer-reviewed articles on his finding, and nobody has replicated his discovery. In the end, experts dismissed his claim.

When I did some additional research, I found that Sir William Ramsay, the late archaeologist and professor at both Oxford and Cambridge Universities in England, believed that Quirinius was a ruler in Syria on two separate occasions, which would cover the time period of an earlier census, which Ramsay dated around 8/7 BC.[8]

However, this earlier census is not mentioned anywhere in the historical record. Still, this would not be surprising if there had been no disturbances that warranted the attention of Josephus or other ancient historians.

Questions have also been raised about the idea that the Romans would have ordered a census in Syria when it wasn't yet fully enfolded into the Roman Empire. But there is precedent for Rome ordering censuses in client states.[9]

Harold W. Hoehner, who earned his doctorate at Cambridge, pointed out that Herod was ill and came into conflict with the Roman emperor Augustus in 8/7 BC. "With such instability and such a bad state of health, it would have been an opportune time for Augustus to have had a census taken in order to assess the situation before Herod's death," he said. "Therefore, a census within the last year or two of Herod's reign would have been reasonable, and in fact, most probable."[10]

Said New Testament professor Darrell L. Bock: "A census in Herod's time requiring a journey by Joseph and Mary is a possibility based upon what we know of Roman practice. That no other source mentions such a census is not a significant problem, since many ancient sources refer to events that are not corroborated elsewhere and since Luke is found to be trustworthy in his handling of facts that one can check. Since the details of this census fit into general Roman tax policy, there is no need to question that it could have occurred in the time of Herod."[11]

But what about Luke's claim concerning Quirinius? Some scholars have pointed out that Luke's text could be translated, "This census took place *before* Quirinius was governing Syria," which would resolve the problem.[12] Said Hoehner: "This gives a good sense to the passage at hand,"[13] although some scholars have disagreed with this rendering.

Other possibilities have been discussed. "The solutions to the Quirinius problem are varied," Bock said. "No candidate is so manifestly superior that it can be regarded as the solution. What one faces is a variety of solutions, any of which could be correct."[14]

But one other fact seemed especially persuasive to me: Luke could not have been referencing the AD 6 census because this would mean he would be contradicting himself.

How? Hoehner points out that Luke was well aware of the AD 6 census, which he references in Acts 5:37.[15] But Luke was also aware that Jesus could not have been born that late, since he and Matthew concur the birth occurred under Herod (see Luke 1:5 and Matthew 2:1). Further, Luke said Jesus was about thirty years old when he started his ministry (Luke 3:23). This would have been shortly after the start of John the Baptist's ministry, which Luke dates around AD 27 to 29 (see Luke 3:1–2).[16]

The implication is clear: if the census had been in AD 6, Jesus would only have been twenty-one to twenty-three years old when he started his ministry. But Luke knew he was older than that. Therefore, said Hoehner, Luke could not have been referencing the AD 6 census when he wrote about Jesus' birth. "Certainly," he said, "Luke was conscious of chronology in his works."[17]

That made sense to me. Luke was an astute historian who would not have made such a fundamental error of contradicting himself. There must have been an earlier census that prompted the journey of Joseph and Mary—a census that would have occurred during the reign of Herod, as Luke reported.

After assessing the various scenarios, Bock concluded: "It is clear that the relegation of [the census account in Luke] to the category of historical error is premature and erroneous."[18]

PUZZLE 2: Existence of Nazareth

Many Christians are unaware that skeptics have been asserting for a long time that Nazareth never existed during the time when the New Testament says Jesus spent his childhood there.

In an article called "Where Jesus Never Walked," atheist Frank Zindler noted that Nazareth is not mentioned in the Old Testament, by the apostle Paul, by the Talmud (although sixty-three other Galilean towns are cited), or by Josephus (who listed forty-five other villages and cities of Galilee, including Japha, which was located just over a mile from present-day Nazareth). No ancient historians or geographers mention Nazareth before the beginning of the fourth century.[19] The name first appears in Jewish literature in a poem written about the seventh century AD.[20]

This absence of evidence paints a suspicious picture. So I put the issue directly to McRay: "Is there any archaeological confirmation that Nazareth was in existence during the first century?"

This issue wasn't new to McRay. "Dr. James Strange of the University of South Florida is an expert on this area, and he describes Nazareth as being a very small place, about sixty acres, with a maximum population of about four hundred and eighty at the beginning of the first century."[21]

In 1962, archaeologists reported the discovery of a list in Aramaic describing the twenty-four "courses," or families, of priests who were relocated after the Jerusalem temple was destroyed in AD 70. One course was moved to Nazareth, which would show that this village must have been in existence. However, other archaeologists later raised questions about this finding.

McRay also mentioned that there have been archaeological digs that uncovered first-century tombs in the vicinity of Nazareth. Two tombs contained objects such as pottery lamps, glass vessels, and vases from the first, third, or fourth centuries.

McRay picked up a copy of a book by archaeologist Jack Finegan, published by Princeton University Press. He leafed through it, then read Finegan's analysis: "From the tombs . . . it can be concluded that Nazareth was a strongly Jewish settlement in the Roman period."[22]

McRay looked up at me. "There has been discussion about the location of some sites from the first century, such as exactly where Jesus' tomb is situated, but among archaeologists there has never really been a big doubt about the location of Nazareth. The burden of proof ought to be on those who dispute its existence."

That burden became more difficult in subsequent years after the discovery of two houses from first-century Nazareth. In 2006, the Nazareth Archaeological Project began excavating beneath the Sisters of Nazareth Convent, a location known since 1880. The director of the project, Ken Dark of the University of Reading, described the remains of a first-century home that was found. "Taken together, the walls conformed to the plan of a so-called courtyard house, one of the typical architectural forms of Early Roman-period settlements in the Galilee," Dark said.[23]

Archaeologists found doors and windows, cooking pottery, and a spindle whorl used in spinning thread. Fragments of limestone vessels, which Jews believed could not become impure, were also found, suggesting a Jewish family lived there.

"The house must date from the first century AD or earlier," Dark concluded. "No stratified pottery earlier or later than the Early Roman period was discovered in layers associated with the house."[24]

Another first-century house, similar in structure, was discovered nearby in an excavation by Yardenna Alexandre of the Israel Antiquities Authority in 2009.[25]

"Such evidence would be consistent with what archaeologists of the Roman provinces elsewhere conventionally term a 'small town'," Dark said. "The evidence suggests that Jesus' boyhood was spent in a conservative Jewish community that had little contact with Hellenistic or Roman culture."

Some people have wondered whether Dark's team may have actually found the very home where Jesus grew up. While clues from later centuries suggest Byzantines may have believed that this was the house where Jesus spent his childhood, Dark concluded that "it is impossible to say on archaeological grounds. On the other hand, there is no good archaeological reason why such an identification should be discounted."

Regardless, the case for the existence of Nazareth in the first century has gotten stronger over the years.

PUZZLE 3: Slaughter at Bethlehem

The gospel of Matthew paints a grisly scene: Herod the Great, the king of Judea, feeling threatened by the birth of a baby whom he feared would eventually seize his throne, dispatches his troops to murder all the children under the age of two in Bethlehem. Warned by an angel, however, Joseph escapes to Egypt with Mary and Jesus. Only after Herod dies do they return to settle in Nazareth, the entire episode having fulfilled three ancient prophecies about the Messiah. (See Matt. 2:13–23.)

The problem: There is no independent confirmation that this mass murder ever took place. There's nothing in the writings of Josephus or other historians. There's no archaeological support. There are no records or documents.

"Certainly an event of this magnitude would have been noticed by someone other than Matthew," I insisted. "With the complete absence of any historical or archaeological corroboration, isn't it logical to conclude that this slaughter never occurred?"

"I can see why you'd say that," McRay replied, "since today an event like that would probably be splashed all over CNN and the rest of the news media."

I agreed. In fact, in 1997 and 1998 there was a steady stream of news accounts about Muslim extremists repeatedly staging commando raids and slaying virtually entire villages, including women and children, in Algeria. The entire world was taking notice.

"But," added McRay, "you have to put yourself back in the first century and keep a few things in mind. First, Bethlehem was probably no bigger than Nazareth, so how many babies of that age would there be in a village of five hundred or six hundred people? Not thousands, not hundreds, although certainly a few.

"Second, Herod the Great was a bloodthirsty king: he killed members of his own family; he executed lots of people who he thought might challenge him. So the fact that he killed some babies in Bethlehem is not going to captivate the attention of people in the Roman world.

"And third, there was no television, no radio, no newspapers. It would have taken a long time for word of this to get out, especially from such a minor village way in the back hills of nowhere, and historians had much bigger stories to write about."

As a journalist, this was still hard to fathom. "This just wasn't much of a story?" I asked, a bit incredulous.

"I don't think it was, at least not in those days," he said. "A madman killing everybody who seems to be a potential threat to him—that was business as usual for Herod. Later, of course, as Christianity developed, this incident became more important, but I would have been surprised if this had made a big splash back then."

Maybe so, but this was difficult to imagine for a journalist who was trained to sniff out news in a highly technological age of rapid and worldwide communications. At the same time, I had to acknowledge that from what I knew of the bloody landscape of ancient Palestine, McRay's explanation did seem reasonable.

This left one other area I wanted to inquire about. And to me, it was the most fascinating of all.

Riddle of the Dead Sea Scrolls

Admittedly, there is an allure to archaeology. Ancient tombs, cryptic inscriptions etched in stone or scratched onto papyrus, bits of broken pottery, worn coins—they're tantalizing clues for an inveterate investigator. But few vestiges of the past have generated as much intrigue as the Dead Sea Scrolls, hundreds of manuscripts dating from 250 BC to AD 68 that were found in caves twenty miles east of Jerusalem in 1947. They apparently had been hidden by a strict sect of Jews called the Essenes before the Romans destroyed their settlement.

Some bizarre claims have been made about the scrolls, including John Marco Allegro's absurd book in which he theorized that Christianity emerged from a fertility cult in which adherents tripped out on hallucinogenic mushrooms![26] In a more legitimate but nevertheless much-questioned assertion, papyri expert Jose O'Callaghan said one Dead Sea fragment is part of the earliest manuscript ever found of the gospel of Mark, dating back to a mere seventeen to twenty years after Jesus was crucified. However, scholars continue to be skeptical of his interpretation.[27]

In any event, no inquiry into the archaeology of the first century would be complete without asking about the scrolls. "Do they tell us anything directly about Jesus?" I asked McRay.

"Well, no, Jesus isn't specifically mentioned in any of the scrolls," he replied. "Primarily these documents give us insights into Jewish life and customs." Then he pulled out some papers and pointed to an article that was published in late 1997. "Although," he added, "there is a very interesting development involving a manuscript called 4Q521 that could tell us something about who Jesus was claiming to be."

That whet my appetite. "Tell me about it," I said with some urgency in my voice.

McRay unfolded the mystery. The gospel of Matthew describes how John the Baptist, imprisoned and wrestling with lingering doubts about Jesus' identity, sent his followers to ask Jesus this monumental question: "Are you the one who is to come, or should we expect someone else?" (Matt. 11:3). He was seeking a straight answer about whether Jesus really was the long-awaited Messiah.

Through the centuries, Christians have wondered about Jesus' rather enigmatic answer. Instead of directly saying yes or no, Jesus replied, "Go back and report to John what you hear and see: The blind receive sight, the lame walk, those who have leprosy are cleansed, the deaf hear, the dead are raised, and the good news is proclaimed to the poor" (Matt. 11:4–5).

Jesus' response was an allusion to Isaiah 35. But for some reason Jesus included the phrase "the dead are raised," which is conspicuously absent from the Old Testament text.

This is where 4Q521 comes in. This nonbiblical manuscript from the Dead Sea collection, written in Hebrew, dates back to thirty years before Jesus was born. It contains a version of Isaiah 61 that does include this missing phrase, "the dead are raised."

"[Scroll scholar Craig] Evans has pointed out that this phrase in 4Q521 is unquestionably embedded in a messianic context," McRay said. "It refers to the wonders that the Messiah will do when he comes and when heaven and earth will obey him. So when Jesus gave his response to John, he was not being ambiguous at all. John would have instantly recognized his words as a distinct claim that Jesus was the Messiah."

McRay tossed me the article in which Evans was quoted as saying, "4Q521 makes it clear that [Jesus'] appeal to Isaiah 35 is indeed messianic. In essence, Jesus is telling John through his messengers that messianic things are happening. So that answers [John's] question: *Yes, he is the one who is to come.*"[28]

I sat back in my chair. To me, Evans' discovery was a remarkable confirmation of Jesus' self-identity. It was staggering to me how modern archaeology could finally unlock the significance of a statement in which Jesus boldly asserted nearly two thousand years ago that he was indeed the anointed one of God.

"A Remarkably Accurate Source Book"

Archaeology's repeated affirmation of the New Testament's accuracy provides important corroboration for its reliability. This is in stark contrast with how archaeology has proved to be devastating for Mormonism.

Although Joseph Smith, the founder of the Mormon church, claimed that his *Book of Mormon* is "the most correct of any book upon the earth,"[29] archaeology has repeatedly failed to substantiate its claims about events that supposedly occurred long ago in the Americas.

I remember writing to the Smithsonian Institute to inquire about whether there was any evidence supporting the claims of Mormonism, only to be told in unequivocal terms that its archaeologists see "no direct connection between the archaeology of the New World and the subject matter of the book."

As authors John Ankerberg and John Weldon concluded in a book on the topic, "In other words, no *Book of Mormon* cities have ever been located, no *Book of Mormon* person, place, nation, or name has ever been found, no *Book of Mormon* artifacts, no *Book of Mormon* scriptures, no *Book of Mormon* inscriptions . . . nothing which demonstrates the *Book of Mormon* is anything other than myth or invention has *ever* been found."[30]

However, the story is totally different for the New Testament. McRay's conclusions have been echoed by many other scientists, including prominent Australian archaeologist Clifford Wilson, who wrote, "Those who know the facts now recognize that the New Testament must be accepted as a remarkably accurate source book."[31]

With Craig Blomberg having established the essential reliability of the New Testament documents, Bruce Metzger having confirmed their accurate transmittal through history, Edwin Yamauchi having demonstrated extensive corroboration by ancient historians and others, and now John McRay having shown how archaeology underscores their trustworthiness, I had to agree with Wilson. The case for Christ, while far from complete, was being constructed on solid bedrock.

At the same time, I knew there were some high-profile professors who would dissent from that assessment. You've seen them quoted in *Newsweek* and being interviewed on the evening news, talking about their radical reassessment of Jesus. The time had come for me to confront their critiques head-on before I went any further in my investigation. That meant a trip to Minnesota to interview a feisty, Yale-educated scholar named Dr. Gregory Boyd.

Deliberations
Questions for Reflection or Group Study

1. What do you see as some of the shortcomings and benefits of using archaeology to corroborate the New Testament?

2. If Luke and other New Testament writers are shown to be accurate in reporting incidental details, does this increase your confidence that they would be similarly careful in recording more important events? Why or why not?

3. Why do you find Dr. McRay's analysis of the puzzles concerning the census, the existence of Nazareth, and the slaughter at Bethlehem to be generally plausible or implausible?

4. After having considered the eyewitness, documentary, corroborating, and scientific evidence in the case for Christ, stop and assess your conclusions so far. On a scale of zero to ten, with zero being "no confidence" in the essential reliability of the gospels and ten being "full confidence," where would you rate yourself at this point? What are some reasons you chose that number?

For Further Evidence
More Resources on This Topic

Evans, Craig A. *Jesus and His World: The Archaeological Evidence*. Louisville, KY: Westminster John Knox Press, 2012.

Free, Joseph P., and Howard F. Vos. *Archaeology and Bible History*. Revised edition. Grand Rapids: Zondervan, 1992.

Hoerth, Alfred, and John McRay. *Bible Archaeology*. Grand Rapids: Baker, 2006.

Holden, Joseph M., and Norman Geisler. *The Popular Handbook of Archaeology and the Bible*. Eugene, OR: Harvest House, 2013.

Kaiser, Walter C. Jr., and Duane Garrett, eds. *NIV Archaeological Study Bible*. Grand Rapids.: Zondervan, 2006.

McRay, John. *Archaeology and the New Testament*. Grand Rapids: Baker Academic, 2008.

CHAPTER 6

The Rebuttal
Evidence

Is the Jesus of History
the Same as the Jesus of Faith?

It happens all the time on *television dramas* and in paperback novels, but it's extremely rare in real-life legal dramas. So when an eyewitness in a murder trial refused to point out the defendant as the slayer and instead confessed that he was the killer, the entire courtroom was stunned—and I had an amazing story for the *Chicago Tribune*.

Richard Moss was accused of shooting a nineteen-year-old Chicagoan to death outside a northwest-side tavern. Moss's lifelong friend, Ed Passeri, was called to the witness stand to describe the altercation that led to the slaying.

Passeri painted the scene that occurred outside the Rusty Nail Pub, and then the defense attorney asked him what happened to the victim.

Without blinking, Passeri replied that after the victim stabbed him with a pair of scissors, "I shot him."

The court transcriber's jaw dropped open. Prosecutors threw up their hands. The judge immediately halted the proceedings to advise Passeri of his constitutional right against self-incrimination. And then the defendant got on the stand to say yes, that's right—it was Passeri who committed the crime.

"What Passeri did [by confessing] was an act of raw courage," crowed the defense attorney.

But prosecutors were unconvinced. "What courage?" asked one of them. "Passeri knows he's not running the risk of prosecution, because the only evidence the state has points to Richard Moss!"

Still overwhelmingly persuaded of Moss's guilt, prosecutors knew they had to present strong testimony to controvert Passeri's claim. In legal terminology, what they needed was "rebuttal evidence," defined as any proof that's offered to "explain, counteract, or disprove" a witness's account.[1]

The next day, prosecutors questioned three other eyewitnesses who said there was no doubt that it was Moss who had committed the slaying. Sure enough, based on this and other evidence, the jurors found Moss guilty.[2]

Prosecutors did the right thing. When the overpowering strength of the evidence clearly pointed toward the guilt of the defendant, they were wise to be skeptical of an essentially unsupported assertion made by someone with a vested interest in helping his friend.

Can the Jesus Seminar Be Refuted?

How does this legal concept of rebuttal evidence fit into my investigation of Jesus?

Now that I had heard powerfully convincing and well-reasoned evidence from the scholars I questioned for this book, I needed to turn my attention to the decidedly contrary opinions of a small group of academics who have been the subject of a whirlwind of news coverage.

I'm sure you've seen the articles. In recent years the news media have been saturated with uncritical reports about the Jesus Seminar, a self-selected group that represents a minuscule percentage of New Testament scholars but that generates coverage vastly out of proportion to the group's influence.

The Seminar's publicity-savvy participants attracted the press by voting with colored beads on whether they thought Jesus said what the gospels quote him as saying. A red bead meant Jesus undoubtedly said this or something like it; a pink bead meant he probably said it; a gray bead meant he didn't say it but the ideas are similar to his own; and a black bead meant he didn't utter these words at all.

In the end they concluded Jesus did not say 82 percent of what the gospels attribute to him. Most of the remaining 18 percent was considered somewhat doubtful, with only 2 percent of Jesus' sayings confidently determined to be authentic.[3] Craving controversy and lacking the expertise to scrutinize the Seminar's methodology, journalists devoted fountains of ink to the story.

Then the Seminar published *The Five Gospels*, containing the four traditional gospels plus the questionable Gospel of Thomas, with Jesus' words color-coded to match the group's findings. Flip through it and you find expanses of black type but precious little in red. For example, the only words in the Lord's Prayer that the Seminar is convinced Jesus said are "Our Father."

But I wanted to go beyond the headlines and to unearth the rest of the story. I needed to know if there was any credible rebuttal evidence to refute these troubling and widely publicized opinions. Were the Jesus Seminar's findings solidly based on unbiased scholarly research, or were they like Passeri's ill-fated testimony: well-meaning but ultimately unsupported?

For answers, I made the six-hour drive to St. Paul, Minnesota, to confer with Dr. Gregory Boyd, the Ivy League–educated theology professor whose books and articles have challenged the Jesus Seminar head-on.

THE FIFTH INTERVIEW:
Gregory A. Boyd, PhD

Boyd first clashed with the Jesus Seminar in 1996, when he wrote a devastating critique of liberal perspectives of Jesus, called *Cynic Sage or Son of God? Recovering the Real Jesus in an Age of Revisionist Replies*. The heavily footnoted, 416-page tome was honored by readers of *Christianity Today* as one of their favorite books of the year. His popular paperback *Jesus under Siege* continues the same themes on a more introductory level.

Boyd's other books include the award-winning *Letters from a Skeptic*, in which he and his then-doubting father wrestle through tough issues involving Christianity (culminating in his father becoming a committed Christian), and *God at War: The Bible and Spiritual Conflict*. He also co-authored *The Jesus Legend: A Case for the Historical Reliability of the Synoptic Jesus Tradition*. In addition, he was a contributing scholar to *The Quest Study Bible*, which was designed for people who are asking intellectual questions about the Christian faith.[4]

After receiving a bachelor's degree in philosophy from the University of Minnesota, Boyd earned a master of divinity degree (*cum laude*) from Yale University Divinity School and a doctorate (*magna cum laude*) from Princeton Theological Seminary.

He is not, however, a stereotypical ivory tower intellectual. With wavy black hair, a wiry frame, and a wry smile, Boyd looks like the academic counterpart of comedian Howie Mandell. And like Mandell, he is pure kinetic energy.

Words gush from him like water from a ruptured pipe. He spins out sophisticated ideas and theological concepts at a dizzying rate. He fidgets, he gestures, he squirms in his chair. There's no time to tuck in his shirt all the way, to file the flurry of papers strewn about his office, or to shelve the books that sit in untidy stacks on his floor. He's too busy thinking, debating, questioning, wondering, dreaming, contemplating, inventing, and tackling one project after another.

In fact, one career can't contain him. In addition to his position as adjunct professor of theology at Bethel University, he's also a pastor at Woodland Hills Church, where his passionate preaching has helped attendance grow from forty-two in 1992 to twenty-five hundred today. This real-world environment helps anchor him in the reality of everyday life.

For fun, he debates atheists. He grappled with the late Gordon Stein on the topic "Does God Exist?" He and pastor-turned-skeptic Dan Barker sparred over "Did Jesus Rise from the Dead?" And in a program sponsored by the Islamic Center of Minnesota, he challenged a Muslim on the issue "Is God a Trinity?" Boyd's agile mind, quick wit, empathy with people, and deep reservoir of biblical and philosophical knowledge make him a formidable foe.

What's more, he blends popular culture and serious scholarship as well as anyone I know. He knows football as well as footnotes. He can start a sentence with an offhand observation about a new movie and end it with a stratospheric reference to a profound philosophical conundrum. He's as comfortable reading a current comic strip or watching a trendy sitcom as he is writing his impressive book *Trinity and Process:*

A Critical Evaluation and Reconstruction of Hartshorne's Di-Polar Theism towards a Trinitarian Metaphysics.

His casual and colloquial style (what other biblical scholar gets away with words like "funky" and "wacko"?) quickly made me feel at home as we squeezed into his second-floor office. It was soon clear that Boyd was wound up and ready to go.

Writings from the Radical Fringe

I decided to start from the perspective of the average consumer of news. "People pick up a magazine or newspaper, read the conclusions of the Jesus Seminar, and assume that this represents the mainstream of New Testament scholarship," I said. "But is that really the case?"

"No," he said, looking as if he had just bitten into something sour. "No, no, that's *not* the case. But you're right—people get that impression."

He rocked in his chair until he got comfortable enough to tell a story. "When *Time* came out with its first major article on the Jesus Seminar," he said, "I happened to be in the process of talking about Christianity with a guy whom I was building a relationship with. He was very skeptical by nature and quite inebriated with New Age ideas.

"We had a mutual friend who was hospitalized, and when I went to visit him, this other guy was already there, reading *Time*. As I walked into the room, he said to me, 'Well, Greg, it looks like the scholars disagree with you,' and he threw the magazine at me!"

Boyd shook his head in both sadness and disbelief. "You see, that article gave him the reason to stop taking me seriously. Even though he knew I was a scholar, he interpreted this article as saying that the majority of scholars—at least, those who aren't wacko fundamentalists—hold these views."

I could empathize with Boyd's story, having heard too many people equate the Jesus Seminar with all scholars. "Do you think that impression is an accident?" I asked.

"Well, the Jesus Seminar certainly portrays itself that way," Boyd replied. "In fact, this is one of its most irritating facets, not just to evangelicals but to other scholars as well.

"If you look at their book *The Five Gospels*, they give 'seven pillars of scholarly wisdom,' as if you must follow their methodology if you're going to be a true scholar. But a lot of scholars, from a wide spectrum of backgrounds, would have serious reservations about one or even most of these pillars. And the Jesus Seminar calls its translation of the Bible 'The Scholars Version'—well, what does that imply? That other versions aren't scholarly?"

He paused for a moment, then cut to the core of the issue. "Here's the truth," he said. "The Jesus Seminar represents an extremely small number of radical-fringe scholars who are on the far, far left wing of New Testament thinking. It does not represent mainstream scholarship.

"And ironically, they have their own brand of fundamentalism. They say they have the right way of doing things, period." He smiled. "In the name of diversity," he added with a chuckle, "they can actually be quite narrow."

Discovering the "Real" Jesus

"At least," I said, "the participants in the Jesus Seminar have been very up-front about their goals, haven't they?"

"Yes, that's right. They're explicit in saying they want to rescue the Bible from fundamentalism and to free Americans from the 'naive' belief that the Jesus of the Bible is the 'real' Jesus. They say they want a Jesus who's relevant for today. One of them said that the traditional Jesus did not speak to the needs of the ecological crisis, the nuclear crisis, the feminist crisis, so we need a new picture of Jesus. As another one said, we need 'a new fiction.'

"One of the twists is that they're going directly to the masses instead of to other scholars. They want to take their findings out of the ivory tower and bring them into the marketplace to influence popular opinion. And what they have in mind is a totally new form of Christianity."

The idea of a new Jesus, a new faith, a new Christianity, was intriguing. "So tell me about this Jesus that people from the Jesus Seminar have discovered," I said. "What's he like?"

"Basically, they've discovered what they set out to find. Some think he was a political revolutionary, some a religious fanatic, some a wonder worker, some a feminist, some an egalitarian, some a subversive—there's a lot of diversity," he said.

Then he zeroed in on the key issue. "But there is one picture that they all agree with: Jesus first of all must be a naturalistic Jesus.

"In other words, whatever else is said about him, Jesus was a man like you or me. Maybe he was an extraordinary man, maybe he tapped into our inherent potential as nobody else ever has, but he was not supernatural.

"So they say Jesus and his early followers didn't see him as God or the Messiah, and they didn't see his death as having any special significance. His crucifixion was unfortunate and untimely, and stories about his resurrection came later as a way of trying to deal with that sad reality."

Giving Evidence a Fair Hearing

I stood and strolled over to his bookshelf as I formulated my next question. "OK, but you personally have faith that Jesus was resurrected, and maybe your faith taints your viewpoint too much," I said. "The Jesus Seminar paints itself as being on an unbiased quest for truth, as compared with religiously committed people—people like you—who have a theological agenda."

Boyd turned in his seat to face me. "Ah, but that's not what's really going on," he insisted. "The participants of the Jesus Seminar are at least as biased as evangelicals—and I would say more so. They bring a whole set of assumptions to their scholarship, which of course we all do to some degree.

"Their major assumption—which, incidentally, is not the product of unbiased scholarly research—is that the gospels are not even generally reliable. They conclude this at the outset because the gospels include things that seem historically unlikely, like miracles—walking on water, raising the dead. These things, they say, just don't happen. That's naturalism, which says that for every effect in the natural or physical world, there is a natural cause."

"Yeah, but isn't that the way people typically live their lives?" I asked. "Are you saying we should be looking for supernatural explanations behind everything that takes place?"

"Everyone would agree that you don't appeal to supernatural causes if you don't have to," Boyd said. "But these scholars go beyond that and say you don't *ever* have to. They operate under the assumption that everything in history has happened according to their own experiences, and since they've never seen the supernatural, they assume miracles have never occurred in history.

"Here's what they do: they rule out the possibility of the supernatural from the beginning, and then they say, 'Now bring on the evidence about Jesus.' No wonder they get the results they do!"[5]

I wanted to turn the tables a bit. "All right, then how would you proceed?" I asked.

"I would grant that you shouldn't appeal to the supernatural until you have to. Yes, first look for a natural explanation. I do that in my own life. A tree falls—OK, maybe there were termites. Now, could an angel have pushed it over? Well, I wouldn't go to that conclusion until there was definite evidence for it.

"So I grant that. But what I can't grant is the tremendous presumption that we know enough about the universe to say that God—if there is a God—can never break into our world in a supernatural way. That's a very presumptuous assumption. That's not a presumption based on history; now you're doing metaphysics.

"I think there should be a certain amount of humility in the historical investigation to say, 'You know what? It is just possible that Jesus Christ did rise from the dead. It's just possible that his disciples actually saw what the gospels say they saw.' And if there's no other way of accounting adequately for the evidence, let's investigate that possibility.'

"That, I think, is the only way to give the evidence a fair hearing."

Critiquing the Criteria

To come up with their conclusion that Jesus never spoke most of the words in the gospels, members of the Jesus Seminar used their own set of assumptions and criteria. But are these standards reasonable and appropriate? Or were they loaded from the outset, like dice that are weighted so they yield the result that was desired all along?

"There are multiple problems with their assumptions and criteria,"

Boyd began in analyzing the group's approach. "For instance, they assume that the later church put these sayings into the mouth of Jesus, unless they have good evidence to think otherwise. That assumption is rooted in their suspicion of the gospels, and that comes from their assumption that the supernatural can't occur.

"Historians usually operate with the burden of proof on the historian to prove falsity or unreliability, since people are generally not compulsive liars. Without that assumption, we'd know very little about ancient history.

"The Jesus Seminar turns this on its head and says you've got to affirmatively prove that a saying came from Jesus. Then they come up with questionable criteria to do that. Now, it's OK for scholars to use appropriate criteria in considering whether Jesus said something. But I'm against the idea that if Jesus doesn't meet these criteria, he must not have said it. That kind of negative conclusion can be a problem."

Dealing in this theoretical realm was starting to bring more murkiness than clarity for me. I needed some concrete examples so I could follow Boyd's point. "Talk about some of the specific criteria they used," I said.

"One is called double dissimilarity," he replied. "This means they can believe Jesus said something if it doesn't look like something a rabbi or the later church would say. Otherwise they assume it got into the gospels from a Jewish or Christian source.

"The obvious problem is that Jesus was Jewish and he founded the Christian church, so it shouldn't be surprising if he sounds Jewish and Christian! Yet they've applied this criterion to reach the negative conclusion that Jesus didn't say a whole lot.

"Then there's the criterion of 'multiple attestation,' which means we can only be sure Jesus said something if it's found in more than one source. Now, this can be a helpful test in confirming a saying. However, why argue in the other direction—if it's only found in one source, it's not valid? In fact, most of ancient history is based on single sources. Generally, if a source is considered reliable—and I would argue that there are plenty of reasons to believe that the gospels are reliable—it should be considered credible, even if it can't be confirmed by other sources.

"Even when Jesus' sayings are found in two or three gospels, they don't consider this as passing the 'multiple attestation' criterion. If a saying is found in Matthew, Mark, and Luke, they consider that only one source, because they assume that Matthew and Luke used Mark in writing their gospels. They're failing to recognize that an increasing number of scholars are expressing serious reservations about the theory that Matthew and Luke used Mark. With this line of thinking, you can see why it's extremely difficult to prove multiple attestation."

Boyd started to go on, but I told him he had already made his point: loaded criteria, like weighted dice, inevitably bring the results that were desired from the beginning.

Jesus the Wonder Worker

One approach taken by naturalistic scholars has been to look for parallels between Jesus and others from ancient history as a way of demonstrating that his claims and deeds were not completely unique. Their goal is to explain away the view that Jesus was one of a kind.

"How do you respond to this?" I asked Boyd. "For example, there were ancient rabbis who did exorcisms or prayed for rain and it came, so some scholars have said Jesus was merely another example of a Jewish wonder worker. Do those parallels hold up?"

I was about to see Boyd the debater in action as he responded point by point to a complex issue without the benefit of notes. I was glad I was taping our conversation; my note taking would never have kept up with his rapid-fire delivery.

"Actually, the parallels break down quickly when you look more closely," he began, picking up speed as he went. "For one thing, the sheer centrality of the supernatural in the life of Jesus has no parallel whatsoever in Jewish history.

"Second, the radical nature of his miracles distinguishes him. It didn't just rain when he prayed for it; we're talking about blindness, deafness, leprosy, and scoliosis being healed, storms being stopped, bread and fish being multiplied, sons and daughters being raised from the dead. This is beyond any parallels.

"Third, Jesus' biggest distinctive is how he did miracles on his own authority. He is the one who says, 'If I, by the finger of God, cast out demons, then the kingdom of God is among you'—he's referring to himself. He says, 'I have been anointed to set the captives free.' He does give God the Father credit for what he does, but you never find him asking God the Father to do it—he does it in the power of God the Father. And for that there is just no parallel.

"This goes right along with the different way Jesus talked about himself—'all authority has been given to me,' 'honor me even as you honor the Father,' 'heaven and earth shall pass away but my word will not pass away.' You don't find rabbis talking like this anywhere."

Having been on the receiving end of that quick burst of arguments, I said with a chuckle, "So what's your point?"

Boyd laughed. "Any parallels with wonder-working rabbis," he said, "are going to be very, very stretched."

Jesus and the Amazing Apollonius

I wasn't going to let Boyd's debating skills intimidate me. I decided to raise a more difficult issue: the seemingly stronger parallels between Jesus and a historical figure named Apollonius of Tyana.

"You know the evidence as well as I do," I said to Boyd. "Here's someone from the first century who was said to have healed people and to have exorcised demons; who may have raised a young girl from the dead; and who appeared to some of his followers after he died. People point to that and say, 'Aha! If you're going to admit that the Apollonius story is legendary, why not say the same thing about the Jesus story?'"

Boyd was nodding to indicate he was tracking with me. "I'll admit that initially this sounds impressive," he said. "When I first heard about Apollonius as a college student, I was really taken aback. But if you do the historical work calmly and objectively, you find that the alleged parallels just don't stand up."

I needed specifics, not generalities. "Go ahead," I said. "Do your best to shoot it down."

"OK. Well, first, his biographer, Philostratus, was writing a century and a half after Apollonius lived, whereas the gospels were written within a generation of Jesus. The closer the proximity to the event, the less chance there is for legendary development, for error, or for memories to get confused.

"Another thing is that we have four gospels, corroborated with Paul, that can be cross-checked to some degree with nonbiblical authors, like Josephus and others. With Apollonius we're dealing with one source. Plus the gospels pass the standard tests used to assess historical reliability, but we can't say that about the stories of Apollonius.

"On top of that, Philostratus was commissioned by an empress to write a biography in order to dedicate a temple to Apollonius. She was a follower of Apollonius, so Philostratus would have had a financial motive to embellish the story and give the empress what she wanted. On the other hand, the writers of the gospels had nothing to gain—and much to lose—by writing Jesus' story, and they didn't have ulterior motives such as financial gain.

"Also, the way Philostratus writes is very different than the gospels. The gospels have a very confident eyewitness perspective, as if they had a camera there. But Philostratus includes a lot of tentative statements, like 'It is reported that . . .' or 'Some say this young girl had died; others say she was just ill.' To his credit, he backs off and treats stories like stories.

"And here's a biggie: Philostratus was writing in the early third century in Cappadocia, where Christianity had already been present for quite a while. So any borrowing would have been done by him, not by Christians. You can imagine the followers of Apollonius seeing Christianity as competition and saying, 'Oh, yeah? Well, Apollonius did the same things Jesus did!' Sort of like, 'My dad can beat up your dad!'

"One final point. I'm willing to admit that Apollonius may have done some amazing things or at least tricked people into thinking he did. But that doesn't in any way compromise the evidence for Jesus. Even if you grant the evidence for Apollonius, you're still left with having to deal with the evidence for Christ."

Jesus and the "Mystery Religions"

OK, I thought to myself, let's give this one more try. A lot of college students are taught that many of the themes seen in the life of Jesus are merely echoes of ancient "mystery religions," in which there are stories about gods dying and rising, and rituals of baptism and Communion. "What about those parallels?" I asked.

"That was a very popular argument at the beginning of the century, but it generally died off because it was so discredited. For one thing, given the timing involved, if you're going to argue for borrowing, it should be from the direction of Christianity to the mystery religions, not vice versa.

"Also, the mystery religions were do-your-own-thing religions that freely borrowed ideas from various places. However, the Jews carefully guarded their beliefs from outside influences. They saw themselves as a separate people and strongly resisted pagan ideas and rituals."

To me, the most interesting potential parallels were the mythological tales of gods dying and rising. "Aren't those stories similar to Christian beliefs?" I asked.

"While it's true that some mystery religions had stories of gods dying and rising, these stories always revolved around the natural life cycle of death and rebirth," Boyd said. "Crops die in the fall and come to life in the spring. People express the wonder of this ongoing phenomenon through mythological stories about gods dying and rising. These stories were always cast in a legendary form. They depicted events that happened 'once upon a time.'

"Contrast that with the depiction of Jesus Christ in the gospels. They talk about someone who actually lived several decades earlier, and they name names—crucified under Pontius Pilate, when Caiaphas was the high priest, and the father of Alexander and Rufus carried his cross, for example. That's concrete historical stuff. It has nothing in common with stories about what supposedly happened 'once upon a time.'

"And Christianity has nothing to do with life cycles or the harvest. It has to do with a very Jewish belief—which is absent from the mystery religions—about the resurrection of the dead and about life eternal and reconciliation with God.

"As for the suggestion that the New Testament doctrines of baptism or Communion come from mystery religions, that's just nonsense. For one thing, the evidence for these supposed parallels comes after the second century, so any borrowing would have come from Christianity, not the other way around.

"And when you look carefully, the similarities vanish. For instance, to get to a higher level in the Mithra cult, followers had to stand under a bull while it was slain, so they could be bathed in its blood and guts. Then they'd join the others in eating the bull.

"Now, to suggest that Jews would find anything attractive about this and want to model baptism and Communion after this barbaric practice is extremely implausible, which is why most scholars don't go for it."[6]

Secret Gospels and Talking Crosses

As disorderly and disorganized as his office was, Boyd's mind was sharp and systematized. His analysis of these much-touted parallels left little room for doubt. So I decided to advance to another area that the media often write about: the "new discoveries" that are often the subject of books by Jesus Seminar participants.

"There has been a lot written in the popular press about the Gospel of Thomas, Secret Mark, the Cross Gospel, and Q," I said. "Have there really been any new discoveries that change the way we should think about Jesus?"

Boyd sighed in exasperation. "No, there are no new discoveries that tell us anything new about Jesus. The Gospel of Thomas was discovered long ago, but it's only now being used to create an alternative Jesus. Some theories about the Gospel of Thomas may be new, but the gospel itself is not.

"As for Q, it's not a discovery but a theory that has been around for one and a half centuries, which tries to account for the material that Luke and Matthew have in common. What's new is the highly questionable way that left-wing scholars are using their presuppositions to slice this hypothetical Q into various layers of legendary development to back up their preconceived theories."

I knew that John Dominic Crossan, perhaps the most influential scholar in the Jesus Seminar, has made some strong claims about a gospel called Secret Mark. In fact, he asserts that Secret Mark may actually be an uncensored version of the gospel of Mark, containing confidential matters for spiritual insiders.[7] Some have used it to claim that Jesus was actually a magician or that a number of early Christians practiced homosexuality. This conspiratorial scenario has captured the media's imagination.

"What proof is there for this?" I asked Boyd.

His answer came quickly. "None," he said.

Though he apparently didn't see the need to elaborate, I asked him to explain what he meant.

"You see, we don't have Secret Mark," he said. "What we have is one scholar who found a quote from Clement of Alexandria, from late in the second century, that supposedly comes from this gospel. And now, mysteriously, even that is gone, disappeared.

"We don't have it, we don't have a quote from it, and even if we did have a quote from it, we don't have any reason to think that it has given us any valid information about the historical Jesus or what early Christians thought about him. On top of that, we already know that Clement had a track record of being very gullible in accepting spurious writings.

"So Secret Mark is a nonexistent work cited by a now nonexistent text by a late second-century writer who's known for being naive about these things. The vast majority of scholars don't give this any credibility. Unfortunately, those who do get a lot of press, because the media love the sensational."

Crossan also gives credence to what he calls the Cross Gospel. "Does that fare any better?" I asked.

"No, most scholars don't give it credibility, because it includes such outlandishly legendary material. For instance, Jesus comes out of his tomb and he's huge—he goes up beyond the sky—and the cross comes out of the tomb and actually talks! Obviously, the much more sober gospels are more reliable than anything found in this account. It fits better with later apocryphal writings. In fact, it's dependent on biblical material, so it should be dated later."

Unlike the overwhelming majority of biblical experts, the Jesus Seminar has accorded extremely high status to the Gospel of Thomas, elevating it to a place alongside the four traditional gospels. In chapter 3 Dr. Bruce Metzger strongly criticized that position as being unwarranted.

I asked Boyd for his opinion. "Why shouldn't Thomas be given that kind of honor?"

"Everyone concedes that this gospel has been significantly influenced by Gnosticism, which was a religious movement in the second, third, and fourth centuries that supposedly had secret insights, knowledge, or revelations that would allow people to know the key to the universe. Salvation was by what you knew—*gnosis* is Greek for 'know,'" he said.

"So most scholars date the Gospel of Thomas to the mid-second century, in which it fits well into the cultural milieu. Let me give you an example: Jesus is quoted as saying, 'Every woman who will make herself male will enter the kingdom of heaven.' That contradicts the attitude that we know Jesus had toward women, but it fits well with the Gnostic mind-set.

"However, the Jesus Seminar has arbitrarily latched onto certain passages of the Gospel of Thomas and has argued that these passages represent an early strand of tradition about Jesus, even earlier than the canonical gospels.

"Because none of these passages include Jesus making exalted claims for himself or doing supernatural feats, they argue that the earliest view of Jesus was that he was only a great teacher. But the whole line of reasoning is circular. The only reason for thinking these passages in Thomas are early in the first place is because they contain a view of Jesus that these scholars already believed was the original Jesus. In truth, there is no good reason for preferring the second-century Gospel of Thomas over the first-century gospels of the New Testament."

History versus Faith

The Jesus of history and the Jesus of faith: the Jesus Seminar believes there's a big gulf between the two. In its view, the historical Jesus was a bright, witty, countercultural man who never claimed to be the Son of God, while the Jesus of faith is a cluster of feel-good ideas that help people live right but are ultimately based on wishful thinking.

"There's not just a gulf between the Jesus of history and the Jesus of faith," Boyd said as I brought up this subject. "If you discredit everything that says Jesus is divine and reconciles people with God, there's an outright contradiction between the two.

"Generally speaking, they define the Jesus of faith this way: there are religious symbols that are quite meaningful to people—the symbol of Jesus being divine, of the cross, of self-sacrificial love, of the resurrection. Even though people don't really believe that those things actually happened, they nevertheless can inspire people to live a good life, to overcome existential angst, to realize new potentialities, to resurrect hope in the midst of despair—blah, blah, blah."

He shrugged his shoulders. "Sorry," he said, "I've heard this stuff so much, it comes out my ears!"

"So these liberals say historical research can't possibly discover the Jesus of faith, because the Jesus of faith is not rooted in history. He's merely a symbol," Boyd continued. "But listen: Jesus is not a symbol of anything unless he's rooted in history. The Nicene Creed doesn't say, 'We wish these things were true.' It says, 'Jesus Christ was crucified under Pontius Pilate, and the third day he rose again from the dead,' and it goes on from there.

"The theological truth is based on historical truth. That's the way the New Testament talks. Look at the sermon of Peter in the second chapter of Acts. He stands up and says, 'You guys are a witness of these things; they weren't done in secret. David's tomb is still with us, but God has raised Jesus from the dead. Therefore we proclaim him to be the Son of God.'

"Take away miracles and you take away the resurrection, and then you've got nothing to proclaim. Paul said that if Jesus wasn't raised from the dead, our faith is futile, it's useless, it's empty."[8]

Boyd stopped for a moment. His voice dropped a notch, from preaching mode to an intense expression of personal conviction.

"I don't want to base my life on a symbol," he said resolutely. "I want reality, and the Christian faith has always been rooted in reality. What's not rooted in reality is the faith of liberal scholars. They're the ones who are following a pipe dream, but Christianity is not a pipe dream."

Combining History and Faith

We had spent a lot of time talking about the Jesus of the Jesus Seminar—a symbolic Jesus, but one who's impotent to offer the world anything except the illusion of hope. But before we left, I wanted to hear about the Jesus of Gregory Boyd. I needed to know whether the Jesus he researches and writes scholarly books about as a theology professor is the same Jesus he preaches about in his church on Sunday mornings.

"Let me get this straight," I said. "Your Jesus—the Jesus you relate to—is both a Jesus of history *and* a Jesus of faith."

Boyd clenched his fist for emphasis, as if I'd just scored a touchdown. "Yes, that's it exactly, Lee!" he exclaimed. Moving to the very edge of his chair, he spelled out precisely what his scholarship—and his heart—have brought him to believe.

"It's like this: If you love a person, your love goes beyond the facts of that person, but it's rooted in the facts about that person. For example, you love your wife because she's gorgeous, she's nice, she's sweet, she's kind. All these things are facts about your wife, and therefore you love her.

"But your love goes beyond that. You can know all these things about your wife and not be in love with her and put your trust in her, but you do. So the decision goes beyond the evidence, yet it is there also on the basis of the evidence.

"So it is with falling in love with Jesus. To have a relationship with Jesus Christ goes beyond just knowing the historical facts about him, yet it's rooted in the historical facts about him. I believe in Jesus on the basis of the historical evidence, but my relationship with Jesus goes way beyond the evidence. I have to put my trust in him and walk with him on a daily basis."

I interrupted to say, "Yes, but will you acknowledge that Christianity makes some claims about Jesus that are just plain hard to believe?"

"Yes, of course I do," he replied. "That's why I'm glad we have such incredibly strong evidence to show us they're true.

"For me," he added, "it comes down to this: There's no competition. The evidence for Jesus being who the disciples said he was—for having done the miracles that he did, for rising from the dead, for making the claims that he did—is just light-years beyond my reasons for thinking that the left-wing scholarship of the Jesus Seminar is correct.

"What do these scholars have? Well, there's a brief allusion to a lost 'secret' gospel in a late-second-century letter that has unfortunately only been seen by one person and has now itself been lost. There's a third-century account of the crucifixion and resurrection that stars a talking cross and that less than a handful of scholars think predates the gospels. There's a second-century Gnostic document, parts of which some scholars now want to date early to back up their own preconceptions. And there is a hypothetical document built on shaky assumptions that is being sliced thinner and thinner by using circular reasoning."

Boyd flopped back in his chair. "No, I'm sorry," he said, shaking his head. "I don't buy it. It's far more reasonable to put my trust in the gospels—which pass the tests of historical scrutiny with flying colors—than to put my hope in what the Jesus Seminar is saying."

A Chorus of Criticism

Back at my motel, I mentally played back my interview with Boyd. I felt the same way he did: If the Jesus of faith is not also the Jesus of history, he's powerless and he's meaningless. Unless he's rooted in reality, unless he established his divinity by rising from the dead, he's just a feel-good symbol who's as irrelevant as Santa Claus.

But there's good evidence that he's more than that. I had already heard well-supported eyewitness, documentary, corroborating, and scientific evidence supporting the New Testament claim that he is God incarnate, and I was getting ready to hit the road again to dig out even more historical material about his character and resurrection.

Meanwhile Greg Boyd isn't a lone voice crying out against the Jesus Seminar. He's part of a growing crescendo of criticism coming not just from prominent conservative evangelicals but also from other well-respected scholars representing a wide variety of theological backgrounds.

An example was as close as my motel's nightstand, where I reached over to pick up a book called *The Real Jesus*, which I had recently purchased. Its author is Dr. Luke Timothy Johnson, the highly regarded professor of New Testament and Christian origins at the Candler School of Theology of Emory University. Johnson is a Roman Catholic who was a Benedictine monk before becoming a biblical scholar and writing a number of influential books.

Johnson systematically skewers the Jesus Seminar, saying it "by no means represents the cream of New Testament scholarship," it follows a process that is "biased against the authenticity of the gospel traditions," and its results were "already determined ahead of time."[9] He concludes, "This is not responsible, or even critical, scholarship. It is a self-indulgent charade."[10]

He goes on to quote other distinguished scholars with similar opinions, including Dr. Howard Clark Kee, who called the Seminar "an academic disgrace," and Richard Hayes of Duke University, whose review of *The Five Gospels* asserted that "the case argued by this book would not stand up in any court."[11]

I closed the book and turned off the light. Tomorrow I'd resume my hunt for evidence that *would* stand up.

Deliberations
Questions for Reflection or Group Study

1. Have you read news accounts of the Jesus Seminar's opinions? What was your response to what was reported? Did the articles give you the impression that the Seminar's findings represent the opinions of the majority of scholars? What dangers do you see in relying on the news media in reporting on issues of this kind?

2. As you conduct your own investigation of Jesus, should you rule out any possibility of the supernatural at the outset, or should you allow yourself to consider all the evidence of history, even if it points toward the miraculous as having occurred? Why?

3. Boyd said, "I don't want to base my life on a symbol. I want reality . . . ." Why do you agree or disagree? Is it enough that Jesus is a symbol of hope, or is it important for you to be confident that his life, teachings, and resurrection are rooted in history? Why?

For Further Evidence
More Resources on This Topic

Bock, Darrell L. *Studying the Historical Jesus: A Guide to Sources and Methods.* Grand Rapids: Baker Academic, 2002.

Boyd, Gregory A. *Cynic Sage or Son of God? Recovering the Real Jesus in an Age of Revisionist Replies.* Wheaton, IL: BridgePoint, 1995.

Boyd, Gregory A., and Paul Rhodes Eddy. *The Jesus Legend: A Case for the Historical Reliability of the Synoptic Jesus Tradition.* Grand Rapids: Baker Academic, 2007.

——————————. *Lord or Legend: Wrestling with the Jesus Dilemma.* Grand Rapids: Baker, 2007.

Evans, Craig A. *Fabricating Jesus: How Modern Scholars Distort the Gospels.* Expanded Edition. Downers Grove, IL: InterVarsity Press, 2006.

Johnson, Luke Timothy. *The Real Jesus.* San Francisco: HarperSanFrancisco, 1996.

Wilkins, Michael J., and J. P. Moreland, eds. *Jesus Under Fire.* Grand Rapids: Zondervan, 1995.

Witherington, Ben III. *What Have They Done With Jesus?* Reprint Edition. New York: HarperOne, 2007.

PART 2

Analyzing Jesus

CHAPTER 7

The Identity Evidence

Was Jesus Really Convinced That
He Was the Son of God?

John Douglas has an uncanny ability to look into the minds of people he has never met.

As the original "psychological profiler" for the Federal Bureau of Investigation, Douglas would gather information at a crime scene and then use his insights to peer inside the personality of the still-at-large perpetrator.

Case in point: Douglas predicted that the "Trailside Killer," a serial murderer who stalked wooded areas near San Francisco from 1979 to 1981, would be someone who had a speech impediment as well as tendencies toward animal cruelty, bed-wetting, and arson. Sure enough, the person finally arrested and convicted in the case fit those descriptions perfectly.[1]

With a doctorate in psychology, years of experience as a detective, and a natural talent for understanding human behavior, Douglas has become renowned for his profiling prowess. He has coauthored several bestsellers on the topic, and when Jodie Foster won the Oscar for her performance in *Silence of the Lambs*, she publicly thanked Douglas for being the real-life figure behind her character's FBI mentor.

How is Douglas able to understand the thinking process of individuals he has never even talked to? "Behavior reflects personality," Douglas explained to *Biography* magazine.[2]

In other words, Douglas closely examines the evidence left behind at the crime scene and, where possible, interviews victims to find out exactly what the criminal said and did. From these clues—the left-behind products of the person's behavior—he deduces the individual's psychological makeup.

Now to Jesus: Without dialoguing with him, how can we possibly delve into his mind to determine what his motivations, intentions, and self-understanding were? How do we know who he thought he was and what he understood his mission to be?

By looking at his behavior, Douglas would say. If we want to figure out whether Jesus thought he was the Messiah or the Son of God—or merely considered himself to be a rabbi or prophet—we need to look at what he did, what he said, and how he related to others.

The question of what Jesus thought about himself is a critical issue. Some professors maintain that the myth of Jesus' deity was superimposed on the Jesus tradition by overzealous supporters years after his death. The real Jesus, these professors believe, would roll over in his grave if he knew people were worshiping him. If you strip away the legends and go back to the earliest material about him, they say you'll find he never aspired to be anything more than an itinerant teacher and occasional rabble-rouser.

But is the evidence of history on their side? To find out, I flew to Lexington, Kentucky, and drove the winding roads past a series of picturesque horse farms to track down the scholar whose acclaimed book *The Christology of Jesus* confronts this very subject.

THE SIXTH INTERVIEW:
Ben Witherington III, PhD

There isn't much to tiny Wilmore, Kentucky, except Asbury Theological Seminary, where I found Ben Witherington's office on the fourth floor of a colonial-style building off the rustic community's main drag. With the gracious hospitality of a Southern gentleman, the North Carolina native offered me a comfortable chair and some coffee as we sat down to discuss who Jesus of Nazareth thought he was.

This topic is familiar territory to Witherington, whose books include *The Christology of Jesus, Jesus the Sage, The Many Faces of the Christ, The Jesus Quest, Jesus, Paul, and the End of the World, Reading and Understanding the Bible, New Testament History*, and commentaries on Mark, John, Acts, and Romans. His articles have been featured in specialized dictionaries and academic journals.

Educated at Gordon-Conwell Theological Seminary (master of divinity degree, *summa cum laude*) and the University of Durham in England (doctorate in theology with a concentration in New Testament), Witherington has taught at Asbury, Ashland Theological Seminary, the Divinity School of Duke University, and Gordon-Conwell. His memberships include the Society for the Study of the New Testament, the Society of Biblical Literature, and the Institute for Biblical Research.

Speaking distinctly and deliberately, weighing his words with care, Witherington definitely sounded like a scholar, yet his voice betrayed an unmistakable undercurrent of fascination—even awe—for his subject. This attitude emerged even further when he took me on a tour of a high-tech studio where he had been mixing images of Jesus with songs whose lyrics illuminate the compassion, the sacrifice, the humanity, and the majesty of his life and ministry.

For a scholar who writes heavily footnoted, cautiously nuanced, and academically precise prose on the technical issues involving Jesus, this artistic wedding of video and music is a poetic outlet for exploring the side of Jesus that only the creative arts can come close to capturing.

Back in Witherington's office, I decided to begin examining the issue of Jesus' self-understanding with a question that often springs to the minds of readers when they're exposed to the gospels for the first time.

"The truth is that Jesus was a bit mysterious about his identity, wasn't he?" I asked as Witherington pulled up a chair across from me. "He tended to shy away from forthrightly proclaiming himself to be the Messiah or the Son of God. Was that because he didn't think of himself in those terms or because he had other reasons?"

"No, it's not because he didn't think of himself in those terms," Witherington said as he settled into his chair and crossed his legs. "If he had simply announced, 'Hi, folks; I'm God,' that would have been heard as 'I'm Yahweh,' because the Jews of his day didn't have any concept of the Trinity. They only knew of God the Father—whom they called Yahweh—and not God the Son or God the Holy Spirit.

"So if someone were to say he was God, that wouldn't have made any sense to them and would have been seen as clear-cut blasphemy. And it would have been counterproductive to Jesus in his efforts to get people to listen to his message.

"Besides, there were already a host of expectations about what the Messiah would look like, and Jesus didn't want to be pigeonholed into somebody else's categories. Consequently, he was very careful about what he said publicly. In private with his disciples—that was a different story, but the gospels primarily tell us about what he did in public."

Exploring the Earliest Traditions

It was a 1977 book by British theologian John Hick and half a dozen like-minded colleagues who prompted a firestorm of controversy by charging that Jesus never thought of himself as God incarnate or the Messiah. These concepts, they wrote, developed later and were written into the gospels so it appeared that Jesus was making these claims about himself.

To explore that allegation, Witherington has gone back to the very earliest traditions about Jesus—the most primitive material, unquestionably safe from legendary development—and discovered persuasive clues concerning how Jesus really regarded himself.

I wanted to delve into that research, starting with this question: "What clues can we find about Jesus' self-understanding from the way he related to others?"

Witherington thought for a moment, then replied, "Look at his relationship with his disciples. Jesus has twelve disciples, yet notice that he's not one of the Twelve."

While that may sound like a detail without a difference, Witherington said it's quite significant.

"If the Twelve represent a renewed Israel, where does Jesus fit in?" he asked. "He's not just part of Israel, not merely part of the redeemed group, he's forming the group—just as God in the Old Testament formed his people and set up the twelve tribes of Israel. That's a clue about what Jesus thought of himself."

Witherington went on to describe a clue that can be found in Jesus' relationship with John the Baptist. "Jesus says, 'Of all people born of woman, John is the greatest man on earth.' Having said that, he then goes even further in his ministry than the Baptist did—by doing miracles, for example. What does that say about what he thinks of himself?

"And his relationship with the religious leaders is perhaps the most revealing. Jesus makes the truly radical statement that it's not what enters a person that defiles him but what comes out of his heart. Frankly, this sets aside huge portions of the Old Testament book of Leviticus, with its meticulous rules concerning purity.

"Now, the Pharisees didn't like this message. They wanted to keep things as they were, but Jesus said, 'No, God has further plans. He's doing a new thing.' We have to ask, What kind of person thinks he has the authority to set aside the divinely inspired Jewish Scriptures and supplant them with his own teaching?

"And what about his relationship—if we can call it that—with the Roman authorities? We have to ask why they crucified him. If he had merely been an innocuous sage telling nice little parables, how did he end up on a cross, especially at a Passover season, when no Jew wants any Jew to be executed? There had to be a reason why the sign above his head said, 'This is the King of the Jews.'"

Witherington let that last comment hang in the air before providing the explanation himself: "Either Jesus had made that verbal claim," he said, "or someone clearly thought he did."

By the Finger of God

While Jesus' relationships provide one window into his self-understanding, Witherington said that Jesus' deeds—especially his miracles—offer additional insights. However, I raised my hand to stop him.

"Certainly you can't say that Jesus' miracles establish that he thought he was God," I said, "since later his own disciples went out and did the same things—and certainly they weren't making claims of deity."

"No, it's not the fact that Jesus did miracles that illuminates his self-understanding," replied Witherington. "What's important is how he interprets his miracles."

"What do you mean?" I asked.

"Jesus says, 'If I, by the finger of God, cast out demons, then you will know that the kingdom of God has come upon you.'[3] He's not like other miracle workers who do amazing things and then life proceeds as it always has. No—to Jesus, his miracles are a sign indicating the coming of the kingdom of God. They are a foretaste of what the kingdom is going to be like. And that sets Jesus apart."

Again I interrupted. "Elaborate on that a bit," I said. "How does it set him apart?"

"Jesus sees his miracles as bringing about something unprecedented— the coming of God's dominion," replied Witherington. "He doesn't merely see himself as a worker of miracles; he sees himself as the one in whom and through whom the promises of God come to pass. And that's a not-too-thinly-veiled claim of transcendence."

I nodded. Now his point made sense to me. With that, I turned to the words of Jesus in search of more clues concerning his self-understanding.

"He was called *Rabbouni*, or 'Rabbi,' by his followers," I said. "Doesn't this imply that he merely taught like the other rabbis of his day?"

Witherington grinned. "Actually," he said, "Jesus taught in a radical new way. He begins his teachings with the phrase 'Amen I say to you,' which is to say, 'I swear in advance to the truthfulness of what I'm about to say.' This was absolutely revolutionary."

"How so?" I asked.

He replied, "In Judaism you needed the testimony of two witnesses, so witness A could witness the truth of witness B and vice versa. But Jesus witnesses to the truth of his own sayings. Instead of basing his teaching on the authority of others, he speaks on his own authority.

"So here is someone who considered himself to have authority above and beyond what the Old Testament prophets had. He believed he possessed not only divine inspiration, as King David did, but also divine authority and the power of direct divine utterance."

In addition to employing the "Amen" phrase in his teaching, Jesus used the term "Abba" when he was relating to God. "What does that tell us about what he thought about himself?" I asked.

"'Abba' connotes intimacy in a relationship between a child and his father," Witherington explained. "Interestingly, it's also the term disciples used for a beloved teacher in early Judaism. But Jesus used it of

God—and as far as I can tell, he and his followers were the only ones praying to God that way."

When I asked Witherington to expand on the importance of this, he said, "In the context in which Jesus operated, it was customary for Jews to work around having to say the name of God. His name was the most holy word you could speak, and they even feared mispronouncing it. If they were going to address God, they might say something like, 'The Holy One, blessed be he,' but they were not going to use his personal name."

"And 'Abba' is a personal term," I said.

"Very personal," he replied. "It's the term of endearment in which a child would say to a parent, 'Father Dearest, what would you have me do?'"

However, I spotted an apparent inconsistency. "Wait a second," I interjected. "Praying 'Abba' must not imply that Jesus thinks he's God, because he taught his disciples to use the same term in their own prayers, and they're not God."

"Actually," came Witherington's reply, "the significance of 'Abba' is that Jesus is the initiator of an intimate relationship that was previously unavailable. The question is, What kind of person can change the terms of relating to God? What kind of person can initiate a new covenantal relationship with God?"

His distinction made sense to me. "So how significant do you consider Jesus' use of 'Abba' to be?" I asked.

"Quite significant," he answered. "It implies that Jesus had a degree of intimacy with God that is unlike anything in the Judaism of his day. And listen, here's the kicker: Jesus is saying that only through having a relationship with him does this kind of prayer language—this kind of 'Abba' relationship with God—become possible. That says volumes about how he regarded himself."

Witherington started to add another important clue—Jesus' repeated reference to himself as the "Son of Man"—but I let him know that a previous expert, Craig Blomberg, had already explained that this was a reference to Daniel 7. This term, Witherington agreed, is extremely important in revealing Jesus' messianic or transcendent self-understanding.

At this point I paused to take stock of what Witherington had said. When I put together the clues from Jesus' relationships, miracles, and words, his perception of his identity came into sharp focus.

There seemed little question, based upon the earliest evidence, that Jesus considered himself to be more than a doer of great deeds, more than a teacher, more than another prophet in a line of many. There was ample evidence to conclude that he thought of himself in unique and supreme terms—but exactly how sweeping was this self-understanding?

John's Portrait of Jesus

In its opening scene the gospel of John uses majestic and unambiguous language to boldly assert the deity of Jesus.

> In the beginning was the Word, and the Word was with God, and the Word was God. He was with God in the beginning. Through him all things were made; without him nothing was made that has been made . . . .The Word became flesh and made his dwelling among us. We have seen his glory, the glory of the one and only Son, who came from the Father, full of grace and truth.
>
> JOHN 1:1–3, 14

I remember reading that regal introduction when I went through the gospel of John for the first time. I recall asking myself, I wonder how Jesus would respond if he were to read John's words about him? Would he recoil and say, "Whoa, John has got me all wrong! He has embellished and mythologized me to the point where I don't even recognize myself"? Or would he nod approvingly and say, "Yep, I'm all that—and more"?

Later I encountered the words of scholar Raymond Brown, who had come to his own conclusion: "I have no difficulty with the thesis that if Jesus . . . could have read John he would have found that gospel a suitable expression of his identity."[4]

Now here was my chance to hear directly from Witherington, who has spent a lifetime analyzing the scholarly minutiae concerning Jesus' self-perception, about whether he agrees with Brown's assessment.

There was no hesitation and no equivocation. "Yes, I do," he said.

"I don't have a problem with that. When you're dealing with the gospel of John, you're dealing with a somewhat interpreted picture of Jesus, but I also believe it's a logical drawing out of what was implicit in the historical Jesus.

"And I'll add this: Even if you eliminate the gospel of John, there's still no non-messianic Jesus to be conjured up out of the material in the other three gospels. It's just not there."

Immediately I thought of the famous exchange, recorded in Matthew, in which Jesus asked his disciples in a private meeting, "Who do you say I am?" Peter replied with clarity, "You are the Messiah, the Son of the living God." Instead of ducking the issue, Jesus affirmed Peter for his observation. "Blessed are you," he said, "for this was not revealed to you by man, but by my Father in heaven." (See Matt. 16:15–17.)

Even so, some popular depictions of Jesus, such as in the movie *The Last Temptation of Christ*, show him as basically uncertain about his identity and mission. He's saddled with ambiguity and angst.

"Is there any evidence," I asked Witherington, "that Jesus ever had an identity crisis?"

"Not an identity crisis, although I do believe he had points of identity confirmation," the professor replied. "At his baptism, at his temptation, at the transfiguration, in the Garden of Gethsemane—these are crisis moments in which God confirmed to him who he was and what his mission was.

"For instance, I don't think it's accidental that his ministry does not begin in earnest until after his baptism, when he hears the voice saying, 'You are my Son, with whom I am well pleased.'"

"What did he think his mission was?"

"He saw his job as coming to free the people of God, so his mission was directed to Israel."

"Specifically to Israel," I stressed.

"Yes, that's correct," Witherington said. "There's very little evidence that he sought out Gentiles during his ministry—that was a mission for the later church. You see, the promises of the prophets had come to Israel—and to Israel he must go."

"I and the Father Are One"

In his book *Reasonable Faith*, William Lane Craig points to a substantial amount of evidence that within twenty years of the crucifixion there was a full-blown Christology proclaiming Jesus as God incarnate.

Church historian Jaroslav Pelikan has pointed out that the oldest Christian sermon, the oldest account of a Christian martyr, the oldest pagan report of the church, and the oldest liturgical prayer (1 Cor. 16:22) all refer to Jesus as Lord and God. Pelikan said, "Clearly, it was the message of what the church believed and taught that 'God' was an appropriate name for Jesus Christ."[5]

In light of this, I asked Witherington, "Do you see any possible way this could have developed—especially so soon—if Jesus had never made transcendent and messianic claims about himself?"

Witherington was adamant. "Not unless you're prepared to argue that the disciples completely forgot what the historical Jesus was like and that they had nothing to do with the traditions that start showing up twenty years after his death," he said. "Frankly, as a historian, this would not make any sense at all."

In dealing with history, he added, all sorts of things are possible, but not all possible things are equally probable.

"Is it probable," he asked, "that all this stuff was conjured up out of thin air within twenty years after Jesus died, when there were still living witnesses to what Jesus the historical figure was really like? I find that just about as unlikely a historical hypothesis as you could possibly come up with.

"The real issue is, what happened after the crucifixion of Jesus that changed the minds of the disciples, who had denied, disobeyed, and deserted Jesus? Very simply, something happened to them that was similar to what Jesus experienced at his baptism—it was confirmed to them that what they had hoped Jesus was, he was."

And what exactly was he? As I was wrapping up my time with Witherington, I wanted him to sum it up for me. Taking all his research into consideration, what was his personal conclusion about who Jesus saw himself to be? I posed the question, sat back, and let him spell it out—which he did, with eloquence and conviction.

"Jesus thought he was the person appointed by God to bring in the climactic saving act of God in human history. He believed he was the agent of God to carry that out—that he had been authorized by God, empowered by God, he spoke for God, and he was directed by God to do this task. So what Jesus said, God said. What Jesus did was the work of God.

"Under the Jewish concept of agency, 'a man's agent is as himself.' Remember how Jesus sent out his apostles and said, 'Whatever they do to you, they've done to me'? There was a strong connection between a man and his agent whom he sends on a mission.

"Well, Jesus believed he was on a divine mission, and the mission was to redeem the people of God. The implication is that the people of God were lost and that God had to do something—as he had always done—to intervene and set them back on the right track. But there was a difference this time. This was the last time. This was the last chance.

"Did Jesus believe he was the Son of God, the anointed one of God? The answer is yes. Did he see himself as the Son of Man? The answer is yes. Did he see himself as the final Messiah? Yes, that's the way he viewed himself. Did he believe that anybody less than God could save the world? No, I don't believe he did.

"And here's where the paradox gets as quizzical as it can possibly get: The way God was going to save the world was by his Son dying. The most human of all human acts—to die.

"Now, God, in his divine nature, doesn't die. So how was God going to get this done? How was God going to be the Savior of the human race? He had to come as a human being to accomplish that task. And Jesus believed he was the one to do it.

"Jesus said in Mark 10:45, 'I did not come to be served but to serve and give my life as a ransom in place of the many.' This is either the highest form of megalomania or it's the example of somebody who really believes, as he said, 'I and the Father are one.'[6] In other words, 'I have the authority to speak for the Father; I have the power to act for the Father; if you reject me, you've rejected the Father.'

"Even if you eliminated the fourth gospel and just read the Synoptics, this would still be the conclusion you would come to. And it is the conclusion that Jesus would have led us to if we had a Bible study and asked him this question.

"We have to ask, Why is there no other first-century Jew who has millions of followers today? Why isn't there a John the Baptist movement? Why, of all first-century figures, including the Roman emperors, is Jesus still worshiped today, while the others have crumbled into the dust of history?

"It's because this Jesus—the historical Jesus—is also the living Lord. That's why. It's because he's still around, while the others are long gone."

In the Very Place of God

Like Witherington, many other scholars have painstakingly picked apart the earliest evidence for Jesus and reached the same conclusions.

Wrote Craig, "Here is a man who thought of himself as the Son of God in a unique sense, who claimed to act and speak with divine authority, who held himself to be a worker of miracles, and who believed that people's eternal destiny hinged on whether or not they believed in him."[7]

Then he added a remark that's especially startling: "The clues sufficient for a high christological self-understanding of Jesus are present even in the attenuated twenty percent of Jesus' sayings recognized by the members of the Jesus Seminar as authentic."[8]

The evidence for concluding that Jesus intended to stand in the very place of God is "absolutely convincing," concurred theologian Royce Gordon Gruenler.[9]

So extraordinary is Jesus' assertion, said Craig, that inevitably the issue of his sanity has to come up. He notes that after James Dunn completed his own epic study of this issue, Dunn was compelled to comment, "One last question cannot be ignored: *Was Jesus mad?*"[10]

At the airport in Lexington, waiting for my flight back to Chicago, I dropped coins into a pay phone and called for an appointment to interview one of the country's leading experts on psychology.

It was time to find out.

Deliberations
Questions for Reflection or Group Study

1. What do you think are some reasons why Jesus was evasive in disclosing who he was to the public? Can you imagine some ways in which an early proclamation of his deity could have harmed his mission?

2. What are some of the difficulties we face in determining what historical figures thought about themselves? What clues would you find most helpful in trying to determine this? Why did the clues offered by Witherington convince or fail to persuade you that Jesus thought he was God and the Messiah?

3. Jesus taught his disciples to use the term "Abba," or "Dearest Father," in addressing God. What does this tell you about Jesus' relationship with the Father? Is that kind of relationship attractive to you? Why or why not?

For Further Evidence
More Resources on This Topic

Bauckham, Richard. *Jesus and the God of Israel: God Crucified and Other Studies on the New Testament's Christology of Divine Identity*. Grand Rapids: Eerdmans, 2008.

Bird, Michael F. "Did Jesus Think He was God?" In *How God Became Jesus: The Real Origins of Belief in Jesus' Divine Nature,* by Michael F. Bird, Craig A. Evans, Simon J. Gathercole, Charles Hill, and Chris Tilling, 45–70. Grand Rapids: Zondervan, 2014.

Bock, Darrell L. *Who Is Jesus? Linking the Historical Jesus with the Christ of Faith*. New York: Howard Books, 2012.

Craig, William Lane. "The Self-Understanding of Jesus." In *Reasonable Faith*, Third edition, by William Lane Craig, 287–332. Wheaton, IL: Crossway, 2008.

Hurtado, Larry W. *How on Earth Did Jesus Become a God? Historical Questions about Earliest Devotion to Jesus*. Grand Rapids: Eerdmans, 2005.

Marshall, Howard I. *The Origins of New Testament Christology*. Downers Grove, IL: InterVarsity Press, 1976.

Moule, C. F. D. *The Origins of Christology*. Cambridge: Cambridge University Press, 1977.

Witherington III, Ben. *The Christology of Jesus*. Minneapolis: Fortress Press, 1990.

Wright, N. T. *Christian Origins and the Question of God*. 3 vols. Minneapolis: Fortress Press, 1992, 1996, 2003.

CHAPTER 8

The Psychological Evidence

*Was Jesus Crazy When He Claimed
to Be the Son of God?*

> When a psychologist or psychiatrist testifies, he shall wear a cone-shaped hat that is not less than two feet tall. The surface of the hat shall be imprinted with stars and lightning bolts. Additionally, he shall be required to don a white beard that is not less than eighteen inches in length and shall punctuate crucial elements of his testimony by stabbing the air with a wand. Whenever a psychologist or psychiatrist provides testimony, the bailiff shall contemporaneously dim the courtroom lights and administer two strikes to a Chinese gong.

By suggesting this amendment to the state statutes in 1997, New Mexico state senator Duncan Scott left no doubt about his attitude toward experts who testify that defendants are insane and therefore not legally responsible for their crimes. Apparently, Scott's cynicism was shared by a majority of his colleagues—they voted to approve his tongue-in-cheek proposal! The joke got as far as the House of Representatives, which eventually blocked it from becoming law.[1]

Admittedly, there's an undercurrent of skepticism in courthouses over psychiatrists and psychologists who testify concerning the mental state of defendants, their ability to cooperate with their attorney in preparing their defense, and whether they were legally insane at the time they committed their crime. Even so, most lawyers recognize that mental health professionals offer important insights for the criminal justice system.

I recall a case in which a mild-mannered housewife stood accused of murdering her husband. At first glance she appeared no different from anybody's mother—well dressed, pleasant, kindly, looking as if she had just emerged from baking a fresh batch of chocolate chip cookies for the neighborhood children. I scoffed when a psychologist testified she was mentally unable to stand trial.

Then her lawyer put her on the witness stand. Initially her testimony was clear, rational, and lucid. However, slowly it became more and more bizarre as she described, calmly and with great seriousness, how she had been assaulted by a succession of famous individuals, including Dwight Eisenhower and the ghost of Napoleon. By the time she finished, nobody in the courtroom doubted that she was totally out of touch with reality. The judge committed her to a mental institution until she was well enough to face the charges against her.

Looks can be deceiving. It's the psychologist's job to peer beneath the defendant's veneer and draw conclusions concerning his or her mental condition. It's an inexact science, which means mistakes and even abuses can occur, but overall psychological testimony provides important safeguards for defendants.

How does all this relate to Jesus? In the preceding chapter Dr. Ben Witherington III offered convincing evidence that even the earliest material about Jesus showed he was claiming to be God incarnate. That naturally raises the issue of whether Jesus was crazy when he made those assertions.

In search of an expert's assessment of Jesus' mental state, I drove to a suburban Chicago office building to elicit testimony from one of the country's leading authorities on psychological issues.

THE SEVENTH INTERVIEW:
Gary R. Collins, PhD

With a master's degree in psychology from the University of Toronto and a doctorate in clinical psychology from Purdue University, Collins has been studying, teaching, and writing about human behavior for almost half a century. He was a professor of psychology at Trinity Evangelical Divinity School for two decades, most of that time as chairman of its psychology division.

A live wire with boundless energy and enthusiasm, Collins is a prolific author. He has written nearly 150 articles for journals and other periodicals and was editor of *Christian Counseling Today* and contributing editor of the *Journal of Psychology and Theology*.

He also has produced an astounding forty-five books on psychology-related topics, including *The Magnificent Mind*; *Family Shock*; *Can You Trust Psychology?*; and the classic textbook *Christian Counseling: A Comprehensive Guide*. In addition, he was general editor of the thirty-volume *Resources for Christian Counseling*, a series of books for mental health professionals.

I found Collins in his bright and airy office at the American Association of Christian Counselors, a fifteen-thousand-member society of which he was the president. With salt-and-pepper hair and silver-rimmed glasses, he was looking dapper in a maroon turtleneck sweater, herringbone sports jacket, and gray slacks (but sorry, no pointy hat or flowing white beard).

I started our interview by gesturing out the window, where snow was gently falling on evergreen trees. "A few miles in that direction is a state mental institution," I said. "If we were to go over there, I'm sure we'd find some people who claim that they're God. We'd say they were insane. Jesus said he was God—was he crazy, too?"

"If you want the short answer," Collins said with a chuckle, "it's no."

But, I insisted, this is a legitimate topic that's worthy of further analysis. Experts say that people suffering from delusional psychosis may appear rational much of the time yet can have grandiose beliefs that they are superlative individuals. Some can even attract followers who believe they're geniuses. Maybe that's what happened with Jesus, I suggested.

"Well, it's true that people with psychological difficulties will often claim to be somebody they're not," Collins replied as he clasped his hands behind his head. "They'll sometimes claim to be Jesus himself or the president of the United States or someone else famous—like Lee Strobel," he quipped.

"However," he continued, "psychologists don't just look at what a person says. They'll go much deeper than that. They'll look at a person's emotions, because disturbed individuals frequently show inappropriate depression, or they might be vehemently angry, or perhaps they're plagued with anxiety. But look at Jesus: He never demonstrated inappropriate emotions. For instance, he cried at the death of his friend Lazarus—that's natural for an emotionally healthy individual."

"He certainly got angry at times," I asserted.

"Yes, he did, but it was a healthy kind of anger at people taking advantage of the downtrodden by lining their pockets at the temple. He wasn't just irrationally ticked off because someone was annoying him; this was a righteous reaction against injustice and the blatant mistreatment of people.

"Other deluded people will have misperceptions," he added. "They think people are watching them or are trying to get them when they're not. They're out of contact with reality. They misperceive the actions of other people and accuse them of doing things they have no intention of ever doing. Again, we don't see this in Jesus. He was obviously in contact with reality. He wasn't paranoid, although he rightfully understood that there were some very real dangers around him.

"Or people with psychological difficulties may have thinking disorders—they can't carry on a logical conversation, they'll jump to faulty conclusions, they're irrational. We don't see this in Jesus. He spoke clearly, powerfully, and eloquently. He was brilliant and had absolutely amazing insights into human nature.

"Another sign of mental disturbances is unsuitable behavior, such as dressing oddly or being unable to relate socially to others. Jesus' behavior was quite in line with what would be expected, and he had deep and abiding relationships with a wide variety of people from different walks of life."

He paused, although I sensed he wasn't finished yet. I prompted him to continue by asking, "What else do you observe about him?"

Collins gazed out the window at the beautiful and peaceful snow-blanketed landscape. When he resumed, it was as if he were reminiscing about an old friend.

"He was loving but didn't let his compassion immobilize him; he didn't have a bloated ego, even though he was often surrounded by adoring crowds; he maintained balance despite an often demanding lifestyle; he always knew what he was doing and where he was going; he cared deeply about people, including women and children, who weren't seen as being important back then; he was able to accept people while not merely winking at their sin; he responded to individuals based on where they were at and what they uniquely needed."

"So, Doctor—your diagnosis?" I asked.

"All in all, I just don't see signs that Jesus was suffering from any known mental illness," he concluded, adding with a smile, "He was much healthier than anyone else I know—including me!"

"Raving Mad"

Granted, as we look back through history, we don't see obvious signs of delusion in Jesus. But what about people who were directly interacting with him? What did they see from their much closer vantage point?

"Some people who were on the scene in the first century would vehemently disagree with you," I pointed out to Collins. "They did conclude that Jesus was crazy. John 10:20 tells us that many Jews thought he was 'demon-possessed and raving mad.' Those are strong words!"

"Yes, but that's hardly a diagnosis by a trained mental health professional," Collins countered. "Look at what prompted those words— Jesus' moving and profound teaching about being the Good Shepherd. They were reacting because his assertions about himself were so far beyond their understanding of the norm, not because Jesus was truly mentally unbalanced.

"And notice that their comments were immediately challenged by others, who said in verse 21, 'These are not the sayings of a man possessed by a demon. Can a demon open the eyes of the blind?'"

"Why is that significant?" I asked.

"Because Jesus wasn't just making outrageous claims about himself. He was backing them up with miraculous acts of compassion, like healing the blind.

"You see, if I claimed to be the president of the United States, that would be crazy. You'd look at me and see none of the trappings of the office of president. I wouldn't look like the president. People wouldn't accept my authority as president. No Secret Service agents would be guarding me. But if the real president claimed to be president, that wouldn't be crazy, because he *is* president and there would be plenty of confirming evidence of that.

"In an analogous way, Jesus didn't just claim to be God—he backed it up with amazing feats of healing, with astounding demonstrations of power over nature, with transcendent and unprecedented teaching, with divine insights into people, and ultimately with his own resurrection from the dead, which absolutely nobody else has been able to duplicate. So when Jesus claimed to be God, it wasn't crazy. It was the truth."

However, Collins' appeal to Jesus' miracles opened the door to other objections. "Some people have tried to shoot down these miracles that supposedly help authenticate Jesus' claim to being the Son of God," I said, pulling out a book from my briefcase. I read him the words of skeptic Charles Templeton.

> Many illnesses, then as now, were psychosomatic, and could be "cured" when the sufferer's perception changed. Just as today a placebo prescribed by a physician in whom the patient has faith can effect an apparent cure, so, in an early time, faith in the healer could banish adverse symptoms. With each success the healer's reputation would grow and his powers would, as a consequence, become more efficacious.[2]

"Does this," I demanded, "explain away the miracles that supposedly back up Jesus' claim to being the Son of God?"

Collins' reaction surprised me. "I wouldn't have a whole lot of disagreement with what Templeton wrote," Collins replied.

"You wouldn't?"

"Not really. Might Jesus have sometimes healed by suggestion? I have no problem with that. Sometimes people can have a psychologically induced illness, and if they get a new purpose for living, a new direction, they don't need the illness anymore.

"The placebo effect? If you think you're going to get better, you often do get better. That's a well-established medical fact. And when people came to Jesus, they believed he could heal them, so he did. But the fact remains: Regardless of how he did it, Jesus did heal them.

"Of course," he quickly added, "that doesn't explain all of Jesus' healings. Often a psychosomatic healing takes time; Jesus' healings were spontaneous. Many times people who are healed psychologically have their symptoms return a few days later, but we don't see any evidence of this. And Jesus healed conditions like lifelong blindness and leprosy, for which a psychosomatic explanation isn't very likely.

"On top of that, he brought people back from the dead—and death is not a psychologically induced state! Plus you have all of his nature miracles—the calming of the sea, turning water into wine. They defy naturalistic answers."

Well . . . maybe. However, Collins' mention of the miracle of turning water into wine brought up another possible explanation of Jesus' amazing feats.

Jesus the Hypnotist

Have you ever seen a stage hypnotist give water to someone they've put in a trance and then suggest to them that they were drinking wine? They smack their lips, they get giddy, they start feeling intoxicated, just as if they were swigging a cheap Bordeaux.

British author Ian Wilson has raised the question of whether this is how Jesus convinced the wedding guests at Cana that he had transformed jugs of water into the finest fermented libation.

In fact, Wilson discusses the possibility that Jesus may have been a master hypnotist, which could explain the supposedly supernatural aspects of his life. For instance, hypnosis could account for his exorcisms; his transfiguration, during which three of his followers saw his face glow and his garments shine as white as light; and even his healings. As evidence, Wilson cites the modern example of a sixteen-year-old boy whose serious skin disorder was inexplicably healed through hypnotic suggestion.

Perhaps Lazarus wasn't really brought back from the dead. Couldn't he have been in a deathlike trance that had been induced by hypnosis? As for the resurrection, Jesus "could have effectively conditioned [the disciples] to hallucinate his appearances in response to certain prearranged cues (the breaking of bread?) for a predetermined period after his death," Wilson speculated.[3]

This would even explain the enigmatic reference in the gospels to Jesus' inability to perform many miracles in his hometown of Nazareth. Said Wilson,

Jesus failed precisely where *as a hypnotist* we would most expect him to fail, among those who knew him best, those who had seen him grow up as an ordinary child. Largely responsible for any hypnotist's success rate are the awe and mystery with which he surrounds himself, and these essential factors would have been entirely lacking in Jesus' home town.[4]

"You have to admit," I said to Collins, "that this is a rather interesting way of trying to explain away Jesus' miracles."

There was a look of incredulity on his face. "This guy has a whole lot more faith in hypnosis than I do!" he exclaimed. "While it's a clever argument, it just doesn't stand up to analysis. It's full of holes."

One by one, Collins began to enumerate them. "First, there's the problem of a whole bunch of people being hypnotized. Not everybody is equally susceptible.

"Stage hypnotists will talk in a certain soothing tone of voice to the audience and watch for people who seem to be responding, and then they'll pick these people as their volunteers, because they're readily susceptible to hypnosis. In a big group many people are resistant. When Jesus multiplied the bread and fish, there were five thousand witnesses. How could he have hypnotized them all?

"Second, hypnosis doesn't generally work on people who are skeptics and doubters. So how did Jesus hypnotize his brother James, who doubted him but later saw the resurrected Christ? How did he hypnotize Saul of Tarsus, the opponent of Christianity who never even met Jesus until he saw him after his resurrection? How did he hypnotize Thomas, who was so skeptical he wouldn't believe in the resurrection until he put his fingers in the nail holes in Jesus' hands?

"Third, concerning the resurrection, hypnosis wouldn't explain the empty tomb."

I jumped in. "I suppose someone could claim that the disciples had been hypnotized to imagine the tomb was empty," I offered.

"Even if that were possible," Collins replied, "Jesus certainly couldn't have hypnotized the Pharisees and Roman authorities, and they would have gladly produced his body if it had remained in the tomb. The fact that they didn't tells us the tomb was really empty.

"Fourth, look at the miracle of turning water into wine. Jesus never addressed the wedding guests. He didn't even suggest to the servants that the water had been turned into wine—he merely told them to take some water to the master of the banquet. He's the one who tasted it and said it was wine, with no prior prompting.

"Fifth, the skin healing that Wilson talks about wasn't spontaneous, was it?"

Actually, I said, the *British Medical Journal* says it took five days after the hypnosis for the reptilian skin, called ichthyosis, to fall off the teenager's left arm, and several more days for the skin to appear normal. The hypnotic success rate for dealing with other parts of his body over a period of several weeks was 50 to 95 percent.[5]

"Compare that," Collins said, "with Jesus healing ten lepers in Luke 17. They were instantaneously healed—and 100 percent. That's not explainable merely by hypnosis. And neither is his healing of a man with a shriveled hand in Mark 3. Even if people were in a trance and merely thought his hand had been healed, eventually they would have found out the truth. Hypnosis doesn't last a real long time.

"And finally, the gospels record all sorts of details about what Jesus said and did, but never once do they portray him as saying or doing anything that would suggest he was hypnotizing people. I could go on and on."

I laughed. "I told you it was an interesting explanation; I didn't say it was convincing!" I said. "Yet books are being written to advance these kinds of ideas."

"It's just amazing to me," Collins replied, "how people will grasp at anything to try to disprove Jesus' miracles."

Jesus the Exorcist

Before we finished our interview, I wanted to tap into Collins' psychological expertise in one more area that skeptics find troubling.

"Jesus was an exorcist," I observed. "He talked to demons and cast them out of the people they supposedly possessed. But is it really rational to believe that evil spirits are responsible for some illnesses and bizarre behavior?"

Collins wasn't disturbed by the question. "From my theological beliefs, I accept that demons exist," he replied. "We live in a society in which many people believe in angels. They know there are spiritual forces out there, and it's not too hard to conclude that some might be malevolent. Where you see God working, sometimes those forces are more active, and that's what was probably going on in the time of Jesus."

I noticed Collins had referred to his theological beliefs and not his clinical experience. "Have you, as a psychologist, ever seen clear evidence of the demonic?" I asked.

"I haven't personally, but then I haven't spent my whole career in clinical settings," he said. "My friends in clinical work have said that sometimes they have seen this, and these are not people who are inclined to see a demon behind every problem. They tend to be skeptical. The psychiatrist M. Scott Peck wrote a bit about this kind of thing in his book *People of the Lie*."[6]

I pointed out that Ian Wilson, in suggesting that Jesus may have used hypnosis to cure people who only believed they were possessed, said dismissively that no "realistic individual" would explain a state of possession "as the work of real demons."[7]

"To some degree, you find what you set out to find," Collins said in response. "People who deny the existence of the supernatural will find some way, no matter how far-fetched, to explain a situation apart from the demonic. They'll keep giving medication, keep drugging the person, but he or she doesn't get better. There are cases that don't respond to normal medical or psychiatric treatment."

"Could Jesus' exorcisms really have been psychosomatic healings?" I asked.

"Yes, in some cases, but again you have to look at the whole context. What about the man who was possessed and Jesus sent the demons into the pigs and the pigs ran off the cliff? What's going on if that was a psychosomatic situation? I think Jesus really did drive out demons, and I think some people do that today.

"At the same time, we shouldn't be too quick to jump to a demonic conclusion when faced with a recalcitrant problem. As C. S. Lewis put it, there are two equal and opposite errors we can fall into concerning demons: 'One is to disbelieve in their existence. The other is to believe, and to feel an excessive and unhealthy interest in them. They themselves are equally pleased with both errors.'"[8]

"You know, Gary, that idea might fly with the American Association of Christian Counselors, but would secular psychologists consider it rational to believe in the demonic?" I asked.

I thought Collins might take offense at the question, which came out sounding more condescending than I had intended, but he didn't.

"It's interesting how things are changing," he mused. "Our society today is caught up in 'spirituality.' That's a term that can mean almost anything, but it does recognize the supernatural. It's very interesting what psychologists are believing in these days. Some are into Eastern mystical stuff; some talk about the power of shamans to influence people's lives.

"Whereas twenty-five years ago the suggestion of demonic activity would have been immediately dismissed, many psychologists are beginning to recognize that maybe there are more things in heaven and earth than our philosophies can account for."

"Preposterous Imagination!"

Collins and I had drifted a bit from the original point of our interview. As I thought about our talk while I was driving home, I returned to the central issue that had brought me to him: Jesus claimed to be God. Nobody is suggesting he was intentionally deceptive. And now Collins has concluded, based on thirty-five years of psychological experience, that he was not mentally impaired.

However, that left me with a new question: Did Jesus fulfill the attributes of God? After all, it's one thing to claim divinity; it's quite another to embody the characteristics that make God God.

At a stoplight, I pulled a notebook out of my briefcase and scrawled a note to myself: *Track down D. A. Carson.* I knew that I'd want to talk to one of the country's leading theologians about this next matter.

In the meantime my talk with Gary Collins prompted me to spend time that night carefully rereading the discourses of Jesus. I could detect no sign of dementia, delusions, or paranoia. On the contrary, I was moved once more by his profound wisdom, his uncanny insights, his poetic eloquence, and his deep compassion. Historian Philip Schaff said it better than I can.

Is such an intellect—clear as the sky, bracing as the mountain air, sharp and penetrating as a sword, thoroughly healthy and vigorous, always ready and always self-possessed—liable to a radical and most serious delusion concerning his own character and mission? *Preposterous imagination!*[9]

Deliberations
Questions for Reflection or Group Study

1. What are some of the differences between a patient in a mental hospital claiming to be God and Jesus making the same assertion about himself?

2. Read Jesus' teaching called the Beatitudes in Matthew 5:1–12. What observations can you make about his intellect, eloquence, compassion, insight into human nature, ability to teach profound truths, and overall psychological health?

3. Having read Collins' response to the theory that hypnosis can account for Jesus' miracles, do you believe this is a viable hypothesis? Why or why not?

For Further Evidence
More Resources on This Topic

Collins, Gary R. *Can You Trust Psychology?* Downers Grove, IL: InterVarsity Press, 1988.

Cramer, Raymond L. *Psychology of Jesus and Mental Health.* Grand Rapids: Zondervan, 1987.

Keener, Craig S. *Miracles: The Credibility of New Testament Accounts.* 2 volumes. Grand Rapids.: Baker Academic, 2011.

Twelftree, Graham H. *Jesus the Exorcist: A Contribution to the Study of the Historical Jesus.* Reprint edition. Eugene, OR: Wipf & Stock, 2011.

—————————. *Jesus the Miracle Worker: A Historical and Theological Study.* Downers Grove, IL: InterVarsity Academic, 1999.

CHAPTER 9

The Profile Evidence

Did Jesus Fulfill
the Attributes of God?

Shortly after eight student nurses were murdered in a Chicago apartment, the trembling lone survivor huddled with a police sketch artist and described in detail the killer she had seen from her secret vantage point beneath a bed.

Quickly the drawing was flashed around the city—to police officers, to hospitals, to transit stations, to the airport. Soon an emergency room physician called detectives to say he was treating a man who looked suspiciously like the flinty-eyed fugitive depicted in the sketch.

That's how police arrested a drifter named Richard Speck, who was promptly convicted of the heinous slayings and ended up dying in prison thirty years later.[1]

Ever since Scotland Yard first turned a witness's recollections into a sketch of a murder suspect in 1889, forensic artists have played an important role in law enforcement. Today more than three hundred sketch artists work with U.S. police agencies, and an increasing number of departments are relying on a computerized system called EFIT (Electronic Facial Identification Technique).

This recently developed technology was successfully used to solve a 1997 kidnapping that occurred at a shopping mall just a few miles from my suburban Chicago home. The victim provided details about the kidnapper's appearance to a technician, who used a computer to create an electronic likeness of the offender by choosing from different styles of noses, mouths, hairlines, and so forth.

Just moments after the drawing was faxed to police agencies throughout the area, an investigator in another suburb recognized the picture as a dead ringer for a criminal he had encountered earlier. Fortunately, this led to a quick arrest of the kidnapping suspect.[2]

Oddly enough, the concept of an artist's drawing can provide a rough analogy that can help us in our quest for the truth about Jesus. Here's how: The Old Testament provides numerous details about God that sketch out in great specificity what he's like. For instance, God is described as omnipresent, or existing everywhere in the universe; as omniscient, or knowing everything that can be known throughout eternity; as omnipotent, or all-powerful; as eternal, or being both beyond time and the source of all time; and as immutable, or unchanging in his attributes. He's loving, he's holy, he's righteous, he's wise, he's just.

Now, Jesus claims to be God. But does he fulfill these characteristics of deity? In other words, if we examine Jesus carefully, does his likeness closely match the sketch of God that we find elsewhere in the Bible? If it doesn't, we can conclude that his claim to being God is false.

This is an extremely complex and mind-stretching issue. For example, when Jesus was delivering the Sermon on the Mount on a hillside outside Capernaum, he wasn't simultaneously standing on Main Street of Jericho, so in what sense could he be called omnipresent? How can he be called omniscient if he readily admits in Mark 13:32 that he doesn't know everything about the future? If he's eternal, why does Colossians 1:15 call him "the firstborn over all creation"?

On the surface these issues seem to suggest that Jesus doesn't resemble the sketch of God. Nevertheless, I've learned over the years that initial impressions can be deceiving. That's why I was glad I would be able to discuss these issues with Dr. D. A. Carson, the theologian who has emerged in recent years as one of the most distinguished thinkers in Christianity.

THE EIGHTH INTERVIEW:
Donald A. Carson, PhD

D. A. Carson, a research professor of New Testament at Trinity Evangelical Divinity School, has written or edited more than forty books, including *The Sermon on the Mount*; *Exegetical Fallacies*; *The Gospel According to John*; and his award-winning *The Gagging of God*.

He can read a dozen languages (his mastery of French stems from a childhood spent in Quebec) and is a member of the Tyndale Fellowship for Biblical Research, the Society for Biblical Literature, and the Institute for Biblical Research. His areas of expertise include the historical Jesus, postmodernism, Greek grammar, and the theology of the apostles Paul and John.

After initially studying chemistry (receiving a bachelor of science degree from McGill University), Carson went on to receive a master of divinity degree before going to England, where he earned a doctorate in New Testament at prestigious Cambridge University. He taught at three other colleges and seminaries before joining Trinity in 1978.

I had never met Carson before I drove onto Trinity's Deerfield, Illinois, campus for our interview. Frankly, I was expecting a starched academic. But while I found Carson to be every bit the scholar I had anticipated, I was taken aback by his warm, sincere, and pastoral tone as he responded to what turned out to be, in some cases, rather caustic questions.

Our conversation was held in an otherwise deserted faculty lounge over Christmas break. Carson was wearing a white windbreaker over a button-down shirt, blue jeans, and Adidas shoes. After some preliminary banter about our mutual appreciation of England (Carson has lived there off and on through the years, and his wife, Joy, is British), I pulled out my notebook, started my recorder, and posed a background question to help determine whether Jesus has "the right stuff" to be God.

Living and Forgiving Like God

My initial question centered on why Carson thinks Jesus is God in the first place. "What did he say or do," I asked, "that convinces you that he is divine?" I wasn't sure how he would respond, although I anticipated he would focus on Jesus' supernatural feats. I was wrong.

"One could point to such things as his miracles," Carson said as he leaned back in the comfortably upholstered chair, "but other people have done miracles, so while this may be indicative, it's not decisive. Of course, the resurrection was the ultimate vindication of his identity. But of the many things he did, one of the most striking to me is his forgiving of sin."

"Really?" I said, shifting in my chair, which was perpendicular to his, in order to face him more directly. "How so?"

"The point is, if you do something against me, I have the right to forgive you. However, if you do something against me and somebody else comes along and says, 'I forgive you,' what kind of cheek is that? The only person who can say that sort of thing meaningfully is God himself, because sin, even if it is against other people, is first and foremost a defiance of God and his laws.

"When David sinned by committing adultery and arranging the death of the woman's husband, he ultimately says to God in Psalm 51, 'Against you, only you, have I sinned and done what is evil in your sight.' He recognized that although he had wronged people, in the end he had sinned against the God who made him in his image, and God needed to forgive him.

"So along comes Jesus and says to sinners, 'I forgive you.' The Jews immediately recognize the blasphemy of this. They react by saying, 'Who can forgive sins but God alone?' To my mind, that is one of the most striking things Jesus did."

"Not only did Jesus forgive sin," I observed, "but he asserted that he himself was without sin. And certainly sinlessness is an attribute of deity."

"Yes," he replied. "Historically in the West, people considered most holy have also been the most conscious of their own failures and sins. They are people who are aware of their shortcomings and lusts and resentments, and they're fighting them honestly by the grace of God. In fact, they're fighting them so well that others take notice and say, 'There is a holy man or woman.'

"But along comes Jesus, who can say with a straight face, 'Which of you can convict me of sin?'³ If I said that, my wife and children and all who know me would be glad to stand up and testify, whereas no one could with respect to Christ."

Although moral perfection and the forgiveness of sin are undoubtedly characteristics of deity, there are several additional attributes that Jesus must fulfill if he is to match the sketch of God. It was time to progress to those. After having started by lobbing softballs at Carson, I got ready to throw some curves.

Mystery of the Incarnation

Using some notes I had brought along, I hit Carson in rapid-fire succession with some of the biggest obstacles to Jesus' claim of deity.

"Dr. Carson, how in the world could Jesus be omnipresent if he couldn't be in two places at once?" I asked. "How could he be omniscient when he says, 'Not even the Son of Man knows the hour of his return'? How could he be omnipotent when the gospels plainly tell us that he was unable to do many miracles in his hometown?"

Pointing my pen at him for emphasis, I concluded by saying, "Let's admit it: The Bible itself seems to argue against Jesus being God."

While Carson didn't flinch, he did concede that these questions have no simple answers. After all, they strike at the very heart of the incarnation—God becoming man, spirit taking on flesh, the infinite becoming finite, the eternal becoming time-bound. It's a doctrine that has kept theologians busy for centuries. And that's where Carson chose to start his answer: by going back to the way scholars have tried to respond to these matters through the years.

"Historically, there have been two or three approaches to this," he began, sounding a bit as if he were beginning a classroom lecture.

"For example, at the end of the last century, the great theologian Benjamin Warfield worked through the gospels and ascribed various bits either to Christ's humanity or to his deity. When Jesus does something that's a reflection of him being God, that's ascribed to Christ's deity. When there's something reflecting his limitations or finiteness or his humanness—for example, his tears; does God cry?—that's ascribed to his humanity."

That explanation was fraught with problems, it seemed to me. "If you do that, wouldn't you end up with a schizophrenic Jesus?" I asked.

"It's easy to slip into that unwittingly," he replied. "All the confessional statements have insisted that both Jesus' humanity and his deity remained distinct, yet they combined in one person. So you want to avoid a solution in which there are essentially two minds—sort of a Jesus human mind and a Christ heavenly mind. However, this is one kind of solution, and there may be something to it.

"The other kind of solution is some form of *kenosis*, which means 'emptying.' This spins out of Philippians 2, where Paul tells us that Jesus, 'being in the form of God, did not think equality with God was something to be exploited'—that's the way it should be translated—'but emptied himself.' He became a nobody."

That seemed a little ambiguous to me. "Can you be more explicit?" I asked. "What exactly did he empty himself of?"

Apparently, I had put my finger on the issue. "Ah, that's the question," Carson replied with a nod. "Through the centuries, people have given various answers to that. For instance, did he empty himself of his deity? Well, then he would no longer be God.

"Did he empty himself of the attributes of his deity? I have a problem with that too, because it's difficult to separate attributes from reality. If you have an animal that looks like a horse, smells like a horse, walks like a horse, and has all the attributes of a horse, you've got a horse. So I don't know what it means for God to empty himself of his attributes and still be God.

"Some have said, 'He didn't empty himself of his attributes, but he emptied himself of the use of his attributes'—a self-limiting type of thing. That's getting closer, although there are times when that was not what he was doing—he was forgiving sins the way only God can, which is an attribute of deity.

"Others go further by saying, 'He emptied himself of the independent use of his attributes.' That is, he functioned like God when his heavenly Father gave him explicit sanction to do so. Now, that's much closer. The difficulty is that there is a sense in which the eternal Son has always acted in line with his Father's commandments. You don't want to lose that, even in eternity past. But it's getting closer."

I sensed we were somewhere in the vicinity of the bull's-eye, but I wasn't sure we were going to get much closer. That seemed to be Carson's sentiment, too.

"Strictly speaking," he said, "Philippians 2 does not tell us precisely what the eternal Son emptied himself of. He emptied himself; he became a nobody. Some kind of emptying is at issue, but let's be frank—you're talking about the incarnation, one of the central mysteries of the Christian faith.

"You're dealing with formless, bodiless, omniscient, omnipresent,

omnipotent Spirit and finite, touchable, physical, time-bound crea-
tures. For one to become the other inevitably binds you up in mysteries.

"So part of Christian theology has been concerned not with 'explaining it all away' but with trying to take the biblical evidence and, retain-
ing all of it fairly, find ways of synthesis that are rationally coherent,
even if they're not exhaustively explanatory."

That was a sophisticated way of saying that theologians can come
up with explanations that seem to make sense, even though they might
not be able to explain every nuance about the incarnation. In a way, that
seemed logical. If the incarnation is true, it's not surprising that finite
minds couldn't totally comprehend it.

It seemed to me that some sort of voluntary "emptying" of Jesus'
independent use of his attributes was reasonable in explaining why he
generally didn't exhibit the "omnis"—omniscience, omnipotence, and
omnipresence—in his earthly existence, even though the New Testament
clearly states that all these qualities are ultimately true of him.

That, however, was only part of the problem. I flipped to the next
page of my notes and began another line of questioning about some
specific biblical passages that seemed to directly contradict Jesus' claim
to being God.

Creator or Created?

Part of the sketch that Jesus must match is that God is an uncreated
being who has existed from eternity past. Isaiah 57:15 describes God as
"he who lives forever." But, I said to Carson, there are some verses that
seem to strongly suggest that Jesus was a created being.

"For instance," I said, "John 3:16 calls Jesus the 'begotten' Son of
God, and Colossians 1:15 says he was the 'firstborn over all creation.'
Don't they clearly imply that Jesus was created, as opposed to being the
Creator?"

One of Carson's areas of expertise is Greek grammar, which he called
upon in responding to both of those verses.

"Let's take John 3:16," he said. "It's the King James Version that
translates the Greek with the words 'his only begotten Son.' Those
who consider this the correct rendering usually bind that up with the

incarnation itself—that is, his begetting in the Virgin Mary. But in fact, that's not what the word in Greek means.

"It really means 'unique one.' The way it was usually used in the first century is 'unique and beloved.' So John 3:16 is simply saying that Jesus is the unique and beloved Son—or as the New International Version translates it, 'the one and only Son'—rather than saying that he's onto-logically begotten in time."

"That only explains that one passage," I pointed out.

"OK, let's look at the Colossians verse, which uses the term 'first-born.' The vast majority of commentators, whether conservative or liberal, recognize that in the Old Testament the firstborn, because of the laws of succession, normally received the lion's share of the estate, or the firstborn would become king in the case of a royal family. The firstborn therefore was the one ultimately with all the rights of the father.

"By the second century before Christ, there are places where the word no longer has any notion of actual begetting or of being born first but carries the idea of the authority that comes with the position of being the rightful heir. That's the way it applies to Jesus, as virtually all scholars admit. In light of that, the very expression 'firstborn' is slightly misleading."

"What would be a better translation?" I asked.

"I think 'supreme heir' would be more appropriate," he responded.

While that would explain the Colossians passage, Carson went even further, with one last point.

"If you're going to quote Colossians 1:15, you have to keep it in context by going on to Colossians 2:9, where the very same author stresses, 'For in Christ all the fullness of the Deity lives in bodily form.' The author wouldn't contradict himself. So the term 'firstborn' cannot exclude Jesus' eternality, since that is part of what it means to possess the fullness of the divine."

For me, that nailed the issue. But there were other troubling pas-sages as well. For example, in Mark 10 someone addresses Jesus as "good teacher," promoting him to reply, "Why do you call me good? No one is good—except God alone."

"Wasn't he denying his divinity by saying this?" I asked.

"No, I think he was trying to get the fellow to stop and think about what he was saying," Carson explained. "The parallel passage in

Matthew is a little more expansive and does not find Jesus downplaying his deity at all.

"I think all he's saying is, 'Wait a minute; why are you calling me good? Is this just a polite thing, like you say, "Good day"? What do you mean by good? You call me good master—is this because you're trying to honey up to me?'

"In a fundamental sense there's only one who is good, and that's God. But Jesus is not implicitly saying, 'So don't call me that.' He's saying, 'Do you really understand what you're saying when you say that? Are you really ascribing to me what should only be ascribed to God?'

"That could be teased out to mean, 'I really am what you say; you speak better than you know' or 'Don't you dare call me that; next time call me "sinner Jesus" like everybody else does.' In terms of all that Jesus says and does elsewhere, which way does it make sense to take it?"

With so many verses that call Jesus "sinless," "holy," "righteous," "innocent," "undefiled," and "separate from sinners," the answer was pretty obvious.

Was Jesus a Lesser God?

If Jesus was God, what kind of God was he? Was he equal to the Father, or some sort of junior God, possessing the attributes of deity and yet somehow failing to match the total sketch that the Old Testament provides of the divine?

That question comes out of another passage that I pointed out to Carson. "Jesus said in John 14:28, 'The Father is greater than I.' Some people look at this and conclude that Jesus must have been a lesser God. Are they right?" I asked.

Carson sighed. "My father was a preacher," he replied, "and a dictum in our home when I was growing up was, 'A text without a context becomes a pretext for a prooftext.' It's very important to see this passage in its context.

"The disciples are moaning because Jesus has said he's going away. Jesus says, 'If you loved me, you'd be glad for my sake when I say I'm going away, because the Father is greater than I.' That is to say, Jesus is returning to the glory that is properly his, so if they really know who he is and really love him properly, they'll be glad that he's going back to the realm where he really is greater. Jesus says in John 17:5, 'Glorify me with the glory that I had with the Father before the world began'—that is, 'the Father is greater than I.'

"When you use a category like 'greater,' it doesn't have to mean ontologically greater. If I say, for example, that the president of the United States is greater than I, I'm not saying he's an ontologically superior being. He's greater in military capability, political prowess, and public acclaim, but he's not more of a man than I am. He's a human being and I'm a human being.

"So when Jesus says, 'The Father is greater than I,' one must look at the context and ask if Jesus is saying, 'The Father is greater than I because he's God and I'm not.' Frankly, that would be a pretty ridiculous thing to say. Suppose I got up on some podium to preach and said, 'I solemnly declare to you that God is greater than I am.' That would be a rather useless observation.

"The comparison is only meaningful if they're already on the same plane and there's some delimitation going on. Jesus is in the limitations of the incarnation—he's going to the cross; he's going to die—but he's about to return to the Father and to the glory he had with the Father before the world began.

"He's saying, 'You guys are moaning for my sake; you ought to be glad because I'm going home.' It's in that sense that 'the Father is greater than I.'"

"So," I said, "this isn't an implicit denial of his deity."

"No," he concluded, "it's really not. The context makes that clear."

While I was ready to accept the fact that Jesus was not a lesser God, I had a different and more sensitive issue to raise: How could Jesus be a compassionate God yet endorse the idea of eternal suffering for those who reject him?

The Disquieting Question of Hell

The Bible says that the Father is loving. The New Testament affirms the same about Jesus. But can they really be loving while at the same time sending people to hell? After all, Jesus teaches more about hell than anyone in the entire Bible. Doesn't that contradict his supposed gentle and compassionate character?

In posing this question to Carson, I quoted the hard-edged words of agnostic Charles Templeton: "How could a loving Heavenly Father create an endless hell and, over the centuries, consign millions of people to it because they do not or cannot or will not accept certain religious beliefs?"[4]

That question, though tweaked for maximum impact, didn't raise Carson's ire. He began with a clarification. "First of all," he said, "I'm not sure that God simply casts people into hell because they don't accept certain beliefs."

He thought for a moment, then backed up to take a run at a more thorough answer by discussing a subject that many modern people consider a quaint anachronism: sin.

"Picture God in the beginning of creation with a man and woman made in his image," Carson said. "They wake up in the morning and think about God. They love him truly. They delight to do what he wants; it's their whole pleasure. They're rightly related to him, and they're rightly related to each other.

"Then, with the entrance of sin and rebellion into the world, these image bearers begin to think that they are at the center of the universe. Not literally, but that's the way they think. And that's the way we think. All the things we call 'social pathologies'—war, rape, bitterness, nurtured envies, secret jealousies, pride, inferiority complexes—are bound up in the first instance with the fact that we're not rightly related with God. The consequence is that people get hurt.

"From God's perspective, that is shockingly disgusting. So what should God do about it? If he says, 'Well, I don't give a rip,' he's saying that evil doesn't matter to him. It's a bit like saying, 'Oh yeah, the Holocaust—I don't care.' Wouldn't we be shocked if we thought God didn't have moral judgments on such matters?

"But in principle, if he's the sort of God who has moral judgments on those matters, he's got to have moral judgments on this huge matter of all these divine image bearers shaking their puny fists at his face and singing with Frank Sinatra, 'I did it my way.' That's the real nature of sin.

"Having said that, hell is not a place where people are consigned because they were pretty good blokes but just didn't believe the right stuff. They're consigned there, first and foremost, because they defy their Maker and want to be at the center of the universe. Hell is not filled with people who have already repented, only God isn't gentle enough or good enough to let them out. It's filled with people who, for all eternity, still want to be at the center of the universe and who persist in their God-defying rebellion.

"What is God to do? If he says it doesn't matter to him, God is no longer a God to be admired. He's either amoral or positively creepy. For him to act in any other way in the face of such blatant defiance would be to reduce God himself."

I interjected, "Yes, but what seems to bother people the most is the idea that God will torment people for eternity. That seems vicious, doesn't it?"

Replied Carson, "In the first place, the Bible says that there are different degrees of punishment, so I'm not sure that it's the same level of intensity for all people.

"In the second place, if God took his hands off this fallen world so that there were no restraints on human wickedness, we would make hell. Thus, if you allow a whole lot of sinners to live somewhere in a confined place where they're not doing damage to anyone but themselves, what do you get but hell? There's a sense in which they're doing it to themselves, and it's what they want because they still don't repent."

I thought Carson was finished with his answer, because he hesitated for a moment. However, he had one more crucial point. "One of the things that the Bible does insist is that in the end not only will justice be done, but justice will be seen to be done, so that every mouth will be stopped."

I grabbed ahold of that last statement. "In other words," I said, "at the time of judgment there is nobody in the world who will walk away from that experience saying that they have been treated unfairly by God. Everyone will recognize the fundamental justice in the way God judges them and the world."

"That's right," Carson said firmly. "Justice is not always done in this world; we see that every day. But on the Last Day it will be done for all to see. And no one will be able to complain by saying, 'This isn't fair.'"

Jesus and Slavery

There was one other issue I wanted to raise with Carson. I glanced at my watch. "Do you have a few more minutes?" I asked. When he indicated he did, I began to address one more controversial topic.

To be God, Jesus must be ethically perfect. But some critics of Christianity have charged that he fell short because, they say, he tacitly approved of the morally abhorrent practice of slavery. As Morton Smith wrote,

> There were innumerable slaves of the emperor and of the Roman state; the Jerusalem Temple owned slaves; the High Priest owned slaves (one of them lost an ear in Jesus' arrest); all of the rich and almost all of the middle class owned slaves. So far as we are told, Jesus never attacked this practice. . . . There seem to have been slave revolts in Palestine and Jordan in Jesus' youth; a miracle-working leader of such a revolt would have attracted a large following. If Jesus had denounced slavery or promised liberation, we should almost certainly have heard of his doing it. We hear nothing, so the most likely supposition is that he said nothing.[5]

How can Jesus' failure to push for the abolition of slavery be squared with God's love for all people? "Why didn't Jesus stand up and shout, 'Slavery is wrong'?" I asked. "Was he morally deficient for not working to dismantle an institution that demeaned people who were made in the image of God?"

Carson straightened up in his chair. "I really think that people who raise that objection are missing the point," he said. "If you'll permit me, I'll set the stage by talking about slavery, ancient and modern, because in our culture the issue is understandably charged with overtones that it didn't have in the ancient world."

I gestured for him to continue. "Please go ahead," I said.

Overthrowing Oppression

"In his book *Race and Culture*,[6] African-American scholar Thomas Sowell points out that every major world culture until the modern period, without exception, has had slavery," Carson explained. "While it could be tied to military conquests, usually slavery served an economic function. They didn't have bankruptcy laws, so if you got yourself into terrible hock, you sold yourself and/or your family into slavery. As it was discharging a debt, slavery was also providing work. It wasn't necessarily all bad; at least it was an option for survival.

"Please understand me: I'm not trying to romanticize slavery in any way. However, in Roman times there were menial laborers who were slaves, and there were also others who were the equivalent of distinguished PhDs, who were teaching families. And there was no association of a particular race with slavery.

"In American slavery, though, all blacks and only blacks were slaves. That was one of the peculiar horrors of it, and it generated an unfair sense of black inferiority that many of us continue to fight to this day.

"Now let's look at the Bible. In Jewish society, under the Law everyone was to be freed every Jubilee. In other words, there was a slavery liberation every seventh year. Whether or not things actually worked out that way, this was nevertheless what God said, and this was the framework in which Jesus was brought up.

"But you have to keep your eye on Jesus' mission. Essentially, he did not come to overturn the Roman economic system, which included slavery. He came to free men and women from their sins. And here's my point: What his message does is transform people so they begin to love God with all their heart, soul, mind, and strength, and to love their neighbor as themselves. Naturally, that has an impact on the idea of slavery.

"Look at what the apostle Paul says in his letter to Philemon concerning a runaway slave named Onesimus. Paul doesn't say to overthrow slavery, because all that would do would be to get him executed. Instead he tells Philemon he'd better treat Onesimus as a brother in Christ, just as he would treat Paul himself. And then, to make matters perfectly clear, Paul emphasizes, 'Remember, you owe your whole life to me because of the gospel.'

"The overthrowing of slavery, then, is through the transformation of men and women by the gospel rather than through merely changing an economic system. We've all seen what can happen when you merely overthrow an economic system and impose a new order. The whole communist dream was to have a 'revolutionary man' followed by the 'new man.' Trouble is, they never found the 'new man.' They got rid of the oppressors of the peasants, but that didn't mean the peasants were suddenly free—they were just under a new regime of darkness. In the final analysis, if you want lasting change, you've got to transform the hearts of human beings. And that was Jesus' mission.

"It's also worth asking the question that Sowell poses: How did slavery stop? He points out that the driving impetus for the abolition of slavery was the evangelical awakening in England. Christians rammed abolition through Parliament in the beginning of the nineteenth century and then eventually used British gunboats to stop the slave trade across the Atlantic.

"While there were about eleven million Africans who were shipped to America—and many didn't make it—there were about thirteen million Africans shipped to become slaves in the Arab world. Again it was the British, prompted by people whose hearts had been changed by Christ, who sent their gunboats to the Persian Gulf to oppose this."

Carson's response made sense not only historically but also in my own experience. For example, years ago I knew a businessman who was a rabid racist with a superior and condescending attitude toward anyone of another color. He hardly made any effort to conceal his contempt for African-Americans, letting his bigoted bile frequently spill out in crude jokes and caustic remarks. No amount of arguments could dissuade him from his disgusting opinions.

Then he became a follower of Jesus. As I watched in amazement, his attitudes, his perspective, and his values changed over time as his heart was renewed by God. He came to realize that he could no longer harbor ill will toward any person, since the Bible teaches that all people are made in the image of God. Today I can honestly say that he's genuinely caring and accepting toward others, including those who are different from him.

Legislation didn't change him. Reasoning didn't change him. Emotional appeals didn't change him. He'll tell you that God changed him from the inside out—decisively, completely, permanently. That's one of many examples I've seen of the power of the gospel that Carson was talking about—the power to transform vengeful haters into humanitarians, hardhearted hoarders into softhearted givers, power mongers into selfless servants, and people who exploit others—through slavery or some other form of oppression—into people who embrace all.

This squares with what the apostle Paul said in Galatians 3:28: "There is neither Jew nor Gentile, neither slave nor free, nor is there male and female, for you are all one in Christ Jesus."

Matching the Sketch of God

Carson and I talked, sometimes in animated tones, for two hours, filling more tapes than would fit in this chapter. I found his answers to be well reasoned and theologically sound. In the end, however, how the incarnation works—how Spirit takes on flesh—remained a mind-boggling concept.

Even so, according to the Bible, the fact that it did occur is not in any doubt. Every attribute of God, says the New Testament, is found in Jesus Christ:

- Omniscience? In John 16:30 the apostle John affirms of Jesus, "Now we can see that you know all things."

- Omnipresence? Jesus said in Matthew 28:20, "Surely I am with you always, to the very end of the age" and in Matthew 18:20, "Where two or three gather in my name, there am I with them."

- Omnipotence? "All authority in heaven and on earth has been given to me," Jesus said in Matthew 28:18.

- Eternality? John 1:1 declares of Jesus, "In the beginning was the Word, and the Word was with God, and the Word was God."

- Immutability? Hebrews 13:8 says, "Jesus Christ is the same yesterday and today and forever."

Also, the Old Testament paints a portrait of God by using such titles and descriptions as Alpha and Omega, Lord, Savior, King, Judge, Light, Rock, Redeemer, Shepherd, Creator, giver of life, forgiver of sin, and speaker with divine authority. It's fascinating to note that in the New Testament each and every one is applied to Jesus.[7]

Jesus said it all in John 14:7: "If you really know me, you will know my Father as well." Loose translation: "When you look at the sketch of God from the Old Testament, you will see a likeness of me."

Deliberations
Questions for Reflection or Group Study

1. Read Philippians 2:5–8, which talks about Jesus emptying himself and being born into humble circumstances, with the cross as his destination. What are some possible motivations for Jesus to do this? Then read verses 9–11. What happens as a result of Jesus' mission? What could prompt everyone to someday conclude that Jesus is Lord?

2. Has the idea of hell been an impediment in your spiritual journey? How do you respond to Carson's explanation of this issue?

3. Carson addressed some verses that on the surface seemed to suggest that Jesus was a created being or a lesser God. Did you find his reasoning persuasive? Why or why not? What did his analysis of these issues teach you in terms of the need for appropriate background information in interpreting Scripture?

For Further Evidence
More Resources on This Topic

Bauckham, Richard. *God Crucified: Monotheism and Christology in the New Testament.* Grand Rapids: Eerdmans, 1999.

Bowman, Robert M. Jr., and J. Ed Komoszewski. *Putting Jesus in His Place.* Grand Rapids: Kregel, 2007.

Gathercole, Simon J. *The Preexistent Son: Recovering the Christologies of Matthew, Mark, and Luke.* Grand Rapids: Eerdmans, 2006.

Harris, Murray J. *Jesus as God.* Grand Rapids: Baker, 1992.

Longnecker, Richard N., ed. *Contours of Christology in the New Testament.* Grand Rapids: Eerdmans, 2005.

Morgan, Christopher W., and Robert A. Peterson. *The Deity of Christ.* Wheaton, IL: Crossway, 2011.

Ware, Bruce A. *The Man Christ Jesus.* Wheaton, IL: Crossway, 2012.

Witherington III, Ben. *The Many Faces of the Christ: The Christologies of the New Testament and Beyond.* New York: Crossroad, 1998.

——————————. *The Christology of Jesus.* Minneapolis: Augsburg Fortress, 1990.

CHAPTER 10

The Fingerprint Evidence
Did Jesus—and Jesus Alone—
Match the Identity of the Messiah?

I t was an uneventful Saturday at the Hiller home in Chicago. Clarence Hiller spent the afternoon painting the trim on the outside of his two-story house on West 104th Street. By early evening he and his family had retired to bed. However, what happened next would change criminal law in America forever.

The Hillers woke in the early morning hours of September 19, 1910, and became suspicious that a gaslight near their daughter's bedroom had gone out. Clarence went to investigate. His wife heard a quick succession of sounds: a scuffle, two men tumbling down the stairs, two gunshots, and the slamming of the front door. She emerged to find Clarence dead at the foot of the stairs.

Police arrested Thomas Jennings, a convicted burglar, less than a mile away. There was blood on his clothes and his left arm had been injured—both, he said, from falling on a streetcar. In his pocket they found the same kind of gun that had been used to shoot Clarence Hiller, but they couldn't determine if it was the murder weapon.

Knowing they needed more to convict Jennings, detectives scoured the inside of Hiller's home in a search for additional clues. One fact soon became obvious: the killer had entered through a rear kitchen window. Detectives went outside, and there, next to that window, forever imprinted in the white paint that the murder victim himself had so carefully applied to a railing only hours before his death, they found four clear fingerprints from someone's left hand.

Fingerprint evidence was a new concept at the time, having been recently introduced at an international police exhibition in St. Louis.

So far, fingerprints had never been used to convict anyone of murder in the United States.

Despite strong objections by defense attorneys that such evidence was unscientific and inadmissible, four officers testified that the fingerprints in the paint perfectly matched those of Thomas Jennings—and him alone. The jury found Jennings guilty, the Illinois Supreme Court upheld his conviction in a historic ruling, and he was later hanged.[1]

The premise behind fingerprint evidence is simple: Each individual has unique ridges on his or her fingers. When a print found on an object matches the pattern of ridges on a person's finger, investigators can conclude with scientific certainty that this specific individual has touched that object.

In many criminal cases, fingerprint identification is the pivotal evidence. I remember covering a trial in which a single thumbprint found on the cellophane wrapper of a cigarette package was the determining factor in convicting a twenty-year-old burglar of murdering a college coed.[2] That's how conclusive fingerprint evidence can be.

OK, but what has this got to do with Jesus Christ? Simply this: There is another kind of evidence that's analogous to fingerprints and establishes to an astounding degree of certainty that Jesus is indeed the Messiah of Israel and the world.

In the Jewish Scriptures, which Christians call the Old Testament, there are several dozen major prophecies about the coming of the Messiah, who would be sent by God to redeem his people. In effect, these predictions formed a figurative fingerprint that only the Anointed One would be able to match. This way, the Israelites could rule out any impostors and validate the credentials of the authentic Messiah.

The Greek word for "Messiah" is *Christ.* But was Jesus really the Christ? Did he miraculously fulfill these predictions that were written hundreds of years before he was born? And how do we know he was the only individual throughout history who fit the prophetic fingerprint?

There are plenty of scholars with long strings of initials after their names whom I could have asked about this topic. However, I wanted to interview someone for whom this was more than just an abstract academic exercise, and that took me to a very unlikely setting in southern California.

THE NINTH INTERVIEW:
Louis S. Lapides, MDiv, ThM

Usually a church would be a natural location in which to question someone about a biblical issue. But there was something different about sitting down with Pastor Louis Lapides in the sanctuary of his congregation on the morning after Sunday worship services. This setting of pews and stained glass was not where you would expect to find a nice Jewish boy from Newark, New Jersey.

Yet that's Lapides' background. For someone with his heritage, the question of whether Jesus is the long-anticipated Messiah goes beyond theory. It's intensely personal, and I had sought out Lapides so I could hear the story of his own investigation of this critical issue.

Lapides earned a bachelor's degree in theology from Dallas Baptist University as well as a master of divinity and a master of theology degree in Old Testament and Semitics from Talbot Theological Seminary. He served for a decade with Chosen People Ministries, talking about Jesus to Jewish college students. He has taught in the Bible department of Biola University and worked for seven years as an instructor for Walk Through the Bible seminars. He is also the former president of a national network of fifteen messianic congregations.

Slender and bespectacled, Lapides is soft-spoken but has a quick smile and a ready laugh. He was upbeat and polite as he ushered me to a chair near the front of Beth Ariel Fellowship in Sherman Oaks, California. I didn't want to begin by debating biblical nuances; instead, I started by inviting Lapides to tell me the story of his spiritual journey.

He folded his hands in his lap, looked at the dark wood walls for a moment as he decided where to start, and then began unfolding an extraordinary tale that took us from Newark to Greenwich Village to Vietnam to Los Angeles, from skepticism to faith, from Judaism to Christianity, from Jesus as irrelevant to Jesus as Messiah.

"As you know, I came from a Jewish family," he began. "I attended a conservative Jewish synagogue for seven years in preparation for bar mitzvah. Although we considered those studies to be very important, our family's faith didn't affect our everyday life very much. We didn't stop work on the Sabbath; we didn't have a kosher home."

He smiled. "However, on the High Holy Days we attended the stricter Orthodox synagogue, because somehow my dad felt that's where you went if you really wanted to get serious with God!"

When I interjected to ask what his parents had taught him about the Messiah, Lapides' answer was crisp. "It never came up," he said matter-of-factly.

I was incredulous. In fact, I thought I had misunderstood him. "You're saying it wasn't even discussed?" I asked.

"Never," he reiterated. "I don't even remember it being an issue in Hebrew school."

This was amazing to me. "How about Jesus?" I asked. "Was he ever talked about? Was his name used?"

"Only derogatorily!" Lapides quipped. "Basically, he was never discussed. My impressions of Jesus came from seeing Catholic churches: There was the cross, the crown of thorns, the pierced side, the blood coming from his head. It didn't make any sense to me. Why would you worship a man on a cross with nails in his hands and his feet? I never once thought Jesus had any connection to the Jewish people. I just thought he was a god of the Gentiles."

I suspected that Lapides' attitudes toward Christians had gone beyond mere confusion over their beliefs. "Did you believe Christians were at the root of anti-Semitism?" I asked.

"Gentiles were looked upon as synonymous with Christians, and we were taught to be cautious because there could be anti-Semitism among the Gentiles," he said, sounding a bit diplomatic.

I pursued the issue further. "Would you say you developed some negative attitudes toward Christians?"

This time he didn't mince words. "Yes, actually I did," he said. "In fact, later, when the New Testament was first presented to me, I sincerely thought it was going to basically be a handbook on anti-Semitism: how to hate Jews, how to kill Jews, how to massacre them. I thought the American Nazi Party would have been very comfortable using it as a guidebook."

I shook my head, saddened at the thought of how many other Jewish children have grown up thinking of Christians as their enemies.

A Spiritual Quest Begins

Lapides said several incidents dimmed his allegiance to Judaism as he was growing up. Curious about the details, I asked him to elaborate, and he immediately turned to what was clearly the most heartrending episode of his life.

"My parents got divorced when I was seventeen," he said—and surprisingly, even after all these years I could still detect hurt in his voice. "That really put a stake in any religious heart I may have had. I wondered, Where does God come in? Why didn't they go to a rabbi for counseling? What good is religion if it can't help people in a practical way? It sure couldn't keep my parents together. When they split up, part of me split as well.

"On top of that, in Judaism I didn't feel as if I had a personal relationship with God. I had a lot of beautiful ceremonies and traditions, but he was the distant and detached God of Mount Sinai who said, 'Here are the rules—you live by them, you'll be OK; I'll see you later.' And there I was, an adolescent with raging hormones, wondering, Does God relate to my struggles? Does he care about me as an individual? Well, not in any way I could see."

The divorce prompted an era of rebellion. Consumed with music and influenced by the writings of Jack Kerouac and Timothy Leary, he spent too much time in Greenwich Village coffeehouses to go to college—making him vulnerable to the draft. By 1967 he found himself on the other side of the world in a cargo boat whose volatile freight— ammunition, bombs, rockets, and other high explosives—made it a tempting target for the Vietcong.

"I remember being told at our orientation in Vietnam, 'Twenty percent of you will probably get killed, and the other eighty percent will probably get a venereal disease or become alcoholics or get hooked on drugs.' I thought, I don't even have a one percent chance of coming out normal!

"It was a very dark period. I witnessed suffering. I saw body bags; I saw the devastation from war. And I encountered anti-Semitism among some of the GIs. A few of them from the South even burned a cross one night. I probably wanted to distance myself from my Jewish identity— maybe that's why I began delving into Eastern religions."

Lapides read books on Eastern philosophies and visited Buddhist temples while in Japan. "I was extremely bothered by the evil I had seen, and I was trying to figure out how faith can deal with it," he told me. "I used to say, 'If there's a God, I don't care if I find him on Mount Sinai or Mount Fuji. I'll take him either way.'"

He survived Vietnam, returning home with a newfound taste for marijuana and plans to become a Buddhist priest. He tried to live an ascetic lifestyle of self-denial in an effort to work off the bad karma for the misdeeds of his past, but soon he realized he'd never be able to make up for all his wrongs.

Lapides was quiet for a moment. "I got depressed," he said. "I remember getting on the subway and thinking, Maybe jumping onto the tracks is the answer. I could free myself from this body and just merge with God. I was very confused. To make matters worse, I started experimenting with LSD."

Looking for a new start, he decided to move to California, where his spiritual quest continued. "I went to Buddhist meetings, but that was empty," he said. "Chinese Buddhism was atheistic, Japanese Buddhism worshiped statues of Buddha, Zen Buddhism was too elusive. I went to Scientology meetings, but they were too manipulative and controlling. Hinduism believed in all these crazy orgies that the gods would have and in gods who were blue elephants. None of it made sense; none of it was satisfying."

He even accompanied friends to meetings that had Satanic undercurrents. "I would watch and think, *Something is going on here, but it's not good*," he said. "In the midst of my drug-crazed world, I told my friends I believed there's a power of evil that's beyond me, that can work in me, that exists as an entity. I had seen enough evil in my life to believe that."

He looked at me with an ironic smile. "I guess I accepted Satan's existence," he said, "before I accepted God's."

"I Can't Believe in Jesus"

It was 1969. Lapides' curiosity prompted him to visit Sunset Strip to gawk at an evangelist who had chained himself to an eight-foot cross to protest the way local tavern owners had managed to get him evicted from his storefront ministry. There on the sidewalk Lapides encountered some Christians who engaged him in an impromptu spiritual debate.

A bit cocky, he started throwing Eastern philosophy at them. "There is no God out there," he said, gesturing toward the heavens. "We're God. I'm God. You're God. You just have to realize it."

"Well, if you're God, why don't you create a rock?" one person replied. "Just make something appear. That's what God does."

In his drug-addled mind Lapides imagined he was holding a rock. "Yeah, well, here's a rock," he said, extending his empty hand.

The Christian scoffed. "That's the difference between you and the true God," he said. "When God creates something, everyone can see it. It's objective, not subjective."

That registered with Lapides. After thinking about it for a while, he said to himself, If I find God, he's got to be objective. I'm through with this Eastern philosophy that says it's all in my mind and that I can create my own reality. God has to be an objective reality if he's going to have any meaning beyond my own imagination.

When one of the Christians brought up the name of Jesus, Lapides tried to fend him off with his stock answer. "I'm Jewish," he said. "I can't believe in Jesus."

A pastor spoke up. "Do you know of the prophecies about the Messiah?" he asked.

Lapides was taken off guard. "Prophecies?" he said. "I've never heard of them."

The minister startled Lapides by referring to some of the Old Testament predictions. Wait a minute! Lapides thought. Those are my Jewish Scriptures he's quoting! How could Jesus be in there?

When the pastor offered him a Bible, Lapides was skeptical. "Is the New Testament in there?" he asked. The pastor nodded. "OK, I'll read the Old Testament, but I'm not going to open up the other one," Lapides told him.

He was taken aback by the minister's response. "Fine," said the pastor. "Just read the Old Testament and ask the God of Abraham, Isaac, and Jacob—the God of Israel—to show you if Jesus is the Messiah.

Because he *is* your Messiah. He came to the Jewish people initially, and then he was also the Savior of the world."

To Lapides, this was new information. Intriguing information. Astonishing information. So he went back to his apartment, opened the Old Testament to its first book, Genesis, and went hunting for Jesus among words that had been written hundreds of years before the carpenter of Nazareth had ever been born.

"Pierced for Our Transgressions"

"Pretty soon," Lapides told me, "I was reading the Old Testament every day and seeing one prophecy after another. For instance, Deuteronomy talked about a prophet greater than Moses who will come and whom we should listen to. I thought, *Who can be greater than Moses?* It sounded like the Messiah—someone as great and as respected as Moses but a greater teacher and a greater authority. I grabbed ahold of that and went searching for him."

As Lapides progressed through the Scriptures, he was stopped cold by Isaiah 53. With clarity and specificity, in a haunting prediction wrapped in exquisite poetry, here was the picture of a Messiah who would suffer and die for the sins of Israel and the world—all written more than seven hundred years before Jesus walked the earth.[3]

> He was despised and rejected by mankind,
>> a man of suffering, and familiar with pain.
> Like one from whom people hide their faces
>> he was despised, and we held him in low esteem.
> Surely he took up our pain
>> and bore our suffering,
> yet we considered him punished by God,
>> stricken by him, and afflicted.
> But he was pierced for our transgressions,
>> he was crushed for our iniquities;
> the punishment that brought us peace was on him,
>> and by his wounds we are healed.
> We all, like sheep, have gone astray,

> each of us has turned to our own way;
> and the Lord has laid on him
>   the iniquity of us all.
>
> He was oppressed and afflicted,
>   yet he did not open his mouth;
> he was led like a lamb to the slaughter,
>   and as a sheep before its shearers is silent,
>   so he did not open his mouth.
> By oppression and judgment he was taken away.
>   Yet who of his generation protested?
> For he was cut off from the land of the living;
>   for the transgression of my people he was punished.
> He was assigned a grave with the wicked,
>   and with the rich in his death,
> though he had done no violence,
>   nor was any deceit in his mouth . . . .
> For he bore the sin of many,
>   and made intercession for the transgressors.

ISAIAH 53:3–9, 12

Instantly Lapides recognized the portrait: this was Jesus of Nazareth! Now he was beginning to understand the paintings he had seen in the Catholic churches he had passed as a child: the suffering Jesus, the crucified Jesus, the Jesus who he now realized had been "pierced for our transgressions" as he "bore the sin of many."

As Jews in the Old Testament sought to atone for their sins through a system of animal sacrifices, here was Jesus, the ultimate sacrificial lamb of God, who paid for sin once and for all. Here was the personification of God's plan of redemption.

So breathtaking was this discovery that Lapides could only come to one conclusion: It was a fraud! He believed that Christians had rewritten the Old Testament and twisted Isaiah's words to make it sound as if the prophet had been foreshadowing Jesus.

Lapides set out to expose the deception. "I asked my stepmother to send me a Jewish Bible so I could check it out myself," he told me. "She did, and guess what? I found that it said the same thing! Now I really had to deal with it."

The Jewishness of Jesus

Over and over Lapides would come upon prophecies in the Old Testament—more than four dozen major predictions in all. Isaiah revealed the manner of the Messiah's birth (of a virgin); Micah pinpointed the place of his birth (Bethlehem); Genesis and Jeremiah specified his ancestry (a descendent of Abraham, Isaac, and Jacob, from the tribe of Judah, the house of David); the Psalms foretold his betrayal, his accusation by false witnesses, his manner of death (pierced in the hands and feet, although crucifixion hadn't been invented yet), and his resurrection (he would not decay but would ascend on high); and on and on.[4] Each one chipped away at Lapides' skepticism until he was finally willing to take a drastic step.

"I decided to open the New Testament and just read the first page," he said. "With trepidation I slowly turned to Matthew as I looked up to heaven, waiting for the lightning bolt to strike!"

Matthew's initial words leaped off the page: "A record of the genealogy of Jesus Christ the son of David, the son of Abraham . . ."

Lapides' eyes widened as he recalled the moment he first read that sentence. "I thought, *Wow! Son of Abraham, son of David—it was all fitting together!* I went to the birth narratives and thought, *Look at this! Matthew is quoting from Isaiah 7:14: 'The virgin will conceive and give birth to a son.'* And then I saw him quoting from the prophet Jeremiah. I sat there thinking, You know, this is about Jewish people. Where do the Gentiles come in? What's going on here?

"I couldn't put it down. I read through the rest of the gospels, and I realized this wasn't a handbook for the American Nazi Party; it was an interaction between Jesus and the Jewish community. I got to the book of Acts and—this was incredible!—they were trying to figure out how the Jews could bring the story of Jesus to the Gentiles. Talk about role reversal!"

So convincing were the fulfilled prophecies that Lapides started telling people that he thought Jesus was the Messiah. At the time, this was merely an intellectual possibility to him, yet its implications were deeply troubling.

"I realized that if I were to accept Jesus into my life, there would have to be some significant changes in the way I was living," he explained. "I'd have to deal with the drugs, the sex, and so forth. I didn't understand that God would help me make those changes; I thought I had to clean up my life on my own."

Epiphany in the Desert

Lapides and some friends headed into the Mojave Desert for a getaway. Spiritually, he was feeling conflicted. He had been unsettled by nightmares of being torn apart by dogs pulling at him from opposite directions. Sitting among the desert scrub, he recalled the words someone had spoken to him on Sunset Strip: "You're either on God's side or on Satan's side."

He believed in the embodiment of evil—and that's not whose side he wanted to be on. So Lapides prayed, "God, I've got to come to the end of this struggle. I have to know beyond a shadow of a doubt that Jesus is the Messiah. I need to know that you, as the God of Israel, want me to believe this."

As he related the story to me, Lapides hesitated, unsure how to put into words what happened next. A few moments passed. Then he told me, "The best I can put together out of that experience is that God objectively spoke to my heart. He convinced me, experientially, that he exists. And at that point, out in the desert, in my heart I said, 'God, I accept Jesus into my life. I don't understand what I'm supposed to do with him, but I want him. I've pretty much made a mess of my life; I need you to change me.'"

And God began to do that in a process that continues to this day. "My friends knew my life had changed, and they couldn't understand it," he said. "They'd say, 'Something happened to you in the desert. You don't want to do drugs anymore. There's something different about you.'

"I would say, 'Well, I can't explain what happened. All I know is that there's someone in my life, and it's someone who's holy, who's righteous, who's a source of positive thoughts about life—and I just feel whole.'"

That last word, it seemed, said everything. "*Whole*," he emphasized to me, "in a way I had never felt before."

Despite the positive changes, he was concerned about breaking the news to his parents. When he finally did, reaction was mixed. "At first they were joyful because they could tell I was no longer dependent on drugs and I sounded much better emotionally," he recalled. "But that began to unravel when they understood the source of all the changes. They winced, as if to say, 'Why does it have to be Jesus? Why can't it be something else?' They didn't know what to do with it."

With a trace of sadness in his voice, he added, "I'm still not sure they really do."

Through a remarkable string of circumstances, Lapides' prayer for a wife was answered when he met Deborah, who was also Jewish and a follower of Jesus. She took him to her church—the same one, it turned out, that was pastored by the minister who many months earlier on Sunset Strip had challenged Lapides to read the Old Testament.

Lapides laughed. "I'll tell you what—his jaw dropped open when he saw me walk into the church!"

That congregation was filled with ex-bikers, ex-hippies, and ex-addicts from the Strip, along with a spattering of transplanted Southerners. For a young Jewish man from Newark who was relationally gun-shy with people who were different from him because of the anti-Semitism he feared he would encounter, it was healing to learn to call such a diverse crowd "brothers and sisters."

Lapides married Deborah a year after they met. Since then she has given birth to two sons. And together they've given birth to Beth Ariel Fellowship, a home for Jews and Gentiles who also are finding wholeness in Christ.

Responding to Objections

Lapides finished his story and relaxed in his chair. I let the moment linger. The sanctuary was peaceful; the stained glass was glowing red and yellow and blue from the California sun. I sat musing over the power of one person's story of a faith found. I marveled at this saga of war and drugs, of Greenwich Village and Sunset Strip and a barren desert, none of which I ever would have associated with the pleasant, well-adjusted minister sitting in front of me.

But I didn't want to ignore the obvious questions that his story raised. With Lapides' permission, I started by asking the one that was foremost on my mind: "If the prophecies were so obvious to you and pointed so unquestionably toward Jesus, why don't more Jews accept him as their Messiah?"

It was a question Lapides has asked himself a lot during the decades since he was challenged by a Christian to investigate the Jewish Scriptures. "In my case, I took the time to read them," he replied. "Oddly enough, even though the Jewish people are known for having high intellects, in this area there's a lot of ignorance.

"Plus you have countermissionary organizations that hold seminars in synagogues to try to disprove the messianic prophecies. Jewish people hear them and use them as an excuse for not exploring the prophecies personally. They'll say, 'The rabbi told me there's nothing to this.'

"I'll ask them, 'Do you think the rabbi just brought up an objection that Christianity has never heard before? I mean, scholars have been working on this for hundreds of years! There's great literature out there and powerful Christian answers to those challenges.' If they're interested, I help them go further."

I wondered about the ostracism a Jewish person faces if he or she becomes a Christian. "That's definitely a factor," he said. "Some people won't let the messianic prophecies grab them because they're afraid of the repercussions—potential rejection by their family and the Jewish community. That's not easy to face. Believe me, I know."

Even so, some of the challenges to the prophecies sound pretty convincing when a person first hears them. So one by one I posed the most common objections to Lapides to see how he would respond.

1. The Coincidence Argument

First, I asked Lapides whether it's possible that Jesus merely fulfilled the prophecies by accident. Maybe he's just one of many throughout history who have coincidentally fit the prophetic fingerprint.

"Not a chance," came his response. "The odds are so astronomical that they rule that out. Someone did the math and figured out that the probability of just eight prophecies being fulfilled is one chance in one hundred million billion. That number is millions of times greater than the total number of people who've ever walked the planet!

"He calculated that if you took this number of silver dollars, they would cover the state of Texas to a depth of two feet. If you marked one silver dollar among them and then had a blindfolded person wander the whole state and bend down to pick up one coin, what would be the odds he'd choose the one that had been marked?"

With that he answered his own question: "The same odds that anybody in history could have fulfilled just eight of the prophecies."

I had studied this same statistical analysis by mathematician Peter W. Stoner when I was investigating the messianic prophecies for myself. Stoner also computed that the probability of fulfilling forty-eight prophecies was one chance in a trillion, trillion, trillion, trillion, trillion, trillion, trillion, trillion, trillion, trillion, trillion, trillion, trillion!5

Our minds can't comprehend a number that big. This is a staggering statistic that's equal to the number of minuscule atoms in a trillion, trillion, trillion, trillion, billion universes the size of our universe!

"The odds alone say it would be impossible for anyone to fulfill the Old Testament prophecies," Lapides concluded. "Yet Jesus—and only Jesus throughout all of history—managed to do it."

The words of the apostle Peter popped into my head: "But the things which God announced beforehand by the mouth of all the prophets, that His Christ would suffer, He has thus fulfilled" (Acts 3:18 NASB).

2. The Altered Gospel Argument

I painted another scenario for Lapides, asking, "Isn't it possible that the gospel writers fabricated details to make it appear that Jesus fulfilled the prophecies?

"For example," I said, "the prophecies say the Messiah's bones would remain unbroken, so maybe John invented the story about the Romans breaking the legs of the two thieves being crucified with Jesus, and not breaking his legs. And the prophecies talk about betrayal for thirty pieces of silver, so maybe Matthew played fast and loose with the facts and said, yeah, Judas sold out Jesus for that same amount."

But that objection didn't fly any further than the previous one. "In God's wisdom, he created checks and balances both inside and outside the Christian community," Lapides explained. "When the gospels were being circulated, there were people living who had been around when all these things happened. Someone would have said to Matthew, 'You know it didn't happen that way. We're trying to communicate a life of righteousness and truth, so don't taint it with a lie.'"

Besides, he added, if traditions are correct that Matthew died as a martyr, then why would he have fabricated fulfilled prophecies and then willingly allowed himself to be put to death for following someone he secretly knew was really not the Messiah? That wouldn't make any sense.

What's more, the Jewish community would have jumped on any opportunity to discredit the gospels by pointing out falsehoods. "They would have said, 'I was there, and Jesus' bones *were* broken by the Romans during the crucifixion,'" Lapides said. "But even though the Jewish Talmud refers to Jesus in derogatory ways, it never once makes the claim that the fulfillment of prophecies was falsified. Not one time."

3. The Intentional Fulfillment Argument

Some skeptics have asserted that Jesus merely maneuvered his life in a way to fulfill the prophecies. "Couldn't he have read in Zechariah that the Messiah would ride a donkey into Jerusalem, and then arrange to do exactly that?" I asked.

Lapides made a small concession. "For a few of the prophecies, yes, that's certainly conceivable," he said. "But there are many others for which this just wouldn't have been possible.

"For instance, how would he control the fact that the Sanhedrin offered Judas thirty pieces of silver to betray him? How could he arrange for his ancestry, or the place of his birth, or his method of execution, or that soldiers gambled for his clothing, or that his legs remained unbroken on the cross? How would he arrange to perform miracles in front of skeptics? How would he arrange for his resurrection? And how would he arrange to be born when he was?"

That last comment piqued my curiosity. "What do you mean by when he was born?" I asked.

"When you interpret Daniel 9:24–26, it foretells that the Messiah would appear a certain length of time after King Artaxerxes I issued a decree for the Jewish people to go from Persia to rebuild the walls in Jerusalem," Lapides replied.

He leaned forward to deliver the clincher: "That puts the anticipated appearance of the Messiah at the exact moment in history when Jesus showed up," he said. "Certainly that's nothing he could have prearranged."[6]

4. The Context Argument

One other objection needed to be addressed: Were the passages that Christians identify as messianic prophecies really intended to point to the coming of the Anointed One, or do Christians rip them out of context and misinterpret them?

Lapides sighed. "You know, I go through the books that people write to try to tear down what we believe. That's not fun to do, but I spend the time to look at each objection individually and then to research the context and the wording in the original language," he said. "And every single time, the prophecies have stood up and shown themselves to be true.

"So here's my challenge to skeptics: Don't accept my word for it, but don't accept your rabbi's either. Spend the time to research it yourself. Today nobody can say, 'There's no information.' There are plenty of books out there to help you.

"And one more thing: Sincerely ask God to show you whether or not Jesus is the Messiah. That's what I did—and without any coaching it became clear to me who fit the fingerprint of the Messiah."

"Everything Must Be Fulfilled . . ."

I appreciated the way Lapides had responded to the objections, but ultimately it was the story of his spiritual journey that kept replaying in my mind as I flew back to Chicago late that night. I reflected on how many times I had encountered similar stories, especially among successful and thoughtful Jewish people who had specifically set out to refute Jesus' messianic claims.

I thought about Stan Telchin, the East Coast businessman who had embarked on a quest to expose the "cult" of Christianity after his daughter went away to college and received *Y'shua* (Jesus) as her

Messiah. He was astonished to find that his investigation led him—and his wife and second daughter—to the same Messiah. He later became a Christian minister, and his book that recounts his story, *Betrayed!*, has been translated into more than twenty languages.[7]

There was Jack Sternberg, a prominent cancer physician in Little Rock, Arkansas, who was so alarmed at what he found in the Old Testament that he challenged three rabbis to disprove that Jesus was the Messiah. They couldn't, and he too has claimed to have found wholeness in Christ.[8]

And there was Peter Greenspan, an obstetrician-gynecologist who practices in the Kansas City area and is a clinical assistant professor at the University of Missouri–Kansas City School of Medicine. Like Lapides, he had been challenged to look for Jesus in Judaism. What he found troubled him, so he went to the Torah and Talmud, seeking to discredit Jesus' messianic credentials. Instead, he concluded that Jesus did miraculously fulfill the prophecies.

For him, the more he read books by those trying to undermine the evidence for Jesus as the Messiah, the more he saw the flaws in their arguments. Ironically, concluded Greenspan, "I think I actually came to faith in *Y'shua* by reading what detractors wrote."[9]

He found, as have Lapides and others, that Jesus' words in the gospel of Luke have proved true: "Everything must be fulfilled that is written about me in the Law of Moses, the Prophets and the Psalms" (Luke 24:44). It was fulfilled, and only in Jesus—the sole individual in history who has matched the prophetic fingerprint of God's anointed one.

Deliberations
Questions for Reflection or Group Study

1. Even if you're not Jewish, is there an aspect of Lapides' spiritual journey that is similar to your own? Were there any lessons you learned from Lapides about how you should proceed?

2. Lapides considered his Jewish heritage and unbiblical lifestyle impediments to becoming a follower of Jesus. Is there anything in your life

that would make it difficult to become a Christian? Do you see any costs that you might incur if you became a Christian? How might they compare with the benefits?

3. Lapides thought Christians were anti-Semitic. In a recent word-association exercise at an East Coast university, the word most often associated with *Christian* was *intolerant*. Do you have negative perceptions of Christians? What do they stem from? How might this influence your receptivity to the evidence about Jesus?

For Further Evidence
More Resources on This Topic

Bock, Darrell L., and Mitch Glaser, eds. *The Gospel According to Isaiah 53.* Grand Rapids: Kregel, 2012.

Brown, Michael L. *Answering Jewish Objections to Jesus.* Vol. 1–5. Grand Rapids: Baker, 2000, 2003, 2006, 2010.

Kaiser, Walter C., Jr. *The Messiah in the Old Testament.* Grand Rapids: Zondervan, 1995.

Porter, Stanley E. *The Messiah in the Old and New Testaments.* Grand Rapids: Eerdmans, 2007.

Rydelnik, Michael. *The Messianic Hope: Is the Hebrew Bible Really Messianic?* Nashville, TN: B&H Academic, 2010.

Strobel, Lee, "Challenge #5: Jesus Was an Imposter Who Failed to Fulfill the Messianic Prophecies," *The Case for the Real Jesus.* Grand Rapids: Zondervan, 2007), 189–226.

Telchin, Stan. *Betrayed!* Grand Rapids: Chosen, 1982.

Wright, Christopher J.H. *Knowing Jesus through the Old Testament.* Downers Grove, IL: InterVarsity, 1995.

PART 3

Researching the Resurrection

CHAPTER 11

The Medical Evidence

Was Jesus' Death a Sham and His Resurrection a Hoax?

I paused to read the plaque hanging in the waiting room of a doctor's office: "Let conversation cease. Let laughter flee. This is the place where death delights to help the living."

Obviously, this was no ordinary physician. I was paying another visit to Dr. Robert J. Stein, one of the world's foremost forensic pathologists, a flamboyant, husky-voiced medical detective who used to regale me with stories about the unexpected clues he had uncovered while examining corpses. For him, dead men *did* tell tales—in fact, tales that would often bring justice to the living.

During his lengthy tenure as medical examiner of Cook County, Illinois, Stein performed more than twenty thousand autopsies, each time meticulously searching for insights into the circumstances surrounding the victim's death. Repeatedly, his sharp eye for detail, his encyclopedic knowledge of the human anatomy, and his uncanny investigative intuition helped this medical sleuth reconstruct the victim's violent demise.

Sometimes innocent people were vindicated as a result of his findings. But more often Stein's work was the final nail in a defendant's coffin. Such was the case with John Wayne Gacy, who faced the executioner after Stein helped convict him of thirty-three grisly murders.

That's how crucial medical evidence can be. It can determine whether a child died of abuse or an accidental fall. It can establish whether a person succumbed to natural causes or was murdered by someone who spiked the person's coffee with arsenic. It can uphold or dismantle a defendant's alibi by pinpointing the victim's time of death, using an ingenious procedure that measures the amount of potassium in the eyes of the deceased.

And yes, even in the case of someone brutally executed on a Roman cross two millennia ago, medical evidence can still make a crucial contribution: It can destroy one of the most persistent arguments used by those who claim that the resurrection of Jesus—the supreme vindication of his claim to deity—was nothing more than an elaborate hoax.

Resurrection or Resuscitation?

The idea that Jesus never really died on the cross can be found in the Qur'an,[1] which was written in the seventh century—in fact, Ahmadiya Muslims contend that Jesus actually fled to India. To this day there's a shrine that supposedly marks his real burial place in Srinagar, Kashmir.[2]

As the nineteenth century dawned, Karl Bahrdt, Karl Venturini, and others tried to explain away the resurrection by suggesting that Jesus only fainted from exhaustion on the cross, or he had been given a drug that made him appear to die, and that he had later been revived by the cool, damp air of the tomb.[3]

Conspiracy theorists bolstered this hypothesis by pointing out that Jesus had been given some liquid on a sponge while on the cross (Mark 15:36) and that Pilate seemed surprised at how quickly Jesus had succumbed (Mark 15:44). Consequently, they said, Jesus' reappearance wasn't a miraculous resurrection but merely a fortuitous resuscitation, and his tomb was empty because he continued to live.

While reputable scholars have repudiated this so-called swoon theory, it keeps recurring in popular literature. In 1929 D. H. Lawrence wove this theme into a short story in which he suggested that Jesus had fled to Egypt, where he fell in love with the priestess Isis.[4]

In 1965 Hugh Schonfield's bestseller *The Passover Plot* alleged that it was only the unanticipated stabbing of Jesus by the Roman soldier that foiled his complicated scheme to escape the cross alive, even though Schonfield conceded, "We are nowhere claiming . . . that [the book] represents what actually happened."[5]

The swoon hypothesis popped up again in Donovan Joyce's 1972 book *The Jesus Scroll*, which "contains an even more incredible string of improbabilities than Schonfield's," according to resurrection expert Gary Habermas.[6] In 1982 *Holy Blood, Holy Grail* added the twist that Pontius Pilate had been bribed to allow Jesus to be taken down from the cross before he was dead. Even so, the authors confessed, "We could not—and still cannot—prove the accuracy of our conclusion."[7]

As recently as 1992 a little-known academic from Australia, Barbara Thiering, caused a stir by reviving the swoon theory in her book *Jesus and the Riddle of the Dead Sea Scrolls*, which was introduced with much fanfare by a well-respected U.S. publisher and then derisively dismissed by Emory University scholar Luke Timothy Johnson as being "the purest poppycock, the product of fevered imagination rather than careful analysis."[8]

Like an urban myth, the swoon theory continues to flourish. I hear it all the time in discussing the resurrection with spiritual seekers. But what does the evidence really establish? What actually happened at the crucifixion? What was Jesus' cause of death? Is there any possible way he could have survived this ordeal? Those are the kinds of questions that I hoped medical evidence could help resolve.

So I flew to southern California and knocked on the door of a prominent physician who has extensively studied the historical, archaeological, and medical data concerning the death of Jesus of Nazareth—although it seems that, due to the mysteriously missing body, no autopsy has ever been performed.

THE TENTH INTERVIEW:
Alexander Metherell, MD, PhD

The plush setting was starkly incongruous with the subject we were discussing. There we were, sitting in the living room of Metherell's comfortable California home on a balmy spring evening, warm ocean breezes whispering through the windows, while we were talking about a topic of unimaginable brutality: a beating so barbarous that it shocks the conscience, and a form of capital punishment so depraved that it stands as wretched testimony to man's inhumanity to man.

I had sought out Metherell because I heard he possessed the medical and scientific credentials to explain the crucifixion. But I also had another motivation: I had been told he could discuss the topic dispassionately as well as accurately. That was important to me, because I wanted the facts to speak for themselves, without the hyperbole or charged language that might otherwise manipulate emotions.

As you would expect from someone with a medical degree (University of Miami in Florida) and a doctorate in engineering (University of Bristol in England), Metherell speaks with scientific precision. He is board certified in diagnosis by the American Board of Radiology and has been a consultant to the National Heart, Lung, and Blood Institute of the National Institutes of Health of Bethesda, Maryland.

A former research scientist who has taught at the University of California, Metherell is editor of five scientific books and has written for publications ranging from *Aerospace Medicine* to *Scientific American*. His ingenious analysis of muscular contraction has been published in *the Physiologist and Biophysics Journal*. He even looks the role of a distinguished medical authority: He's an imposing figure with silver hair and a courteous yet formal demeanor.

I'll be honest: At times I wondered what was going on inside Metherell. With scientific reserve, speaking slowly and methodically, he gave no hint of any inner turmoil as he calmly described the chilling details of Jesus' demise. Whatever was going on underneath, whatever distress it caused him as a Christian to talk about the cruel fate that befell Jesus, he was able to mask with a professionalism born out of decades of laboratory research.

He just gave me the facts—and after all, that was what I had traveled halfway across the country to get.

The Torture before the Cross

Initially I wanted to elicit from Metherell a basic description of the events leading up to Jesus' death. So after a time of social chat, I put down my iced tea and shifted in my chair to face him squarely. "Could you paint a picture of what happened to Jesus?" I asked.

He cleared his throat. "It began after the Last Supper," he said.

"Jesus went with his disciples to the Mount of Olives—specifically, to the Garden of Gethsemane. And there, if you remember, he prayed all night. Now, during that process he was anticipating the coming events of the next day. Since he knew the amount of suffering he was going to have to endure, he was quite naturally experiencing a great deal of psychological stress."

I raised my hand to stop him. "Whoa—here's where skeptics have a field day," I told him. "The gospels tell us he began to sweat blood at this point. Now, c'mon, isn't that just a product of some overactive imaginations? Doesn't that call into question the accuracy of the gospel writers?"

Unfazed, Metherell shook his head. "Not at all," he replied. "This is a known medical condition called hematidrosis. It's not very common, but it is associated with a high degree of psychological stress.[9]

"What happens is that severe anxiety causes the release of chemicals that break down the capillaries in the sweat glands. As a result, there's a small amount of bleeding into these glands, and the sweat comes out tinged with blood. We're not talking about a lot of blood; it's just a very, very small amount."

Though a bit chastened, I pressed on. "Did this have any other effect on the body?"

"What this did was set up the skin to be extremely fragile so that when Jesus was flogged by the Roman soldier the next day, his skin would be very, very sensitive."

Well, I thought, here we go. I braced myself for the grim images I knew were about to flood my mind. I had seen plenty of dead bodies as a journalist—casualties of car accidents, fires, and crime-syndicate retribution—but there was something especially unnerving in hearing about someone being intentionally brutalized by executioners determined to extract maximum suffering.

"Tell me," I said, "what was the flogging like?"

Metherell's eyes never left me. "Roman floggings were known to be terribly brutal. They usually consisted of thirty-nine lashes but frequently were a lot more than that, depending on the mood of the soldier applying the blows.

"The soldier would use a whip of braided leather thongs with metal balls woven into them. When the whip would strike the flesh, these balls would cause deep bruises or contusions, which would break open with further blows. And the whip had pieces of sharp bone as well, which would cut the flesh severely.

"The back would be so shredded that part of the spine was sometimes exposed by the deep, deep cuts. The whipping would have gone all the way from the shoulders down to the back, the buttocks, and the back of the legs. It was just terrible."

Metherell paused. "Go on," I said.

"One physician who has studied Roman beatings said, 'As the flogging continued, the lacerations would tear into the underlying skeletal muscles and produce quivering ribbons of bleeding flesh.' A third-century historian by the name of Eusebius described a flogging by saying, 'The sufferer's veins were laid bare, and the very muscles, sinews, and bowels of the victim were open to exposure.'

"We know that many people would die from this kind of beating even before they could be crucified. At the least, the victim would experience tremendous pain and go into hypovolemic shock."

Metherell had thrown in a medical term I didn't know. "What does hypovolemic shock mean?" I asked.

"*Hypo* means 'low,' *vol* refers to volume, and *emic* means 'blood,' so hypovolemic shock means the person is suffering the effects of losing a large amount of blood," the doctor explained. "This does four things. First, the heart races to try to pump blood that isn't there; second, the blood pressure drops, causing fainting or collapse; third, the kidneys stop producing urine to maintain what volume is left; and fourth, the person becomes very thirsty as the body craves fluids to replace the lost blood volume."

"Do you see evidence of this in the gospel accounts?"

"Yes, most definitely," he replied. "Jesus was in hypovolemic shock as he staggered up the road to the execution site at Calvary, carrying the horizontal beam of the cross. Finally Jesus collapsed, and the Roman soldier ordered Simon to carry the cross for him. Later we read that Jesus said, 'I thirst,' at which point a sip of vinegar was offered to him.

"Because of the terrible effects of this beating, there's no question that Jesus was already in serious-to-critical condition even before the nails were driven through his hands and feet."

The Agony of the Cross

As distasteful as the description of the flogging was, I knew that even more repugnant testimony was yet to come. That's because historians are unanimous that Jesus survived the beating that day and went on to the cross—which is where the real issue lies.

These days when condemned criminals are strapped down and injected with poisons, or secured to a wooden chair and subjected to a surge of electricity, the circumstances are highly controlled. Death comes quickly and predictably. Medical examiners carefully certify the victim's passing. From close proximity witnesses scrutinize everything from beginning to end.

But how certain was death by this crude, slow, and rather inexact form of execution called crucifixion? In fact, most people aren't sure how the cross kills its victims. And without a trained medical examiner to officially attest that Jesus had died, might he have escaped the experience brutalized and bleeding but nevertheless alive?

I began to unpack these issues. "What happened when he arrived at the site of the crucifixion?" I asked.

"He would have been laid down, and his hands would have been nailed in the outstretched position to the horizontal beam. This crossbar was called the patibulum, and at this stage it was separate from the vertical beam, which was permanently set in the ground."

I was having difficulty visualizing this; I needed more details. "Nailed with what?" I asked. "Nailed where?"

"The Romans used spikes that were five to seven inches long and tapered to a sharp point. They were driven through the wrists," Metherell said, pointing about an inch or so below his left palm.

"Hold it," I interrupted. "I thought the nails pierced his palms. That's what all the paintings show. In fact, it's become a standard symbol representing the crucifixion."

"Through the wrists," Metherell repeated. "This was a solid position that would lock the hand; if the nails had been driven through the palms, his weight would have caused the skin to tear and he would have fallen off the cross. So the nails went through the wrists, although this was considered part of the hand in the language of the day.

"And it's important to understand that the nail would go through the place where the median nerve runs. This is the largest nerve going out to the hand, and it would be crushed by the nail that was being pounded in."

Since I have only a rudimentary knowledge of the human anatomy, I wasn't sure what this meant. "What sort of pain would that have produced?" I asked.

"Let me put it this way," he replied. "Do you know the kind of pain you feel when you bang your elbow and hit your funny bone? That's actually another nerve, called the ulna nerve. It's extremely painful when you accidentally hit it.

"Well, picture taking a pair of pliers and squeezing and crushing that nerve," he said, emphasizing the word *squeezing* as he twisted an imaginary pair of pliers. "That effect would be similar to what Jesus experienced."

I winced at the image and squirmed in my chair.

"The pain was absolutely unbearable," he continued. "In fact, it was literally beyond words to describe; they had to invent a new word: *excruciating*. Literally, *excruciating* means 'out of the cross.' Think of that: They needed to create a new word, because there was nothing in the language that could describe the intense anguish caused during the crucifixion.

"At this point Jesus was hoisted as the crossbar was attached to the vertical stake, and then nails were driven through Jesus' feet. Again, the nerves in his feet would have been crushed, and there would have been a similar type of pain."

Crushed and severed nerves were certainly bad enough, but I needed to know about the effect that hanging from the cross would have had on Jesus. "What stresses would this have put on his body?"

Metherell answered, "First of all, his arms would have immediately been stretched, probably about six inches in length, and both shoulders would have become dislocated—you can determine this with simple mathematical equations.

"This fulfilled the Old Testament prophecy in Psalm 22, which foretold the crucifixion hundreds of years before it took place and says, 'My bones are out of joint.'"

The Cause of Death

Metherell had made his point—graphically—about the pain endured as the crucifixion process began. But I needed to get to what finally claims the life of a crucifixion victim, because that's the pivotal issue in determining whether death can be faked or eluded. So I put the cause-of-death question directly to Metherell.

"Once a person is hanging in the vertical position," he replied, "crucifixion is essentially an agonizingly slow death by asphyxiation.

"The reason is that the stresses on the muscles and diaphragm put the chest into the inhaled position; basically, in order to exhale, the individual must push up on his feet so the tension on the muscles would be eased for a moment. In doing so, the nail would tear through the foot, eventually locking up against the tarsal bones.

"After managing to exhale, the person would then be able to relax down and take another breath in. Again he'd have to push himself up to exhale, scraping his bloodied back against the coarse wood of the cross. This would go on and on until complete exhaustion would take over, and the person wouldn't be able to push up and breathe anymore.

"As the person slows down his breathing, he goes into what is called respiratory acidosis—the carbon dioxide in the blood is dissolved as carbonic acid, causing the acidity of the blood to increase. This eventually leads to an irregular heartbeat. In fact, with his heart beating erratically, Jesus would have known that he was at the moment of death, which is when he was able to say, 'Lord, into your hands I commit my spirit.' And then he died of cardiac arrest."

It was the clearest explanation I had ever heard of death by crucifixion—but Metherell wasn't done.

"Even before he died—and this is important, too—the hypovolemic shock would have caused a sustained rapid heart rate that would have contributed to heart failure, resulting in the collection of fluid in the membrane around the heart, called a pericardial effusion, as well as around the lungs, which is called a pleural effusion."

"Why is that significant?"

"Because of what happened when the Roman soldier came around and, being fairly certain that Jesus was dead, confirmed it by thrusting a spear into his right side. It was probably his right side; that's not certain, but from the description it was probably the right side, between the ribs.

"The spear apparently went through the right lung and into the heart, so when the spear was pulled out, some fluid—the pericardial effusion and the pleural effusion—came out. This would have the appearance of a clear fluid, like water, followed by a large volume of blood, as the eyewitness John described in his gospel."

John probably had no idea why he saw both blood and a clear fluid come out—certainly that's not what an untrained person like him would have anticipated. Yet John's description is consistent with what modern medicine would expect to have happened. At first this would seem to give credibility to John being an eyewitness; however, there seemed to be one big flaw in all this.

I pulled out my Bible and flipped to John 19:34. "Wait a minute, Doc," I protested. "When you carefully read what John said, he saw 'blood and water' come out; he intentionally put the words in that order. But according to you, the clear fluid would have come out first. So there's a significant discrepancy here."

Metherell smiled slightly. "I'm not a Greek scholar," he replied, "but according to people who are, the order of words in ancient Greek was determined not necessarily by sequence but by prominence. This means that since there was a lot more blood than water, it would have made sense for John to mention the blood first."

I conceded the point but made a mental note to confirm it myself later. "At this juncture," I said, "what would Jesus' condition have been?"

Metherell's gaze locked with mine. He replied with authority, "There was absolutely no doubt that Jesus was dead."

Answering the Skeptics

Dr. Metherell's assertion seemed well supported by the evidence. But there were still some details I wanted to address—as well as at least one soft spot in his account that could very well undermine the credibility of the biblical account.

"The gospels say the soldiers broke the legs of the two criminals being crucified with Jesus," I said. "Why would they have done that?"

"If they wanted to speed up death—and with the Sabbath and Passover coming, the Jewish leaders certainly wanted to get this over before sundown—the Romans would use the steel shaft of a short Roman spear to shatter the victim's lower leg bones. This would prevent him from pushing up with his legs so he could breathe, and death by asphyxiation would result in a matter of minutes.

"Of course, we're told in the New Testament that Jesus' legs were not broken, because the soldiers had already determined that he was dead, and they just used the spear to confirm it. This fulfilled another Old Testament prophecy about the Messiah, which is that his bones would remain unbroken."

Again I jumped in. "Some people have tried to cast doubt on the gospel accounts by attacking the crucifixion story," I said. "For instance, an article in the *Harvard Theological Review* concluded many years ago that there was 'astonishing little evidence that the feet of a crucified person were ever pierced by nails.' Instead, the article said, the victim's hands and feet were tied to the cross by ropes.[10] Won't you concede that this raises credibility problems with the New Testament account?"

Dr. Metherell moved forward until he was sitting on the edge of his chair. "No," he said, "because archaeology has now established that the use of nails was historical—although I'll certainly concede that ropes were indeed sometimes used."

"What's the evidence?"

"In 1968 archaeologists in Jerusalem found the remains of about three dozen Jews who had died during the uprising against Rome around AD 70. One victim, whose name was apparently Yohanan, had been crucified. And sure enough, they found a seven-inch nail still driven into his feet, with small pieces of olive wood from the cross still attached. This was excellent archaeological confirmation of a key detail in the gospel's description of the crucifixion."

Touché, I thought. "But one other point of dispute concerns the expertise of the Romans to determine whether Jesus was dead," I pointed out. "These people were very primitive in terms of their understanding of medicine and anatomy and so forth. How do we know they weren't just mistaken when they declared that Jesus was no longer living?"

"I'll grant you that these soldiers didn't go to medical school. But remember that they were experts in killing people—that was their job, and they did it very well. They knew without a doubt when a person was dead, and really it's not so terribly difficult to figure out.

"Besides, if a prisoner somehow escaped, the responsible soldiers would be put to death themselves, so they had a huge incentive to make absolutely sure that each and every victim was dead when he was removed from the cross."

The Final Argument

Appealing to history and medicine, to archaeology and even Roman military rules, Metherell had closed every loophole: Jesus could not have come down from the cross alive. But still, I pushed him further. "Is there any possible way—*any possible way*—that Jesus could have survived this?"

Metherell shook his head and pointed his finger at me for emphasis. "Absolutely not," he said. "Remember that he was already in hypovolemic shock from the massive blood loss even before the crucifixion started. He couldn't possibly have faked his death, because you can't fake the inability to breathe for long. Besides, the spear thrust into his heart would have settled the issue once and for all. And the Romans weren't about to risk their own death by allowing him to walk away alive."

"So," I said, "when someone suggests to you that Jesus merely swooned on the cross . . ."

"I tell them it's impossible. It's a fanciful theory without any possible basis in fact."

Yet I wasn't quite ready to let go of the issue. At the risk of frustrating the doctor, I said, "Let's speculate that the impossible happened and that Jesus somehow managed to survive the crucifixion. Let's say he was able to escape from his linen wrappings, roll the huge rock away from the mouth of his tomb, and get past the Roman soldiers who were standing guard. Medically speaking, what condition would he have been in after he tracked down his disciples?"

Metherell was reluctant to play that game. "Again," he stressed, becoming a bit more animated, "there's just no way he could have survived the cross.

"But if he had, how could he walk around after nails had been driven through his feet? How could he have appeared on the road to Emmaus just a short time later, strolling for long distances? How could he have used his arms after they were stretched and pulled from their joints? Remember, he also had massive wounds on his back and a spear wound to his chest."

Then he paused. Something clicked in his mind, and now he was ready to make a closing point that would drive a final stake through the heart of the swoon theory once and for all. It was an argument that nobody has been able to refute ever since it was first advanced by German theologian David Strauss in 1835.

"Listen," Metherell said, "a person in that kind of pathetic condition would never have inspired his disciples to go out and proclaim that he's the Lord of life who had triumphed over the grave.

"Do you see what I'm saying? After suffering that horrible abuse, with all the catastrophic blood loss and trauma, he would have looked so pitiful that the disciples would never have hailed him as a victorious conqueror of death; they would have felt sorry for him and tried to nurse him back to health.

"So it's preposterous to think that if he had appeared to them in that awful state, his followers would have been prompted to start a world-wide movement based on the hope that someday they too would have a resurrection body like his. There's just no way."

A Question for the Heart

Convincingly, masterfully, Metherell had established his case beyond a reasonable doubt. He had done it by focusing exclusively on the "how" question: How was Jesus executed in a way that absolutely ensured his death? But as we ended, I sensed that something was missing. I had tapped into his knowledge, but I hadn't touched his heart. So as we stood to shake hands, I felt compelled to ask the "why" question that begged to be posed.

"Alex, before I go, let me ask your opinion about something—not your medical opinion, not your scientific evaluation, just something from your heart."

I felt him let down his guard a bit. "Yes," he said, "I'll try."

"Jesus intentionally walked into the arms of his betrayer, he didn't resist arrest, he didn't defend himself at his trial—it was clear that he was willingly subjecting himself to what you've described as a humiliating and agonizing form of torture. And I'd like to know why. What could possibly have motivated a person to agree to endure this sort of punishment?"

Alexander Metherell—the man this time, not the doctor—searched for the right words.

"Frankly, I don't think a typical person could have done it," he finally replied. "But Jesus knew what was coming, and he was willing to go through it, because this was the only way he could redeem us—by serving as our substitute and paying the death penalty that we deserve because of our rebellion against God. That was his whole mission in coming to earth."

Having said that, I could still sense that Metherell's relentlessly rational and logical and organized mind was continuing to crunch down my question to its most basic, irreducible answer.

"So when you ask what motivated him," he concluded, "well . . . I suppose the answer can be summed up in one word—and that would be *love*."

Driving away that night, it was this answer that played over and over in my mind.

All in all, my trip to California had been thoroughly helpful. Metherell had persuasively established that Jesus could not have survived the ordeal of the cross, a form of cruelty so vile that the Romans exempted their own citizens from it, except for cases of high treason.

Metherell's conclusions were consistent with the findings of other physicians who have carefully studied the issue. Among them is Dr. William D. Edwards, whose 1986 article in the *Journal of the American Medical Association* concluded, "Clearly, the weight of the historical and medical evidence indicates that Jesus was dead before the wound to his side was inflicted. . . . Accordingly, interpretations based on the assumption that Jesus did not die on the cross appear to be at odds with modern medical knowledge."[11]

Those who seek to explain away the resurrection of Jesus by claiming that he somehow escaped the clutches of death at Golgotha need to offer a more plausible theory that fits the facts.

And then they too must end up pondering the haunting question that all of us need to consider: What could possibly have motivated Jesus to willingly allow himself to be degraded and brutalized the way that he did?

Deliberations
Questions for Reflection or Group Study

1. After considering Metherell's account, do you see any validity to the swoon theory? Why or why not?

2. For two millennia the cross has been a symbol for Christians. Now that you've read Metherell's testimony, how might your own view of that symbol be different in the future?

3. Would you be willing to suffer for the sake of another person? For whom and why? What would it take to motivate you to endure torture in the place of someone else?

4. How would you react to the soldiers if they were abusing, humiliating, and torturing you, as they did Jesus? What could possibly account for Jesus' reaction, which was to utter in the midst of his agony, "Father, forgive them"?

For Further Evidence
More Resources on This Topic

Cook, John Granger. *Crucifixion in the Mediterranean World.* Tuebingen, Germany: Mohr Siebeck, 2015.

Edwards, William D., et al. "On the Physical Death of Jesus Christ." *Journal of the American Medical Association* (March 21, 1986), 1455–63.

Evans, Craig A., and N. T. Wright. *Jesus, the Final Days: What Really Happened.* Louisville, KY: Westminster John Knox Press, 2009.

Foreman, Dale. *Crucify Him*. Grand Rapids: Zondervan, 1990.

Gibson, Shimon. *The Final Days of Jesus: The Archaeological Evidence*. Reprint edition. New York: HarperOne, 2010.

Hengel, M. *Crucifixion in the Ancient World*. Philadelphia: Fortress, 1977.

Köstenberger, Andreas J., and Justin Taylor. *The Final Days of Jesus*. Wheaton, IL: Crossway, 2014.

CHAPTER 12

The Evidence
of the Missing Body

Was Jesus' Body Really Absent
from His Tomb?

Candy heiress Helen Vorhees Brach flew into the world's busiest airport on a crisp autumn afternoon, stepped into a crowd, and promptly disappeared without a trace. For decades the mystery of what happened to this red-haired, animal-loving philanthropist has baffled police and journalists alike.

While investigators are convinced she was murdered, they haven't been able to determine the specific circumstances, largely because they've never found her body. Police have floated some speculation, leaked tantalizing possibilities to the press, and even got a judge to declare that a con man was responsible for her disappearance. But absent a corpse, her murder officially remains unsolved. Nobody has ever been charged with her slaying.

The Brach case is one of those frustrating enigmas that keep me awake from time to time as I mentally sift through the sparse evidence and try to piece together what happened. Ultimately it's an unsatisfying exercise; I want to *know* what happened, and there just aren't enough facts to chase away the conjecture.

Occasionally bodies turn up missing in pulp fiction and in real life, but rarely do you encounter an empty tomb. Unlike the case of Helen Brach, the issue with Jesus isn't that he was nowhere to be seen. It's that he *was* seen, alive; he *was* seen, dead; and he *was* seen, alive once more. If we believe the gospel accounts, this isn't a matter of a missing body. No, it's a matter of Jesus still being alive, even to this day, even

223

after publicly succumbing to the horrors of crucifixion so graphically depicted in the preceding chapter.

The empty tomb, as an enduring symbol of the resurrection, is the ultimate representation of Jesus' claim to being God. The apostle Paul said in 1 Corinthians 15:17 that the resurrection is the very linchpin of the Christian faith: "If Christ has not been raised, your faith is futile; you are still in your sins."

Theologian Gerald O'Collins put it this way: "In a profound sense, Christianity without the resurrection is not simply Christianity without its final chapter. It is not Christianity at all."[1]

The resurrection is the supreme vindication of Jesus' divine identity and his inspired teaching. It's the proof of his triumph over sin and death. It's the foreshadowing of the resurrection of his followers. It's the basis of Christian hope. It's the miracle of all miracles.

If it's true. Skeptics claim that what happened to Jesus' body is still a mystery akin to Helen Brach's disappearance—there's not enough evidence, they say, to reach a firm conclusion.

But others assert that the case is effectively closed, because there is conclusive proof that the tomb was vacant on that first Easter morning. And if you want someone to compellingly present that case, your best bet is to visit with William Lane Craig, widely considered to be among the world's foremost experts on the resurrection.

THE ELEVENTH INTERVIEW:
William Lane Craig, PhD, DTh

I had an unusual perspective the first time I saw Bill Craig in action: I was seated behind him as he defended Christianity before a crowd of nearly eight thousand people, with countless others listening on more than one hundred radio stations across the country.

As moderator of a debate between Craig and an atheist selected by the national spokesman for American Atheists, Inc., I marveled as Craig politely but powerfully built the case for Christianity while simultaneously dismantling the arguments for atheism. From where I was sitting, I could watch the faces of people as they discovered—many for the first time—that Christianity can stand up to rational analysis and rugged scrutiny.

In the end it was no contest. Among those who had entered the auditorium that evening as avowed atheists, agnostics, or skeptics, an overwhelming 82 percent walked out concluding that the case for Christianity had been the most compelling. Forty-seven people entered as nonbelievers and exited as Christians—Craig's arguments for the faith were that persuasive, especially compared with the paucity of evidence for atheism. Incidentally, nobody became an atheist.[2]

So when I flew down to Atlanta to interview him for this book, I was anxious to see how he'd respond to the challenges concerning the empty tomb of Jesus.

He hadn't changed since I had seen him a few years earlier. With his close-cropped black beard, angular features, and riveting gaze, Craig still looks the role of a serious scholar. He speaks in cogent sentences, never losing his train of thought, always working through an answer methodically, point by point, fact by fact.

Yet he isn't a dry theologian. Craig has a refreshing enthusiasm for his work. His pale blue eyes dance as he weaves elaborate propositions and theories; he punctuates his sentences with hand gestures that beckon for understanding and agreement; his voice modulates from near giddiness over some arcane theological point that he finds fascinating to hushed sincerity as he ponders why some scholars resist the evidence that he finds so compelling.

In short, his mind is fully engaged, but so is his heart. When he talks about skeptics he has debated, it isn't with a smug or adversarial tone. He goes out of his way to mention their endearing qualities when he can—this one was a wonderful speaker, that one was charming over dinner.

In the subtleties of our conversation, I sensed that he isn't out to pummel opponents with his arguments; he's sincerely seeking to win over people whom he believes matter to God. He seems genuinely perplexed why some people cannot, or will not, recognize the reality of the empty tomb.

Defending the Empty Tomb

Wearing blue jeans, white socks, and a dark-blue sweater with a red turtleneck collar, Craig lounged on a floral couch in his living room. On the wall behind him was a large framed scene of Munich.

It was there, fresh with a master of arts degree from Trinity Evangelical Divinity School and a doctorate in philosophy from the University of Birmingham, England, that Craig studied the resurrection for the first time, while earning another doctorate, this one in theology from the University of Munich. Later he taught at Trinity Evangelical Divinity School and then served as a visiting scholar at the Higher Institute of Philosophy at the University of Louvain near Brussels.

His books include *Reasonable Faith*; *No Easy Answers*; *Knowing the Truth about the Resurrection*; *The Only Wise God*; *The Existence of God and the Beginning of the Universe*; and (with Quentin Smith) *Theism, Atheism, and Big Bang Cosmology*, published by Oxford University Press.

He also contributed to *The Intellectuals Speak Out about God*; *Jesus under Fire*; *In Defense of Miracles*; and *Does God Exist?* In addition, his scholarly articles have appeared in such journals as *New Testament Studies*; *Journal for the Study of the New Testament*; *Gospel Perspectives*; *Journal of the American Scientific Affiliation*; and *Philosophy*. He is a member of nine professional societies, including the American Academy of Religion and the American Philosophical Association.

While he is internationally known for his writings about the intersection of science, philosophy, and theology, he needed no prompting to discuss the subject that still makes his heart beat fast: the resurrection of Jesus.

Was Jesus Really Buried in the Tomb?

Before looking at whether the tomb of Jesus was empty, I needed to establish whether his body had been there in the first place. History tells us that as a rule, crucified criminals were left on the cross to be devoured by birds or were thrown into a common grave. This has prompted John Dominic Crossan of the Jesus Seminar to conclude that Jesus' body probably was dug up and consumed by wild dogs.

"Based on these customary practices," I said to Craig, "wouldn't you admit that this is most likely what happened?"

"If all you looked at was customary practice, yes, I'd agree," came his reply. "But that would ignore the specific evidence in this case."

"OK, then let's look at the specific evidence," I said. With that, I pointed out an immediate problem: The gospels say Jesus' corpse was turned over to Joseph of Arimathea, a member of the very council—the Sanhedrin—that voted to condemn Jesus. "That's rather implausible, isn't it?" I demanded in a tone that sounded more pointed than I had intended.

Craig shifted on the couch as if he were getting ready to pounce on my question. "No, not when you look at all the evidence for the burial," he said. "So let me go through it. For one thing, the burial is mentioned by the apostle Paul in 1 Corinthians 15:3–7, where he passes on a very early creed of the church."

I acknowledged this with a nod, since Dr. Craig Blomberg had already described this creed in some detail during our earlier interview. Craig agreed with Blomberg that the creed undoubtedly goes back to within a few years of Jesus' crucifixion, having been given to Paul, after his conversion, in Damascus or in his subsequent visit to Jerusalem when he met with the apostles James and Peter.

Since Craig was going to be referring to the creed, I opened the Bible in my lap and quickly reviewed the passage: "For what I received I passed on to you as of first importance: that Christ died for our sins according to the Scriptures, that he was buried, that he was raised on the third day according to the Scriptures . . ." The creed then goes on to list several appearances of the resurrected Jesus.

"This creed is incredibly early and therefore trustworthy material," Craig said. "Essentially, it's a four-line formula. The first line refers to the crucifixion, the second to the burial, the third to the resurrection, and the fourth to Jesus' appearances. As you can see, the second line affirms that Jesus was buried."

That was too vague for me. "Wait a minute," I interjected. "He may have been buried, but was it in a tomb? And was it through Joseph of Arimathea, this mysterious character who comes out of nowhere to claim the body?"

Craig remained patient. "This creed is actually a summary that corresponds line by line with what the gospels teach," he explained. "When we turn to the gospels, we find multiple, independent attestation of this burial story, and Joseph of Arimathea is specifically named in all four accounts. On top of that, the burial story in Mark is so extremely early that it's simply not possible for it to have been subject to legendary corruption."

"How can you tell it's early?" I asked.

"Two reasons," he said. "First, Mark is generally considered to be the earliest gospel. Second, his gospel basically consists of short anecdotes about Jesus, more like pearls on a string than a smooth, continuous narrative.

"But when you get to the last week of Jesus' life—the so-called passion story—then you do have a continuous narrative of events in sequence. This passion story was apparently taken by Mark from an even earlier source—and this source included the story of Jesus being buried in the tomb."

Is Joseph of Arimathea Historical?

While those were good arguments, I spotted a problem with Mark's account of what happened. "Mark says that the entire Sanhedrin voted to condemn Jesus," I said. "If that's true, this means Joseph of Arimathea cast his ballot to kill Jesus. Isn't it highly unlikely that he would have then come to give Jesus an honorable burial?"

Apparently, my observation put me in good company. "Luke may have felt this same discomfort," Craig said, "which would explain why he added one important detail—Joseph of Arimathea wasn't present when the official vote was taken. So that would explain things. But the significant point about Joseph of Arimathea is that he would not be the sort of person who would have been invented by Christian legend or Christian authors."

I needed more than merely a conclusion on that matter; I wanted some solid reasoning. "Why not?" I asked.

"Given the early Christian anger and bitterness toward the Jewish leaders who had instigated the crucifixion of Jesus," he said, "it's highly improbable that they would have invented one who did the right thing by giving Jesus an honorable burial—especially while all of Jesus' disciples deserted him! Besides, they wouldn't make up a specific member of a specific group, whom people could check out for themselves and ask about this. So Joseph is undoubtedly a historical figure."

Before I could ask a follow-up question, Craig continued. "I'll add that if this burial by Joseph were a legend that developed later, you'd expect to find other competing burial traditions about what happened to Jesus' body. However, you don't find these at all.

"As a result, the majority of New Testament scholars today agree that the burial account of Jesus is fundamentally reliable. John A. T. Robinson, the late Cambridge University New Testament scholar, said the honorable burial of Jesus is one of the earliest and best-attested facts that we have about the historical Jesus."

Craig's explanations satisfied me that Jesus' body was indeed placed in Joseph's tomb. But the creed left an ambiguity: Perhaps, even after the resurrection, his body remained entombed.

"While the creed says Jesus was crucified, buried, and then resurrected, it doesn't specifically say the tomb was empty," I pointed out. "Doesn't this leave room for the possibility that the resurrection was only spiritual in nature and that Jesus' body was still in the tomb?"

"The creed definitely implies the empty tomb," Craig countered. "You see, the Jews had a physical concept of resurrection. For them, the primary object of the resurrection was the bones of the deceased—not even the flesh, which was thought to be perishable. After the flesh rotted away, the Jews would gather the bones of their deceased and put them in boxes to be preserved until the resurrection at the end of the world, when God would raise the righteous dead of Israel and they would come together in the final kingdom of God.

"In light of this, it would have been simply a contradiction of terms for an early Jew to say that someone was raised from the dead but his body still was left in the tomb. So when this early Christian creed says Jesus was buried and then raised on the third day, it's saying implicitly but quite clearly: An empty tomb was left behind."

How Secure Was the Tomb?

Having heard convincing evidence that Jesus had been in the tomb, it seemed important to know how secure his grave was from outside influences. The tighter the security, the less likely the body could have been tampered with. "How protected was Jesus' tomb?" I asked.

Craig proceeded to describe how this kind of tomb looked, as best as archaeologists have been able to determine from excavations of first-century sites.

"There was a slanted groove that led down to a low entrance, and a large disk-shaped stone was rolled down this groove and lodged into place across the door," he said, using his hands to illustrate what he was saying. "A smaller stone was then used to secure the disk. Although it would be easy to roll this big disk down the groove, it would take several men to roll the stone back up in order to reopen the tomb. In that sense it was quite secure."

However, was Jesus' tomb also guarded? I knew that some skeptics have attempted to cast doubt on the popular belief that Jesus' tomb was carefully watched around the clock by highly disciplined Roman soldiers, who faced death themselves if they failed in their duty.

"Are you convinced there were Roman guards?" I asked.

"Only Matthew reports that guards were placed around the tomb," he replied. "But in any event, I don't think the guard story is an important facet of the evidence for the resurrection. For one thing, it's too disputed by contemporary scholarship. I find it's prudent to base my arguments on evidence that's most widely accepted by the majority of scholars, so the guard story is better left aside."

I was surprised by his approach. "Doesn't that weaken your case?" I asked.

Craig shook his head. "Frankly, the guard story may have been important in the eighteenth century, when critics were suggesting that the disciples stole Jesus' body, but nobody espouses that theory today," he responded.

"When you read the New Testament," he continued, "there's no doubt that the disciples sincerely believed the truth of the resurrection. The idea that the empty tomb is the result of some hoax, conspiracy, or theft is simply dismissed today. So the guard story has become sort of incidental."

Were Any Guards Present?

Even so, I was interested in whether there was any evidence to back up Matthew's assertion about the guards. Although I understood Craig's reasons for setting aside the issue, I pressed ahead by asking whether there was any good evidence that the guard story is historical.

"Yes, there is," he said. "Think about the claims and counterclaims about the resurrection that went back and forth between the Jews and Christians in the first century.

"The initial Christian proclamation was, 'Jesus is risen.' The Jews responded, 'The disciples stole his body.' To this Christians said, 'Ah, but the guards at the tomb would have prevented such a theft.' The Jews responded, 'Oh, but the guards at the tomb fell asleep.' To that the Christians replied, 'No, the Jews bribed the guards to say they fell asleep.'

"Now, if there had not been any guards, the exchange would have gone like this: In response to the claim Jesus is risen, the Jews would say, 'No, the disciples stole his body.' Christians would reply, 'But the guards would have prevented the theft.' Then the Jewish response would have been, 'What guards? You're crazy! There were no guards!' Yet history tells us that's not what the Jews said.

"This suggests the guards really were historical and that the Jews knew it, which is why they had to invent the absurd story about the guards having been asleep while the disciples took the body."

Again a nagging question prompted me to jump in. "There seems to be another problem here," I said, pausing as I tried to formulate my objection as succinctly as I could.

"Why would the Jewish authorities have placed guards at the tomb in the first place? If they were anticipating a resurrection or the disciples faking one, this would mean they had a better understanding of Jesus' predictions about his resurrection than the disciples did! After all, the disciples were surprised by the whole thing."

"You've hit on something there," Craig conceded. "However, maybe they placed the guards there to prevent any sort of tomb robbery or other disturbances from happening during Passover. We don't know. That's a good argument; I grant its full force. But I don't think it's insuperable."

Yes, but it does raise some question concerning the guard story. Plus another objection came to mind. "Matthew says the Roman guards reported to the Jewish authorities," I said. "But doesn't that seem unlikely, since they were responsible to Pilate?"

A slight smile came to Craig's face. "If you look carefully," he said, "Matthew doesn't say the guards are Romans. When the Jews go to Pilate and ask for a guard, Pilate says, 'You have a guard.' Now, does he mean, 'All right, here's a detachment of Roman soldiers'? Or does he mean, 'You've got your own temple guards; use them'?

"Scholars have debated whether or not it was a Jewish guard. I was initially inclined, for the reason you mentioned, to think that the guard was Jewish. I've rethought that, however, because the word Matthew uses to refer to the guards is often used with respect to Roman soldiers rather than just temple officers.

"And remember, John tells us it was a Roman centurion who led Roman soldiers to arrest Jesus under the direction of Jewish leadership. So there is precedent for Roman guards reporting to Jewish religious leaders. It seems plausible that they could also be involved in the guarding of the tomb."

Weighing the evidence, I felt persuaded that guards had been present, but I decided to drop this line of questioning, since Craig doesn't rely on the guard story anyway. Meanwhile, I was anxious to confront Craig with what seems to be the most persuasive argument against the idea that Jesus' tomb was vacant on Easter Morning.

What About the Contradictions?

Through the years, critics of Christianity have attacked the empty tomb story by pointing out apparent discrepancies among the gospel accounts. For example, skeptic Charles Templeton said, "The four descriptions of events . . . differ so markedly at so many points that, with all the good will in the world, they cannot be reconciled."[3]

Taken at face value, this objection seems to penetrate to the heart of the reliability of the empty tomb narratives. Consider this summary by Dr. Michael Martin of Boston University, which I read to Craig that morning:

In Matthew, when Mary Magdalene and the other Mary arrived toward dawn at the tomb there is a rock in front of it, there is a violent earthquake, and an angel descends and rolls back the stone. In Mark, the women arrive at the tomb at sunrise and the stone had been rolled back. In Luke, when the women arrive at early dawn they find the stone had already been rolled back.

In Matthew, an angel is sitting on the rock outside the tomb and in Mark a youth is inside the tomb. In Luke, two men are inside.

In Matthew, the women present at the tomb are Mary Magdalene and the other Mary. In Mark, the women present at the tomb are the two Marys and Salome. In Luke, Mary Magdalene, Mary the mother of James, Joanna, and the other women are present at the tomb.

In Matthew, the two Marys rush from the tomb in great fear and joy, run to tell the disciples, and meet Jesus on the way. In Mark, they run out of the tomb in fear and say nothing to anyone. In Luke, the women report the story to the disciples who do not believe them and there is no suggestion that they meet Jesus.[4]

"And," I said to Craig, "Martin points out that John conflicts with much of the other three gospels. He concludes, 'In sum, the accounts of what happened at the tomb are either inconsistent or can only be made consistent with the aid of implausible interpretations.'"[5]

I stopped reading and looked up from my notes. My eyes locking with Craig's, I asked him point-blank, "In light of all this, how in the world can you possibly consider the empty tomb story to be credible?"

Immediately I noticed something about Craig's demeanor. In casual conversation or when discussing tepid objections to the empty tomb, he's rather mellow. But the tougher the question and the more piercing the challenge, the more animated and focused he gets. And at this point his body language told me he couldn't wait to dive into these seemingly dangerous waters.

Clearing his throat, Craig began. "With all due respect," he said, "Michael Martin is a philosopher, not a historian, and I don't think he understands the historian's craft. For a philosopher, if something is inconsistent, the law of contradiction says, 'This cannot be true, throw it out!' However, the historian looks at these narratives and says, 'I see some inconsistencies, but I notice something about them: They're all in the secondary details.'

"The core of the story is the same: Joseph of Arimathea takes the body of Jesus, puts it in a tomb, the tomb is visited by a small group of women followers of Jesus early on the Sunday morning following his crucifixion, and they find that the tomb is empty. They see a vision of angels saying that Jesus is risen.

"The careful historian, unlike the philosopher, doesn't throw out the baby with the bathwater. He says, 'This suggests that there is a historical core to this story that is reliable and can be depended upon, however conflicting the secondary details might be.'

"So we can have great confidence in the core that's common to the narratives and that would be agreed upon by the majority of New Testament scholars today, even if there are some differences concerning the names of the women, the exact time of the morning, the number of the angels, and so forth. Those kinds of secondary discrepancies wouldn't bother a historian."

Even the usually skeptical historian Michael Grant, a fellow of Trinity College, Cambridge, and professor at Edinburgh University, concedes in his book *Jesus: An Historian's Review of the Gospels*, "True, the discovery of the empty tomb is differently described by the various gospels, but if we apply the same sort of criteria that we would apply to any other ancient literary sources, then the evidence is firm and plausible enough to necessitate the conclusion that the tomb was, indeed, found empty."[6]

Can Discrepancies Be Harmonized?

Sometimes while covering criminal trials, I've seen two witnesses give the exact same testimony, down to the nitty-gritty details, only to find themselves ripped apart by the defense attorney for having colluded before the trial. So I remarked to Craig, "I suppose if all four gospels were identical in all their minutiae, that would have raised the suspicion of plagiarism."

"Yes, that's a very good point," he said. "The differences between the empty tomb narratives suggest that we have multiple, independent attestation of the empty tomb story. Sometimes people say, 'Matthew and Luke just plagiarized from Mark,' but when you look at the narratives closely, you see divergences that suggest that even if Matthew and Luke did know Mark's account, nevertheless they also had separate, independent sources for the empty tomb story.

"So with these multiple and independent accounts, no historian would disregard this evidence just because of secondary discrepancies. Let me give you a secular example.

"We have two narratives of Hannibal crossing the Alps to attack Rome, and they're incompatible and irreconcilable. Yet no classical historian doubts the fact that Hannibal did mount such a campaign. That's a nonbiblical illustration of discrepancies in secondary details failing to undermine the historical core of a historical story."

I conceded the power of that argument. And as I reflected on Martin's critique, it seemed to me that some of his alleged contradictions could be rather easily reconciled. I mentioned this to Craig by saying, "Aren't there ways to harmonize some of the differences among these accounts?"

"Yes, that's right, there are," Craig replied. "For example, the time of the visit to the tomb. One writer might describe it as still being dark, the other might be saying it was getting light, but that's sort of like the optimist and the pessimist arguing over whether the glass was half empty or half full. It was around dawn, and they were describing the same thing with different words.

"As for the number and names of the women, none of the gospels pretend to give a complete list. They all include Mary Magdalene and other women, so there was probably a gaggle of these early disciples that included those who were named and probably a couple of others. I think it would be pedantic to say that's a contradiction."

"What about the different accounts of what happened afterward?" I asked. "Mark said the women didn't tell anybody, and the other gospels say they did."

Craig explained, "When you look at Mark's theology, he loves to emphasize awe and fright and terror and worship in the presence of the divine. So this reaction of the women—of fleeing with fear and trembling, and saying nothing to anyone because they were afraid—is all part of Mark's literary and theological style.

"It could well be that this was a temporary silence, and then the women went back and told the others what had happened. In fact," he concluded with a grin, "it *had* to be a temporary silence; otherwise Mark couldn't be telling the story about it!"

I wanted to ask about one other commonly cited discrepancy. "Jesus said in Matthew 12:40, 'For as Jonah was three days and three nights in the belly of a huge fish, so the Son of Man will be three days and three nights in the heart of the earth.' However, the gospels report that Jesus was really in the tomb one full day, two full nights, and part of two days. Isn't this an example of Jesus being wrong in not fulfilling his own prophecy?"

"Some well-meaning Christians have used this verse to suggest Jesus was crucified on Wednesday rather than on Friday, in order to get the full time in there!" Craig said. "But most scholars recognize that according to early Jewish time-reckoning, any part of a day counted as a full day. Jesus was in the tomb Friday afternoon, all day Saturday, and on Sunday morning—under the way the Jews conceptualized time back then, this would have counted as three days.[7]

"Again," he concluded, "that's just another example of how many of these discrepancies can be explained or minimized with some background knowledge or by just thinking them through with an open mind."

Can the Witnesses Be Trusted?

The gospels agree that the empty tomb was discovered by women who were friends and followers of Jesus. But that, in Martin's estimation, makes their testimony suspect, since they were "probably not objective observers."

So I put the question to Craig: "Does the women's relationship with Jesus call the reliability of their testimony into question?"

Unwittingly, I had played right into Craig's hand. "Actually, this argument backfires on people who use it," Craig said in response. "Certainly these women were friends of Jesus. But when you understand the role of women in first-century Jewish society, what's really extraordinary is that this empty tomb story should feature women as the discoverers of the empty tomb in the first place.

"Women were on a very low rung of the social ladder in first-century Palestine. There are old rabbinical sayings that said, 'Let the words of the Law be burned rather than delivered to women' and 'Blessed is he whose children are male, but woe to him whose children are female.' Women's testimony was regarded as so worthless that they weren't generally allowed to serve as legal witnesses in a Jewish court of law.

"In light of this, it's absolutely remarkable that the chief witnesses to the empty tomb are these women who were friends of Jesus. Any later legendary account would have certainly portrayed male disciples as discovering the tomb—Peter or John, for example. The fact that women are the first witnesses to the empty tomb is most plausibly explained by the reality that—like it or not—they *were* the discoverers of the empty tomb! This shows that the gospel writers faithfully recorded what happened, even if it was embarrassing. This bespeaks the historicity of this tradition rather than its legendary status."

Why Did the Women Visit the Tomb?

Craig's explanation, however, left yet another question lingering: Why were the women going to anoint the body of Jesus if they already knew that his tomb was securely sealed? "Do their actions really make sense?" I asked.

Craig thought for a moment before he answered—this time not in his debater's voice but in a more tender tone. "Lee, I strongly feel that scholars who have not known the love and devotion that these women felt for Jesus have no right to pronounce cool judgments upon the feasibility of what they wanted to do.

"For people who are grieving, who have lost someone they desperately loved and followed, to want to go to the tomb in a forlorn hope of anointing the body—I just don't think some later critic can treat them like robots and say, 'They shouldn't have gone.'"

He shrugged his shoulders. "Maybe they thought there would be men around who could move the stone. If there were guards, maybe they thought they would. I don't know.

"Certainly the notion of visiting a tomb to pour oils over a body is a historical Jewish practice; the only question is the feasibility of who would move the stone for them. And I don't think we're in the right position to pronounce judgment on whether or not they should have simply stayed at home."

Why Didn't Christians Cite the Empty Tomb?

In preparing for my interview with Craig, I had heard more than one skeptic claim that a major argument against the empty tomb is that none of the apostles, including Peter, bothered to point it out in their preaching. But when I asked Craig about this issue, his eyed widened.

"I just don't think that's true," he replied, a bit of astonishment in his voice, as he picked up his Bible and turned to the second chapter of Acts, which records Peter's sermon at Pentecost.

"The empty tomb *is* found in Peter's speech," Craig insisted. "He proclaims in verse 24 that 'God raised him from the dead, freeing him from the agony of death.'

"Then he quotes from a psalm about how God would not allow his Holy One to undergo decay. This had been written by David, and Peter says, 'I can tell you confidently that the patriarch David died and was buried, and his tomb is here to this day.' But, he says, Christ 'was not abandoned to the realm of the dead, nor did his body see decay. God has raised this Jesus to life, and we are all witnesses of it.'"

Craig looked up from the Bible. "This speech contrasts David's tomb, which remained to that day, with the prophecy in which David says Christ would be raised up—his flesh wouldn't suffer decay. It's clearly implicit that the tomb was left empty."

Then he turned to a later chapter in the book of Acts. "In Acts 13:29–31, Paul says, 'When they had carried out all that was written about him, they took him down from the cross and laid him in a tomb. But God raised him from the dead, and for many days he was seen by those who had traveled with him from Galilee to Jerusalem.' Certainly the empty tomb is implicit there."

He shut his Bible, then added, "I think it's rather wooden and unreasonable to contend that these early preachers didn't refer to the empty tomb, just because they didn't use the two specific words *empty tomb*. There's no question that they knew—and their audiences understood from their preaching—that Jesus' tomb was vacant."

What's the Affirmative Evidence?

I had spent the first part of our interview peppering Craig with objections and arguments challenging the empty tomb. But I suddenly realized that I hadn't given him the opportunity to spell out his affirmative case. While he had already alluded to several reasons why he believes Jesus' tomb was unoccupied, I said, "Why don't you give me your best shot? Convince me with your top four or five reasons that the empty tomb is a historical fact."

Craig rose to the challenge. One by one he spelled out his arguments concisely and powerfully.

"First," he said, "the empty tomb is definitely implicit in the early tradition that is passed along by Paul in 1 Corinthians 15, which is a very old and reliable source of historical information about Jesus.

"Second, the site of Jesus' tomb was known to Christian and Jew alike. So if it weren't empty, it would be impossible for a movement founded on belief in the resurrection to have come into existence in the same city where this man had been publicly executed and buried.

"Third, we can tell from the language, grammar, and style that Mark got his empty tomb story—actually, his whole passion narrative—from an earlier source. In fact, there's evidence it was written before AD 37, which is much too early for legend to have seriously corrupted it.

"A. N. Sherwin-White, the respected Greco-Roman classical historian from Oxford University, said it would have been without precedent anywhere in history for legend to have grown up that fast and significantly distorted the gospels.

"Fourth, there's the simplicity of the empty tomb story in Mark.

Fictional apocryphal accounts from the second century contain all kinds of flowery narratives, in which Jesus comes out of the tomb in glory and power, with everybody seeing him, including the priests, Jewish authorities, and Roman guards. Those are the way legends read, but these don't come until generations after the events, which is after eyewitnesses have died off. By contrast, Mark's account of the story of the empty tomb is stark in its simplicity and unadorned by theological reflection.

"Fifth, the unanimous testimony that the empty tomb was discovered by women argues for the authenticity of the story, because this would have been embarrassing for the disciples to admit and most certainly would have been covered up if this were a legend.

"Sixth, the earliest Jewish polemic presupposes the historicity of the empty tomb. In other words, there was nobody who was claiming that the tomb still contained Jesus' body. The question always was, 'What happened to the body?'

"The Jews proposed the ridiculous story that the guards had fallen asleep. Obviously, they were grasping at straws. But the point is this: They started with the assumption that the tomb was vacant! Why? Because they knew it was!"

What About Alternative Theories?

I listened intently as Craig articulated each point, and to me the six arguments added up to an impressive case. However, I still wanted to see if there were any loopholes before concluding it was airtight.

"Kirsopp Lake suggested in 1907 that the women merely went to the wrong tomb," I said. "He says they got lost and a caretaker at an unoccupied tomb told them, 'You're looking for Jesus of Nazareth. He is not here,' and they ran away, afraid. Isn't that a plausible explanation?"[8]

Craig sighed. "Lake didn't generate any following with this," he said. "The reason is that the site of Jesus' tomb was known to the Jewish authorities. Even if the women had made this mistake, the authorities would have been only too happy to point out the tomb and correct the disciples' error when they began to proclaim that Jesus had risen from the dead. I don't know anybody who holds to Lake's theory today."

Frankly, other options didn't sound very likely, either. Obviously, the disciples had no motive to steal the body and then endure deprivation and suffering as a result, and certainly the Jewish authorities wouldn't have removed the body. I said, "We're left with the theory that the empty tomb was a later legend and that by the time it developed, people were unable to disprove it, because the location of the tomb had been forgotten."

"That has been the issue ever since 1835, when David Strauss claimed these stories are legendary," Craig replied. "And that's why in our conversation today we've focused so much on this legendary hypothesis by showing that the empty tomb story goes back to within a few years of the events themselves. This renders the legend theory worthless. Even if there are some legendary elements in the secondary details of the story, the historical core of the story remains securely established."

Yes, there were answers for these alternative explanations. Upon analysis, every theory seemed to crumble under the weight of evidence and logic. But the only remaining option was to believe that the crucified Jesus returned to life—a conclusion some people find too extraordinary to swallow.

I thought for a moment about how I could phrase this in a question to Craig. Finally I said, "Even though these alternative theories admittedly have holes in them, aren't they more plausible than the absolutely incredible idea that Jesus was God incarnate who was raised from the dead?"

"This, I think, is the issue," he said, leaning forward. "I think people who push these alternative theories would admit, 'Yes, our theories are implausible, but they're not as improbable as the idea that this spectacular miracle occurred.' However, at this point the matter is no longer a historical issue; instead it's a philosophical question about whether miracles are possible."

"And what," I asked, "would you say to that?"

"I would argue that the hypothesis that God raised Jesus from the dead is not at all improbable. In fact, based on the evidence, it's the best explanation for what happened. What is improbable is the hypothesis that Jesus rose naturally from the dead. That, I would agree, is outlandish. Any hypothesis would be more probable than saying the corpse of Jesus spontaneously came back to life.

"But the hypothesis that God raised Jesus from the dead doesn't contradict science or any known facts of experience. All it requires is the hypothesis that God exists, and I think there are good independent reasons for believing that he does."[9]

With that Craig added this clincher: "As long as the existence of God is even possible, it's possible that he acted in history by raising Jesus from the dead."

Conclusion: The Tomb Was Vacant

Craig was convincing: The empty tomb—admittedly, a miracle of staggering proportions—did make sense in light of the evidence. And it was only part of the case for the resurrection. From Craig's Atlanta home I was getting ready to go to Virginia to interview a renowned expert on the evidence for the appearances of the resurrected Jesus, and then to California to speak with another scholar about the considerable circumstantial evidence.

As I thanked Craig and his wife, Jan, for their hospitality, I reflected to myself that up close, in his blue jeans and white socks, Craig didn't look like the kind of formidable adversary who would devastate the best resurrection critics in the world. But I had heard the tapes of the debates for myself.

In the face of the facts, they have been impotent to put Jesus' body back into the tomb. They flounder, they struggle, they snatch at straws, they contradict themselves, they pursue desperate and extraordinary theories to try to account for the evidence. Yet each time, in the end, the tomb remains vacant.

I was reminded of the assessment by one of the towering legal intellects of all time, the Cambridge-educated Sir Norman Anderson, who lectured at Princeton University, was offered a professorship for life at Harvard University, and served as dean of the Faculty of Laws at the University of London.

His conclusion, after a lifetime of analyzing this issue from a legal perspective, was summed up in one sentence: "The empty tomb, then, forms a veritable rock on which all rationalistic theories of the resurrection dash themselves in vain."[10]

Deliberations
Questions for Reflection or Group Study

1. What's your own conclusion concerning whether Jesus' tomb was empty on Easter morning? What evidence did you find most convincing in coming to that judgment?

2. As Craig pointed out, everyone in the ancient world admitted the tomb was empty; the issue was how it got that way. Can you think of any logical explanation for the vacant tomb other than the resurrection of Jesus? If so, how do you imagine someone like Bill Craig might respond to your theory?

3. Read Mark 15:42–16:8, the earliest account of Jesus' burial and empty tomb. Do you agree with Craig that it is "stark in its simplicity and unadorned by theological reflection"? Why or why not?

For Further Evidence
More Resources on This Topic

Copan, Paul, and Ronald K. Tacelli, eds. *Jesus' Resurrection: Fact or Figment? A Debate Between William Lane Craig and Gerd Lüdemann*. Downers Grove, IL: InterVarsity Academic, 2000.

Craig, William Lane. "The Empty Tomb of Jesus." In R. Douglas Geivett and Gary R. Habermas, eds., *In Defense of Miracles*, 247–61. Downers Grove, IL: InterVarsity Press, 1997.

——————. "Did Jesus Rise from the Dead?" In Michael J. Wilkins and J. P. Moreland, eds., *Jesus Under Fire*, 147–82. Grand Rapids: Zondervan, 1995.

——————. "The Resurrection of Jesus." In *Reasonable Faith*, Third edition, ed. William Lane Craig, 333–400. Wheaton, IL: Crossway, 2008.

——————. *The Son Rises: Historical Evidence for the Resurrection of Jesus*. Reprint edition. Eugene, OR: Wipf & Stock, 2000.

—————————. "Objection #2: Since Miracles Contradict Science, They Cannot Be True." In Lee Strobel, *The Case for Faith*, 57–86. Grand Rapids: Zondervan, 2000.

Evans, Craig A. "Getting the Burial Traditions and Evidences Right." In Michael F. Bird, Craig A. Evans, Simon J. Gathercole, Charles Hill, and Chris Tilling, *How God Became Jesus: The Real Origins of Belief in Jesus' Divine Nature*, 71–93. Grand Rapids: Zondervan, 2014.

Morison, Frank. *Who Moved the Stone?* Reprint edition. Grand Rapids: Zondervan, 1987.

CHAPTER 13

The Evidence
of Appearances

Was Jesus Seen Alive
after His Death on the Cross?

In 1963 the body of fourteen-year-old Addie Mae Collins, one of four African-American girls tragically murdered in an infamous church bombing by white racists, was buried in Birmingham, Alabama. For years family members kept returning to the grave to pray and leave flowers. In 1998 they made the decision to disinter the deceased for reburial at another cemetery.

When workers were sent to dig up the body, however, they returned with a shocking discovery: The grave was empty.

Understandably, family members were terribly distraught. Hampered by poorly kept records, cemetery officials scrambled to figure out what had happened. Several possibilities were raised, the primary one being that her tombstone had been erected in the wrong place.[1]

Yet in the midst of determining what happened, one explanation was never proposed: Nobody suggested that young Addie Mae had been resurrected to walk the earth again. Why? Because by itself an empty grave does not a resurrection make.

My conversation with Dr. William Lane Craig has already elicited powerful evidence that the tomb of Jesus was empty the Sunday after his crucifixion. While I knew that this was important and necessary evidence for his resurrection, I was also aware that a missing body is not conclusive proof by itself. More facts would be needed to establish that Jesus really did return from the dead.

That's what prompted my plane trip to Virginia. As my flight gently banked over the wooded hills below, I was doing some last-minute reading of a book by Michael Martin, the Boston University professor who has sought to discredit Christianity. I smiled at his words: "Perhaps the most sophisticated defense of the resurrection to date has been produced by Gary Habermas."[2]

I glanced at my watch. I would land with just enough time to rent a car, drive to Lynchburg, and make my two o'clock appointment with Habermas himself.

THE TWELFTH INTERVIEW:
Gary Habermas, PhD, DD

Two autographed photos of hockey players, shown in flat-out combat on ice, hang on the walls of Habermas's austere office. One features the immortal Bobby Hull of the Chicago Blackhawks; the other depicts Dave "The Hammer" Schultz, the brawling, tough-as-nails forward for the Philadelphia Flyers.

"Hull is my favorite hockey player," explains Habermas. "Schultz is my favorite fighter." He grinned, then added, "There's a difference."

Habermas—bearded, straight-talking, rough-hewn—is also a fighter, an academic pit bull who looks more like a nightclub bouncer than an ivory tower intellectual. Armed with razor-sharp arguments and historical evidence to back them up, he's not afraid to come out swinging.

Antony Flew, one of the leading philosophical atheists in the world, found that out when he tangled with Habermas in a major debate on the topic "Did Jesus Rise from the Dead?" The results were decidedly one-sided. Of the five independent philosophers from various colleges and universities who served as judges of the debate's content, four concluded that Habermas had won. One called the contest a draw. None cast a ballot for Flew. Commented one judge, "I was surprised (shocked might be a more accurate word) to see how weak Flew's own approach was. . . . I was left with this conclusion: Since the case against the resurrection was no stronger than that presented by Antony Flew, I would think it was time I began to take the resurrection seriously."[3]

One of five other professional debate judges who evaluated the contestants' argumentation techniques (again Habermas was the victor) felt compelled to write, "I conclude that the historical evidence, though flawed, is strong enough to lead reasonable minds to conclude that Christ did indeed rise from the dead . . . .Habermas does end up providing 'highly probable evidence' for the historicity of the resurrection 'with no plausible naturalistic evidence against it.' Habermas, therefore, in my opinion, wins the debate."[4]

After earning a doctorate from Michigan State University, where he wrote his dissertation on the resurrection, Habermas received a doctor of divinity degree from Emmanuel College in Oxford, England. He has authored seven books dealing with Jesus rising from the dead, including *The Resurrection of Jesus: A Rational Inquiry; The Resurrection of Jesus: An Apologetic; The Historical Jesus;* and *Did Jesus Rise from the Dead? The Resurrection Debate,* which was based on his debate with Flew. Among his other books are *Dealing with Doubt* and (with J. P. Moreland) *Beyond Death: Exploring the Evidence for Immortality.*

In addition, he coedited *In Defense of Miracles* and contributed to *Jesus under Fire* and *Living Your Faith: Closing the Gap between Mind and Heart.* His one hundred articles have appeared in popular publications (such as the *Saturday Evening Post*), scholarly journals (including *Faith and Philosophy* and *Religious Studies*), and reference books (for example, *The Evangelical Dictionary of Theology*). He's also the former president of the Evangelical Philosophical Society.

I don't mean to suggest by my earlier description that Habermas is unnecessarily combative; he's friendly and self-effacing in casual conversations. I just wouldn't want to be on the other side of a hockey puck—or an argument—from him. He has an innate radar that helps him zero in on his opponent's vulnerable points. He also has a tender side, which I would discover—quite unexpectedly—before our interview was over.

I found Habermas in his no-nonsense office at Liberty University, where he is currently distinguished research professor of apologetics and philosophy at the school of divinity. The room, with its black file cabinets, metal desk with simulated wood top, threadbare carpet, and folding guest chairs, is certainly no showplace. Like its occupant, it's free from pretension.

"Dead People Don't Do That"

Habermas, sitting behind his desk, rolled up the sleeves of his blue button-down shirt as I turned on my tape recorder and started our interview.

"Isn't it true," I began with prosecutorial bluntness, "that there are absolutely no eyewitnesses to Jesus' resurrection?"

"That's exactly right—there's no descriptive account of the resurrection," Habermas replied in an admission that might surprise people who only have a casual knowledge of the subject.

"When I was young, I was reading a book by C. S. Lewis, who wrote that the New Testament says nothing about the resurrection. I wrote a real big 'No!' in the margin. Then I realized what he was saying: Nobody was sitting inside the tomb and saw the body start to vibrate, stand up, take the linen wrappings off, fold them, roll back the stone, wow the guards, and leave."

That, it seemed to me, might pose some problems. "Doesn't this hurt your efforts to establish that the resurrection is a historical event?" I asked.

Habermas pushed back his chair to get more comfortable. "No, this doesn't hurt our case one iota, because science is all about causes and effects. We don't see dinosaurs; we study the fossils. We may not know how a disease originates, but we study its symptoms. Maybe nobody witnesses a crime, but police piece together the evidence after the fact.

"So," he continued, "here's how I look at the evidence for the resurrection: First, did Jesus die on the cross? And second, did he appear later to people? If you can establish those two things, you've made your case, because dead people don't normally do that."

Historians agree there's plenty of evidence that Jesus was crucified, and Dr. Alexander Metherell demonstrated in an earlier chapter that Jesus could not have survived the rigors of that execution. That leaves the second part of the issue: Did Jesus really appear later?

"What evidence is there that people saw him?" I asked.

"I'll start with evidence that virtually all critical scholars will admit," he said, opening the Bible in front of him. "Nobody questions that Paul wrote 1 Corinthians, and we have him affirming in two places that he personally encountered the resurrected Christ. He says in 1 Corinthians 9:1, 'Am I not an apostle? Have I not seen Jesus our Lord?' And he says in 1 Corinthians 15:8, 'Last of all he appeared to me also.'"

I recognized that last quote as being attached to the early church creed that Craig Blomberg and I have already discussed. As William Lane Craig indicated, the first part of the creed (verses 3–4) refers to Jesus' execution, burial, and resurrection.

The final part of the creed (verses 5–8) deals with his post-resurrection appearances: "[Christ] appeared to Cephas, and then to the Twelve. After that, he appeared to more than five hundred of the brothers and sisters at the same time, most of whom are still living, though some have fallen asleep. Then he appeared to James, then to all the apostles." In the next verse, Paul adds, "And last of all he appeared to me also, as to one abnormally born."

On the face of it, this is incredibly influential testimony that Jesus did appear alive after his death. Here were names of specific individuals and groups of people who saw him, written at a time when people could still check them out if they wanted confirmation. Since I knew that the creed would be pivotal in establishing the resurrection, I decided to subject it to greater scrutiny: Why are historians convinced it's a creed? How trustworthy is it? How far back does it go?

"Do you mind if I cross-examine you on this creed?" I asked Habermas.

He extended his hand as if to invite the inquiry. "Please," he said politely, "go ahead."

"Convince Me It's a Creed"

Initially I wanted to determine why Habermas, Craig, Blomberg, and others are convinced that this passage is a creed of the early church and not just the words of Paul, who wrote the letter to the Corinthian church in which it's contained.

My challenge to Habermas was simple and direct: "Convince me it's a creed."

"Well, I can give you several solid reasons. First, Paul introduces it with the words received and delivered [or passed on in the NIV], which are technical rabbinic terms indicating he's passing along holy tradition.

"Second," Habermas said, looking down at his hands as he grabbed a finger at a time to emphasize each point he was making, "the text's parallelism and stylized content indicate it's a creed. Third, the original text uses Cephas for Peter, which is his Aramaic name. In fact, the Aramaic itself could indicate a very early origin. Fourth, the creed uses several other primitive phrases that Paul would not customarily use, like 'the Twelve,' 'the third day,' 'he was raised,' and others. Fifth, the use of certain words is similar to Aramaic and Mishnaic Hebrew means of narration."

Having run out of fingers, he looked up at me. "Should I go on?" he asked.

"OK, OK," I said. "You're saying that these facts convince you, as a conservative evangelical Christian, that this is an early creed."

Habermas seemed a bit offended by that admittedly barbed remark. "It's not just conservative Christians who are convinced," he insisted indignantly. "This is an assessment that's shared by a wide range of scholars from across a broad theological spectrum. The eminent scholar Joachim Jeremias refers to this creed as 'the earliest tradition of all,' and Ulrich Wilckens says it 'indubitably goes back to the oldest phase of all in the history of primitive Christianity.'"

That raised the question of how primitive the creed is. "How far back can you date it?" I asked.

"We know that Paul wrote 1 Corinthians between AD 55 and 57. He indicates in 1 Corinthians 15:1–4 that he has already passed on this creed to the church at Corinth, which would mean it must predate his visit there in AD 51. Therefore the creed was being used within twenty years of the resurrection, which is quite early.

"However, I'd agree with the various scholars who trace it back even further, to within two to eight years of the resurrection, or from about AD 32 to 38, when Paul received it in either Damascus or Jerusalem. So this is incredibly early material—primitive, unadorned testimony to the fact that Jesus appeared alive to skeptics like Paul and James, as well as to Peter and the rest of the disciples."[5]

In fact, I would learn later that prominent New Testament scholar

James D. G. Dunn of the University of Durham, a fellow of the British Academy, said: "This tradition, we can be entirely confident, *was formulated as tradition within months of Jesus' death*."[6]

"But," I protested, "it's not really a firsthand account. Paul is providing the list second- or thirdhand. Doesn't that diminish its value as evidence?"

Not to Habermas. "Keep in mind that Paul personally affirms that Jesus appeared to him as well, so this provides firsthand testimony. And Paul didn't just pick up this list from strangers on the street. The leading view is that he got it directly from the eyewitnesses Peter and James themselves, and he took great pains to confirm its accuracy."

That was a strong claim. "How do you know that?" I asked.

"I would concur with the scholars who believe Paul received this material three years after his conversion, when he took a trip to Jerusalem and met with Peter and James. Paul describes that trip in Galatians 1:18–19, where he uses a very interesting Greek word—*historeo*."

I wasn't familiar with the meaning of the word. "Why is that significant?"

"Because this word indicates that he didn't just casually shoot the breeze when he met with them. It shows this was an investigative inquiry. Paul was playing the role of an examiner, someone who was carefully checking this out. So the fact that Paul personally confirmed matters with two eyewitnesses who are specifically mentioned in the creed—Peter and James—gives this extra weight."

One of the few Jewish New Testament scholars, Pinchas Lapide, said the evidence in support of the creed is so strong that it "may be considered as a statement of eyewitnesses."[7] Richard Bauckham, senior scholar at Ridley Hall in Cambridge, said: "There can be no doubt that . . . Paul is citing the eyewitness testimony of those who were recipients of resurrection appearances."[8]

Before I could jump in, Habermas added, "And later, in 1 Corinthians 15:11, Paul emphasizes that the other apostles agreed in preaching the same gospel, this same message about the resurrection. This means that what the eyewitness Paul is saying is the exact same thing as what the eyewitnesses Peter and James are saying."

I'll admit it: All this sounded pretty convincing. Still, I had some reservations about the creed, and I didn't want Habermas's confident assertions to deter me from probing further.

The Mystery of the Five Hundred

The creed in 1 Corinthians 15 is the only place in ancient literature where it is claimed that Jesus appeared to five hundred people at once. The gospels don't corroborate it. No secular historian mentions it. And to me, that raises a yellow flag.

"If this really happened, why doesn't anyone else talk about it?" I asked Habermas. "You'd think the apostles would cite this as evidence wherever they went. As the atheist Michael Martin says, 'One must conclude that it is extremely unlikely that this incident really occurred' and that this therefore 'indirectly casts doubt on Paul as a reliable source.'"[9]

That remark bothered Habermas. "Well, it's just plain silliness to say this casts doubt on Paul," he replied, sounding both astonished and annoyed that someone would make that claim.

"I mean, give me a break! First, even though it's only reported in one source, it just so happens to be the earliest and best-authenticated passage of all! That counts for something.

"Second, Paul apparently had some proximity to these people. He says, 'most of whom are still living, though some have fallen asleep.' Paul either knew some of these people or was told by someone who knew them that they were still walking around and willing to be interviewed.

"Now, stop and think about it: You would never include this phrase unless you were absolutely confident that these folks would confirm that they really did see Jesus alive. I mean, Paul was virtually inviting people to check it out for themselves! He wouldn't have said this if he didn't know they'd back him up.

"Third, when you have only one source, you can ask, 'Why aren't there more?' But you can't say, 'This one source is crummy on the grounds that someone else didn't pick up on it.' You can't downgrade this one source that way. So this doesn't cast any doubt on Paul at all—believe me, Martin would love to be able to do that, but he can't do it legitimately.

"This is an example of how some critics want it both ways. Generally, they denigrate the gospel resurrection accounts in favor of Paul, since he is taken to be the chief authority. But on this issue, they're questioning Paul for the sake of texts that they don't trust as much in the first place! What does this say about their methodology?"

I was still having trouble envisioning this appearance by Jesus to such a large crowd. "Where would this encounter with five hundred people have taken place?" I asked.

"Well, the Galilean countryside," Habermas speculated. "If Jesus could feed five thousand, he could preach to five hundred. And Matthew does say Jesus appeared on a hillside; maybe more than just the eleven disciples were there."

Picturing that scene in my mind, I still couldn't help but wonder why someone else didn't report on this event. "Wouldn't it be likely that the historian Josephus would have mentioned something of that magnitude?"

"No, I don't think that's necessarily true. Josephus was writing sixty years afterward. How long do local stories circulate before they start to die out?" Habermas asked. "So either Josephus didn't know about it, which is possible, or he chose not to mention it, which would make sense because we know Josephus was not a follower of Jesus. You can't expect Josephus to start building the case for him."

When I didn't respond for a moment, Habermas continued. "Look, I'd love to have five sources for this. I don't. But I do have one excellent source—a creed that's so good that German historian Hans von Campenhausen says, 'This account meets all the demands of historical reliability that could possibly be made of such a text.' Besides, you don't need to rely on the reference to the five hundred to make the case for the resurrection. Usually I don't even use it."

Habermas's answer carried some logic. Still, there was another aspect of the creed that weighed on me: It says Jesus appeared first to Peter, whereas John said he appeared first to Mary Magdalene. In fact, the creed doesn't mention any women, even though they're prominently featured in the gospel accounts.

"Don't these contradictions hurt its credibility?" I asked.

"Ah, no," came the reply. "First of all, look at the creed carefully: It doesn't say Jesus appeared first to Peter. All it does is put Peter's name first on the list. And since women were not considered competent as witnesses in first-century Jewish culture, it's not surprising that they're not mentioned here. In the first-century scheme of things, their testimony wouldn't carry any weight. So placing Peter first could indicate logical priority rather than temporal priority.

"Again," he concluded, "the creed's credibility remains intact. You've raised some questions, but wouldn't you concede that they don't undermine the persuasive evidence that the creed is early, that it's free from legendary contamination, that it's unambiguous and specific, and that it's ultimately rooted in eyewitness accounts?"

All in all, I was forced to agree that he was right. The weight of the evidence clearly and convincingly supports the creed as being powerful evidence for Jesus' post-resurrection appearances.

So powerful that William Lane Craig, the resurrection expert I interviewed in the previous chapter, said that the late Wolfhart Pannenberg, perhaps the greatest living systematic theologian in the world, "rocked modern, skeptical German theology by building his entire theology precisely on the historical evidence for the resurrection of Jesus as supplied in Paul's list of appearances."[10]

Having satisfied myself about the essential reliability of the 1 Corinthians 15 creed, it was time to begin looking at the four gospels, which recount the various appearances by the resurrected Jesus in more detail.

The Testimony of the Gospels

I started this line of inquiry by asking Habermas to describe the post-resurrection appearances in Matthew, Mark, Luke, and John.

"There are several different appearances to a lot of different people in the gospels and Acts—some individually, some in groups, sometimes indoors, sometimes outdoors, to softhearted people like John and skeptical people like Thomas," he began.

"At times they touched Jesus or ate with him, with the texts teaching that he was physically present. The appearances occurred over several weeks. And there are good reasons to trust these accounts—for example, they're lacking in many typical mythical tendencies."

"Can you enumerate these appearances for me?"

From memory, Habermas described them one at a time. Jesus appeared

- to Mary Magdalene, in John 20:10–18;
- to the other women, in Matthew 28:8–10;
- to Cleopas and another disciple on the road to Emmaus, in Luke 24:13–32;
- to eleven disciples and others, in Luke 24:33–49;
- to ten apostles and others, with Thomas absent, in John 20:19–23;
- to Thomas and the other apostles, in John 20:26–30;
- to seven apostles, in John 21:1–14;
- to the disciples, in Matthew 28:16–20.
- And he was with the apostles at the Mount of Olives before his ascension, in Luke 24:50–52 and Acts 1:4–9.

"It's particularly interesting," Habermas added, "that C. H. Dodd, the Cambridge University scholar, has carefully analyzed these appearances and concluded that several of them are based on especially early material, including Jesus' encounter with the women, in Matthew 28:8–10; his meeting with the eleven apostles, in which he gave them the Great Commission, in Matthew 28:16–20; and his meeting with the disciples, in John 20:19–23, in which he showed them his hands and side."

Again, here was a wealth of sightings of Jesus. This was not merely a fleeting observance of a shadowy figure by one or two people. There were multiple appearances to numerous people, several of the appearances being confirmed in more than one gospel or by the 1 Corinthians 15 creed.

"Is there any further corroboration?" I asked.

"Just look at Acts," replied Habermas, referring to the New Testament book that records the launch of the church. Not only are Jesus' appearances mentioned regularly, but details are provided, and the theme of the disciples being a witness of these things is found in almost every context.

"The key," Habermas said, "is that a number of the accounts in Acts 1–5, 10, and 13 also include some creeds that, like the one in 1 Corinthians 15, report some very early data concerning the death and resurrection of Jesus."

With that Habermas picked up a book and read the conclusion of scholar John Drane.

> The earliest evidence we have for the resurrection almost certainly goes back to the time immediately after the resurrection event is alleged to have taken place. This is the evidence contained in the early sermons in the Acts of the Apostles . . . there can be no doubt that in the first few chapters of Acts its author has preserved material from very early sources.[11]

Indeed, Acts is littered with references to Jesus' appearances. The apostle Peter was especially adamant about it. He says in Acts 2:32, "God has raised this Jesus to life, and we are all witnesses of it." In Acts 3:15 he repeats, "You killed the author of life, but God raised him from the dead. We are witnesses of this." He confirms to Cornelius in Acts 10:41 that he and others "ate and drank with him after he rose from the dead."

Not to be outdone, Paul said in a speech recorded in Acts 13:31, "For many days he was seen by those who had traveled with him from Galilee to Jerusalem. They are now his witnesses to our people."

Asserted Habermas, "The resurrection was undoubtedly the central proclamation of the early church from the very beginning. The earliest Christians didn't just endorse Jesus' teachings; they were convinced they had seen him alive after his crucifixion. That's what changed their lives and started the church. Certainly, since this was their centermost conviction, they would have made absolutely sure that it was true."

All of the gospel and Acts evidence—incident after incident, witness after witness, detail after detail, corroboration on top of corroboration—was extremely impressive. Although I tried, I couldn't think of any more thoroughly attested event in ancient history.

However, there was another question that needed to be raised, this one concerning the gospel that most scholars believe was the first account of Jesus to be written.

Mark's Missing Conclusion

When I first began investigating the resurrection, I encountered a troubling comment in the margin of my Bible: "The most reliable early manuscripts and other ancient witnesses do not have Mark 16:9–20." In other words, most scholars believe that the gospel of Mark ends at 16:8, with the women discovering the tomb empty but without Jesus having appeared alive to anyone at all. That seemed perplexing.

"Doesn't it bother you that the earliest gospel doesn't even report any post-resurrection appearances?" I asked Habermas.

On the contrary, he didn't seemed disturbed at all. "I don't have a problem with that whatsoever," he said. "Sure, it would be nice if he had included a list of appearances, but here are some things for you to think about:

"Even if Mark does end there, which not everyone believes, you still have him reporting that the tomb is empty, and a young man proclaiming, 'He is risen!' and telling the women that there will be appearances. So you have, first, a proclamation that the resurrection has occurred, and second, a prediction that appearances will follow.

"You can close your favorite novel and say, 'I can't believe the author's not telling me the next episode,' but you can't close the book and say, 'The writer doesn't believe in the next episode.' Mark definitely does. He obviously believed the resurrection had taken place. He ends with the women being told that Jesus will appear in Galilee, and then others later confirm that he did."

According to church tradition, Mark was a companion of the eyewitness Peter. "Isn't it odd," I asked, "that Mark wouldn't mention that Jesus appeared to Peter, if he really had?"

"Mark doesn't mention any appearances, so it wouldn't be peculiar that Peter's isn't listed," he said. "However, note that Mark does single out Peter. Mark 16:7 says, 'But go, tell his disciples and Peter, "He is going ahead of you into Galilee. There you will see him, just as he told you."'

"This agrees with 1 Corinthians 15:5, which confirms that Jesus did appear to Peter, and Luke 24:34, another early creed, which says, 'It is true! The Lord has risen and has appeared to Simon,' or Peter.

"So what Mark predicts about Peter is reported to have been fulfilled, in two early and very reliable creeds of the church—as well as by Peter himself in Acts."

Are There Any Alternatives?

Without question, the amount of testimony and corroboration of Jesus' post-resurrection appearances is staggering. To put it into perspective, if you were to call each one of the witnesses to a court of law to be cross-examined for just fifteen minutes each, and you went around the clock without a break, it would take you from breakfast on Monday until dinner on Friday to hear them all. After listening to 129 straight hours of eyewitness testimony, who could possibly walk away unconvinced?

Having been a legal affairs journalist who has covered scores of trials, both criminal and civil, I had to agree with the assessment of Sir Edward Clarke, a British High Court judge who conducted a thorough legal analysis of the first Easter: "To me the evidence is conclusive, and over and over again in the High Court I have secured the verdict on evidence not nearly so compelling. As a lawyer I accept the gospel evidence unreservedly as the testimony of truthful men to facts that they were able to substantiate."[12]

However, could there be any plausible alternatives that could explain away these encounters with the risen Jesus? Could these accounts be legendary in nature? Or might the witnesses have experienced hallucinations? I decided to raise those issues with Habermas to get his response.

POSSIBILITY 1: The Appearances Are Legendary

If it's true that the gospel of Mark originally ended before any appearances were reported, it could be argued that there's evolutionary development in the gospels: Mark records no appearances, Matthew has some, Luke has more, and John has the most.

"Doesn't that demonstrate that the appearances are merely legends that grew up over time?" I asked.

"For a lot of reasons, no, it doesn't," Habermas assured me. "First, not everybody believes Mark is the earliest gospel. There are scholars, admittedly in the minority, who believe Matthew was written first.

"Second, even if I accept your thesis as true, it only proves that legends grew up over time—it can't explain away the original belief that Jesus was risen from the dead. Something happened that prompted the apostles to make the resurrection the central proclamation of the earliest church. Legend can't explain those initial eyewitness accounts. In other words, legend can tell you how a story got bigger; it can't tell you how it originated when the participants are both eyewitnesses and reported the events early.

"Third, you're forgetting that the 1 Corinthians 15 creed predates any of the gospels, and it makes huge claims about the appearances. In fact, the claim involving the biggest number—that he was seen alive by five hundred people at once—goes back to this earliest source! That creates problems for the legendary-development theory. The best reasons for rejecting the legend theory come from the early creedal accounts in 1 Corinthians 15 and Acts, both of which predate the gospel material."

"And fourth, what about the empty tomb? If the resurrection were merely a legend, the tomb would be filled. However, it was empty on Easter morning. That demands an additional hypothesis."

POSSIBILITY 2: The Appearances Were Hallucinations

Maybe the witnesses were sincere in believing they saw Jesus. Perhaps they accurately recorded what took place. But could they have been seeing a hallucination that convinced them they were encountering Jesus when they really weren't?

Habermas smiled at the question. "Do you know Gary Collins?" he asked.

That question took me off guard. Sure, I replied, I know him. "I was in his office just recently to interview him for this same book," I said.

"Do you believe he's qualified as a psychologist?" Habermas asked.

"Yes," I answered warily, since I could tell he was setting me up for something. "A doctorate, a professor for twenty years, the author of dozens of books on psychological issues, president of a national association of psychologists—yeah, sure, I'd consider him qualified."

Habermas handed me a piece of paper. "I asked Gary about the possibility that these were hallucinations, and this is his professional opinion," he told me. I looked at the document.

Hallucinations are individual occurrences. By their very nature only one person can see a given hallucination at a time. They certainly aren't something which can be seen by a group of people. Neither is it possible that one person could somehow induce an hallucination in somebody else. Since an hallucination exists only in this subjective, personal sense, it is obvious that others cannot witness it.[13]

"That," said Habermas, "is a big problem for the hallucination theory, since there are repeated accounts of Jesus appearing to multiple people who reported the same thing.

"And there are several other arguments why hallucinations can't explain away his appearances," he continued. "The disciples were fearful, doubtful, and in despair after the crucifixion, whereas people who hallucinate need a fertile mind of expectancy or anticipation. Peter was hardheaded, for goodness' sake; James was a skeptic—certainly not good candidates for hallucinations.

"Also, hallucinations are comparably rare. They're usually caused by drugs or bodily deprivation. Chances are, you don't know anybody who's ever had a hallucination not caused by one of those two things. Yet we're supposed to believe that over a course of many weeks, people from all sorts of backgrounds, all kinds of temperaments, in various places, all experienced hallucinations? That strains the hypothesis quite a bit, doesn't it?

"Besides, if we establish the gospel accounts as being reliable, how do you account for the disciples eating with Jesus and touching him? How does he walk along with two of them on the road to Emmaus? And what about the empty tomb? If people only thought they saw Jesus, his body would still be in his grave."

OK, I thought, if it wasn't a hallucination, maybe it was something more subtle.

"Could this have been an example of groupthink, in which people talk each other into seeing something that doesn't exist?" I asked. "As Michael Martin observed, 'A person full of religious zeal may see what he or she wants to see, not what is really there.'"[14]

Habermas laughed. "You know, one of the atheists I debated, Antony Flew, told me he doesn't like it when other atheists use that last argument, because it cuts both ways. As Flew said, 'Christians believe because they want to, but atheists don't believe because they don't want to!'

"Actually, there are several reasons why the disciples couldn't have talked each other into this. As the center of their faith, there was too much at stake. Wouldn't some of them rethink the groupthink at a later date and recant or just quietly fall away? And what about James, who didn't believe in Jesus, and Paul, who was a persecutor of Christians—how did they get talked into seeing something? Further, what about the empty tomb?

"And on top of that, this view doesn't account for the forthright language of sight in the 1 Corinthians 15 creed and other passages. The eyewitnesses were at least convinced that they had seen Jesus alive, and groupthink doesn't explain this aspect very well."

Habermas paused long enough to pull out a book and cap his argument with a quote from prominent theologian and historian Carl Braaten: "Even the more skeptical historians agree that for primitive Christianity . . . the resurrection of Jesus from the dead was a real event in history, the very foundation of faith, and not a mythical idea arising out of the creative imagination of believers."[15]

"Sometimes," concluded Habermas, "people just grasp at straws trying to account for the appearances. But nothing fits all the evidence better than the explanation that Jesus was alive."

"No Rational Doubt"

Jesus was killed on the cross—Alexander Metherell has made that graphically clear. His tomb was empty on Easter morning—William Lane Craig left no doubt about that. His disciples and others saw him, touched him, and ate with him after the resurrection—Gary Habermas has built that case with abundant evidence. As prominent British theologian Michael Green said, "The appearances of Jesus are as well authenticated as anything in antiquity. . . . There can be no rational doubt that they occurred, and that the main reason why Christians became sure of the resurrection in the earliest days was just this. They could say with assurance, 'We have seen the Lord.' They knew it was he."[16]

And all this doesn't even exhaust the evidence. I had already made plane reservations for a trip to the other side of the country to interview one more expert on the final category of proof that the resurrection is a real event of history.

Before I left Habermas's office, however, I had one more question. Frankly, I hesitated to ask it, because it was a bit too predictable and I thought I'd get an answer that was a little too pat.

The question concerned the importance of the resurrection. I figured if I asked Habermas about that, he'd give the standard reply about it being at the center of Christian doctrine, the axis around which the Christian faith turned. And I was right—he did give a stock answer like that.

But what surprised me was that this wasn't all he said. This nuts-and-bolts scholar, this burly and straight-shooting debater, this combat-ready defender of the faith, allowed me to peer into his soul as he gave an answer that grew out of the deepest valley of despair he had ever walked through.

The Resurrection of Debbie

Habermas rubbed his graying beard. The quick-fire cadence and debater's edge to his voice were gone. No more quoting of scholars, no more citing of Scripture, no more building a case. I had asked about the importance of the resurrection, and Habermas decided to take a risk by harkening back to 1995, when his wife, Debbie, slowly died of stomach cancer. Caught off guard by the tenderness of the moment, all I could do was listen.

"I sat on our porch," he began, looking off to the side at nothing in particular. He sighed deeply, then went on. "My wife was upstairs dying. Except for a few weeks, she was home through it all. It was an awful time. This was the worst thing that could possibly happen."

He turned and looked straight at me. "But do you know what was amazing? My students would call me—not just one but several of them—and say, 'At a time like this, aren't you glad about the resurrection?' As sober as those circumstances were, I had to smile for two reasons. First, my students were trying to cheer me up with my own teaching. And second, it worked.

"As I would sit there, I'd picture Job, who went through all that terrible stuff and asked questions of God, but then God turned the tables and asked him a few questions.

"I knew if God were to come to me, I'd ask only one question: 'Lord, why is Debbie up there in bed?' And I think God would respond by asking gently, 'Gary, did I raise my Son from the dead?'

"I'd say, 'Come on, Lord, I've written seven books on that topic! Of course he was raised from the dead. But I want to know about Debbie!'

"I think he'd keep coming back to the same question—'Did I raise my Son from the dead?' 'Did I raise my Son from the dead?'—until I got his point: The resurrection says that if Jesus was raised two thousand years ago, there's an answer to Debbie's death in 1995. And do you know what? It worked for me while I was sitting on the porch, and it still works today.

"It was a horribly emotional time for me, but I couldn't get around the fact that the resurrection is the answer for her suffering. I still worried; I still wondered what I'd do raising four kids alone. But there wasn't a time when that truth didn't comfort me.

"Losing my wife was the most painful experience I've ever had to face, but if the resurrection could get me through that, it can get me through anything. It was good for 30 AD, it's good for 1995, it's good for 1998, and it's good beyond that."

Habermas locked eyes with mine. "That's not some sermon," he said quietly. "I believe that with all my heart. If there's a resurrection, there's a heaven. If Jesus was raised, Debbie will be raised. And I will be someday, too.

"Then I'll see them both."

Deliberations
Questions for Reflection or Group Study

1. Habermas reduced the issue of the resurrection down to two questions: Did Jesus die? And was he later seen alive? Based on the evidence so far, how would you answer those questions and why?

2. How influential is the 1 Corinthians 15 creed in your assessment of whether Jesus was seen alive? What are your reasons for concluding that it's significant or insignificant in your investigation?

3. Spend a few minutes to look up some of the gospel appearances cited by Habermas. Do they have the ring of truth to you? How would you evaluate them as evidence for the resurrection?

4. Habermas spoke about how the resurrection had a personal meaning for him. Have you faced a loss in your life? How would belief in the resurrection affect the way you view it?

For Further Evidence
More Resources on This Topic

Habermas, Gary R., and Michael R. Licona. *The Case for the Resurrection of Jesus*. Grand Rapids: Kregel, 2004.

Habermas, Gary R., and Antony Flew. *Did the Resurrection Happen? A Conversation with Gary Habermas and Antony Flew*. Downers Grove, IL: InterVarsity Press, 2009.

Habermas, Gary R. *The Risen Jesus and Future Hope*. Lanham, MD: Rowman and Littlefield, 2003.

————————. "The Resurrection Appearances of Jesus." In R. Douglas Geivett and Gary R. Habermas, eds., *In Defense of Miracles*, 262–275. Downers Grove, IL: InterVarsity Press, 1997.

————————. "The Resurrection of Jesus Time Line." In Paul Copan and William Lane Craig, eds., *Contending With Christianity's Critics*, 113–125. Nashville, TN: B&H Academic, 2009.

Licona, Michael R. *The Resurrection of Jesus: A New Historiographical Approach*. Downers Grove, IL: InterVarsity Press, 2010.

Swinburne, Richard. *The Resurrection of God Incarnate*. Oxford: Oxford Press, 2003.

Wright, N.T. *The Resurrection of the Son of God*. Minneapolis: Fortress, 2003.

CHAPTER 14

The Circumstantial Evidence

Are There Any Supporting Facts
That Point to the Resurrection?

No witnesses watched Timothy McVeigh load two tons of fertilizer-based explosives into a Ryder rental truck. Nobody saw him drive the vehicle to the front of the federal building in Oklahoma City and detonate the bomb, killing 168 people. No video camera captured an image of him fleeing the scene.

Yet a jury was able to conclude beyond a reasonable doubt that McVeigh was guilty of the worst act of domestic terrorism in U.S. history. Why? Because fact by fact, exhibit by exhibit, witness by witness, prosecutors used circumstantial evidence to build an airtight case against him.

While none of the 137 people called to the witness stand had seen McVeigh commit the crime, their testimony did provide indirect evidence of his guilt: A businessman said McVeigh rented a Ryder truck, a friend said McVeigh talked about bombing the building out of anger against the government, and a scientist said McVeigh's clothes contained a residue of explosives when he was arrested.

Prosecutors buttressed this with more than seven hundred exhibits, ranging from motel and taxi receipts to telephone records to a truck key to a bill from a Chinese restaurant. Over eighteen days they skillfully wove a convincing web of evidence from which McVeigh was woefully unable to extricate himself.

Eyewitness testimony is called direct evidence because people describe under oath how they personally saw the defendant commit the crime.

While this is often compelling, it can sometimes be subject to faded memories, prejudices, and even outright fabrication. In contrast, circumstantial evidence is made up of indirect facts from which inferences can be rationally drawn.[1] Its cumulative effect can be every bit as strong—and in many instances even more potent—than eyewitness accounts.

Timothy McVeigh may have thought he committed the perfect crime by avoiding eyewitnesses, but he nevertheless landed on death row due to the circumstantial facts that pointed toward him as devastatingly as any firsthand witness could have.

Having already considered the persuasive evidence for the empty tomb, and eyewitness accounts of the risen Jesus, now it was time for me to seek out any circumstantial evidence that might bolster the case for the resurrection. I knew that if an event as extraordinary as the resurrection of Jesus had really occurred, history would be littered with indirect evidence backing it up.

That quest took me once more to southern California, this time to the office of a professor who masterfully blends expertise in history, philosophy, and science.

THE THIRTEENTH INTERVIEW:
J. P. Moreland, PhD

J. P. Moreland is brimming with energy. He spoke in animated and enthusiastic tones, frequently leaning forward in his swivel chair to emphasize his points, actually bouncing a bit at times, almost as if he were going to leap out and throttle me with his arguments.

"I love this stuff," he exclaimed during one brief break—the only time during our conversation when he stated the obvious.

Moreland's highly organized mind works so systematically, so logically, that he seems to effortlessly construct his case in complete sentences and whole paragraphs, without wasted words or extraneous thoughts, ready for proofreading and printing. When my tape recorder would stop, he would pause, give me time to slip in a new cassette, and then pick up exactly where he had left off, without missing a beat.

While Moreland is a well-known philosopher (with a doctorate from the University of Southern California) and is comfortable navigating the conceptual worlds of Kant and Kierkegaard, he doesn't dwell exclusively in the abstract. His background in science (he has a chemistry degree from the University of Missouri) and mastery of history (as demonstrated by his excellent book *Scaling the Secular City*) anchor him in the everyday world and prevent him from floating into purely ethereal thinking.

Moreland, who also has a master's degree in theology from Dallas Theological Seminary, currently is a distinguished professor of philosophy at the Talbot School of Theology, where he teaches in the master's program in philosophy and ethics.

His articles have been published in more than thirty professional journals, such as *American Philosophical Quarterly, Metaphilosophy,* and *Philosophy and Phenomenological Research.* He has written, coauthored, or edited a dozen books, including *Christianity and the Nature of Science; Does God Exist?* (a debate with Kai Nielsen); *The Life and Death Debate; The Creation Hypothesis; Beyond Death: Exploring the Evidence for Immortality; Jesus under Fire;* and *Love Your God with All Your Mind.*

Sitting down with Moreland in his small but homey office, I already knew that circumstantial evidence is plural rather than singular. In other words, it's built brick by brick by brick until there's a sturdy foundation on which conclusions can be confidently based.

So I began our interview with a point-blank challenge: "Can you give me five pieces of circumstantial evidence that convince you Jesus rose from the dead?"

Moreland listened intently to my question. "Five examples?" he asked. "Five things that are not in dispute by anybody?"

I nodded. With that, Moreland pushed his chair back from his desk and launched into his first piece of evidence: the changed lives of the disciples and their willingness to die for their conviction that Jesus had risen from the dead.

EXHIBIT 1: The Disciples Died for Their Beliefs

"When Jesus was crucified," Moreland began, "his followers were discouraged and depressed. They no longer had confidence that Jesus had been sent by God, because they believed anyone crucified was accursed by God. They also had been taught that God would not let his Messiah suffer death. So they dispersed. The Jesus movement was all but stopped in its tracks.

"Then, after a short period of time, we see them abandoning their occupations, regathering, and committing themselves to spreading a very specific message—that Jesus Christ was the Messiah of God who died on a cross, returned to life, and was seen alive by them.

"And they were willing to spend the rest of their lives proclaiming this, without any payoff from a human point of view. It's not as though there were a mansion awaiting them on the Mediterranean. They faced a life of hardship. They often went without food, slept exposed to the elements, were ridiculed, beaten, imprisoned. And finally, most of them were executed in torturous ways.

"For what? For good intentions? No, because they were convinced beyond a shadow of a doubt that they had seen Jesus Christ alive from the dead. What you can't explain is how this particular group of men came up with this particular belief without having had an experience of the resurrected Christ. There's no other adequate explanation."

I interrupted with a "Yes, but . . ." objection. "Yes," I agreed, "they were willing to die for their beliefs. But," I added, "so have Muslims and Mormons and followers of Jim Jones and David Koresh. This may show that they were fanatical, but let's face it: It doesn't prove that what they believed is true."

"Wait a minute—think carefully about the difference," Moreland insisted as he swiveled to face me head-on, planting both of his feet firmly on the floor.

"Muslims might be willing to die for their belief that Allah revealed himself to Muhammad, but this revelation was not done in a publicly observable way. So they could be wrong about it. They may sincerely think it's true, but they can't know for a fact, because they didn't witness it themselves.

"However, the apostles were willing to die for something they had seen with their own eyes and touched with their own hands. They were in a unique position not to just believe Jesus rose from the dead but to know for sure. And when you've got eleven credible people with no ulterior motives, with nothing to gain and a lot to lose, who all agree they observed something with their own eyes—now you've got some difficulty explaining that away."

I smiled because I had been playing devil's advocate by raising my objection. Actually, I knew he was right. In fact, this critical distinction was pivotal in my own spiritual journey.

It had been put to me this way: People will die for their religious beliefs if they sincerely believe they're true, but people won't die for their religious beliefs if they know their beliefs are false.

While most people can only have faith that their beliefs are true, the disciples were in a position to know without a doubt whether or not Jesus had risen from the dead. They claimed that they saw him, talked with him, and ate with him. If they weren't absolutely certain, they wouldn't have allowed themselves to be tortured to death for proclaiming that the resurrection had happened.[2]

"OK, I'm convinced on that one," I said. "But what else do you have?"

EXHIBIT 2: The Conversion of Skeptics

"Another piece of circumstantial evidence," Moreland went on, "is that there were hardened skeptics who didn't believe in Jesus before his crucifixion—and were to some degree dead-set against Christianity—who turned around and adopted the Christian faith after Jesus' death. There's no good reason for this apart from them having experienced the resurrected Christ."

"You're obviously talking about James, the brother of Jesus, and Saul of Tarsus, who became the apostle Paul," I said. "But do you really have any credible evidence that James had been a skeptic of Jesus?"

"Yes, I do," he said. "The gospels tell us Jesus' family, including James, were embarrassed by what he was claiming to be. They didn't believe in him; they confronted him. In ancient Judaism it was highly embarrassing for a rabbi's family not to accept him. Therefore the gospel writers would have no motive for fabricating this skepticism if it weren't true.

"Later the historian Josephus tells us that James, the brother of Jesus, who was the leader of the Jerusalem church, was stoned to death because of his belief in his brother. Why did James's life change? Paul tells us: The resurrected Jesus appeared to him. There's no other explanation."

Indeed, none jumped to mind. "And Saul?" I asked.

"As a Pharisee, he hated anything that disrupted the traditions of the Jewish people. To him, this new countermovement called Christianity would have been the height of disloyalty. In fact, he worked out his frustration by executing Christians when he had a chance," Moreland replied.

"Suddenly he doesn't just ease off Christians but joins their movement! How did this happen? Well, everyone agrees Paul wrote Galatians, and he tells us himself in that letter what caused him to take a 180-degree turn and become the chief proponent of the Christian faith. By his own pen he says he saw the risen Christ and heard Christ appoint him to be one of his followers."

I was waiting for Moreland to make this point, so I could challenge him with an objection by Christianity critic Michael Martin. He said that if you count Paul's conversion as being evidence for the truth of the resurrection, you should count Muhammad's conversion to Islam as being evidence for the truth that Jesus was not resurrected, since Muslims deny the resurrection.

"Basically, he says the evidential values of Paul's conversion and Muhammad's conversion cancel each other out," I told Moreland. "Frankly, that seems like a good point. Won't you admit that he's right?"

Moreland didn't bite. "Let's take a look at Muhammad's conversion," he said with confidence in his voice. "No one knows anything about it. Muhammad claims he went into a cave and had a religious experience in which Allah revealed the Qur'an to him. There's no other eyewitness to verify this. Muhammad offered no publicly miraculous signs to certify anything.

"And someone easily could have had ulterior motives in following Muhammad, because in the early years Islam was spread largely by warfare. Followers of Muhammad gained political influence and power over the villages that were conquered and 'converted' to Islam by the sword.

"Contrast that with the claims of the early followers of Jesus, including Paul. They claimed to have seen public events that other people saw as well. These were things that happened outside their minds, not just in their minds.

"Furthermore, when Paul wrote 2 Corinthians—which nobody disputes he did—he reminded the people in Corinth that he performed miracles when he was with them earlier. He'd certainly be foolish to make this statement if they knew he hadn't."

"And your point?" I asked.

"Remember," he said, "it's not the simple fact that Paul changed his views. You have to explain how he had this particular change of belief that completely went against his upbringing; how he saw the risen Christ in a public event that was witnessed by others, even though they didn't understand it; and how he performed miracles to back up his claim to being an apostle."

"All right, all right," I said. "I see your point. And I'll admit, it's a good one." With that I gestured for him to go on to his next piece of evidence.

EXHIBIT 3: Changes to Key Social Structures

In order to explain his next category of circumstantial proof, Moreland had to provide some important background information about Jewish culture.

"At the time of Jesus, the Jews had been persecuted for seven hundred years by the Babylonians, Assyrians, Persians, and now by the Greeks and the Romans," Moreland explained. "Many Jews had been scattered and lived as captives in these other nations.

"However, we still see Jews today, while we don't see Hittites, Perizzites, Ammonites, Assyrians, Persians, Babylonians, and other people who had been living in that time. Why? Because these people got captured by other nations, intermarried, and lost their national identity.

"Why didn't that happen to the Jews? Because the things that made the Jews Jews—the social structures that gave them their national identity—were unbelievably important to them. The Jews would pass these structures down to their children, celebrate them in synagogue meetings every Sabbath, and reinforce them with their rituals, because they knew if they didn't, there soon would be no Jews left. They would be assimilated into the cultures that captured them.

"And there's another reason why these social institutions were so important: They believed these institutions were entrusted to them by

God. They believed that to abandon these institutions would be to risk their souls being damned to hell after death.

"Now a rabbi named Jesus appears from a lower-class region. He teaches for three years, gathers a following of lower-and middle-class people, gets in trouble with the authorities, and gets crucified along with thirty thousand other Jewish men who are executed during this time period.

"But five weeks after he's crucified, over ten thousand Jews are following him and claiming that he is the initiator of a new religion. And get this: They're willing to give up or alter all five of the social institutions that they have been taught since childhood have such importance both sociologically and theologically."

"So the implication is that something big was going on," I said.

Moreland exclaimed, "Something *very* big was going on!"

Revolutionizing Jewish Life

I invited Moreland to go through these five social structures and explain how the followers of Jesus had changed or abandoned them.

"First," he said, "they had been taught ever since the time of Abraham and Moses that they needed to offer an animal sacrifice on a yearly basis to atone for their sins. God would transfer their sins to that animal, and their sins would be forgiven so they could be in right standing with him. But all of a sudden, after the death of this Nazarene carpenter, these Jewish people no longer offer sacrifices.

"Second, Jews emphasized obeying the laws that God had entrusted to them through Moses. In their view, this is what separated them from pagan nations. Yet within a short time after Jesus' death, Jews were beginning to say that you don't become an upstanding member of their community merely by keeping Moses' laws.

"Third, Jews scrupulously kept the Sabbath by not doing anything except religious devotion every Saturday. This is how they would earn right standing with God, guarantee the salvation of their family, and be in right standing with the nation. However, after the death of this Nazarene carpenter, this fifteen-hundred-year tradition is abruptly changed. These Christians worship on Sunday—why? Because that's when Jesus rose from the dead.

"Fourth, they believed in monotheism—only one God. While Christians teach a form of monotheism, they say that the Father, Son, and Holy Spirit are one God. This is radically different from what the Jews believed. They would have considered it the height of heresy to say someone could be God and man at the same time. Yet Jews begin to worship Jesus as God within the first decade of the Christian religion.

"And fifth, these Christians pictured the Messiah as someone who suffered and died for the sins of the world, whereas Jews had been trained to believe that the Messiah was going to be a political leader who would destroy the Roman armies."

With that context established, Moreland went in for the rhetorical kill, drilling me with his intense and unwavering gaze. "Lee," he said, "how can you possibly explain why in a short period of time not just one Jew but an entire community of at least ten thousand Jews were willing to give up these five key practices that had served them sociologically and theologically for so many centuries? My explanation is simple: They had seen Jesus risen from the dead."

While Moreland's point was extremely impressive, I saw a problem in people understanding it today. I told him that it's very difficult for twentieth-century Americans to appreciate the radical nature of this transformation.

"These days people are fluid in their faith," I said. "They bounce back and forth between Christianity and New Age beliefs. They dabble in Buddhism, they mix and match and create their own spirituality. For them, making the kind of changes you mentioned wouldn't seem like a big deal."

Moreland nodded. He had apparently heard this objection before. "I'd ask a person like that, 'What's your most cherished belief? That your parents were good people? That murder is immoral? Think about how radical something must be to get you to change or give up that belief you treasure so much. Now we're starting to get close.'

"Keep in mind that this is an entire community of people who are abandoning treasured beliefs that have been passed on for centuries and that they believed were from God himself. They were doing it even though they were jeopardizing their own well-being, and they also believed they were risking the damnation of their souls to hell if they were wrong.

"What's more, they were not doing this because they had come upon better ideas. They were very content with the old traditions. They gave them up because they had seen miracles that they could not explain and that forced them to see the world another way."

"We're Western individualists who like technological and sociological change," I observed. "Traditions don't mean as much to us."

"I'll grant that," Moreland replied. "But these people did value tradition. They lived in a period in which the older something was, the better. In fact, for them, the farther back they could trace an idea, the more likely it was to be true. So to come up with new ideas was opposite of the way we are today.

"Believe me," he concluded, "these changes to the Jewish social structures were not just minor adjustments that were casually made— they were absolutely monumental. This was nothing short of a social earthquake! And earthquakes don't happen without a cause."

EXHIBIT 4: Communion and Baptism

Moreland pointed to the emergence of the sacraments of Communion and baptism in the early church as more circumstantial evidence that the resurrection is true. But I had some doubts.

"Isn't it only natural that religions would create their own rituals and practices?" I asked. "All religions have them. So how does that prove anything about the resurrection?"

"Ah, but let's consider Communion for a moment," he replied. "What's odd is that these early followers of Jesus didn't get together to celebrate his teachings or how wonderful he was. They came together regularly to have a celebration meal for one reason: to remember that Jesus had been publicly slaughtered in a grotesque and humiliating way.

"Think about this in modern terms. If a group of people loved John F. Kennedy, they might meet regularly to remember his confrontation with Russia, his promotion of civil rights, and his charismatic personality. But they're not going to celebrate the fact that Lee Harvey Oswald murdered him!

"However, that's analogous to what these early Christians did. How do you explain that? I explain it this way: They realized that Jesus' slaying was a necessary step to a much greater victory. His murder wasn't the last word—the last word was that he had conquered death for all of us by rising from the dead. They celebrated his execution because they were convinced that they had seen him alive from the tomb."

"What about baptism?" I asked.

"The early church adopted a form of baptism from their Jewish upbringing, called proselyte baptism. When Gentiles wanted to take upon themselves the laws of Moses, the Jews would baptize those Gentiles in the authority of the God of Israel. But in the New Testament, people were baptized in the name of God the Father, God the Son, and God the Holy Spirit—which meant they had elevated Jesus to the full status of God.

"Not only that, but baptism was a celebration of the death of Jesus, just as Communion was. By going under the water, you're celebrating his death, and by being brought out of the water, you're celebrating the fact that Jesus was raised to newness of life."

I interrupted by saying, "You're assuming that these sacraments weren't merely adapted from the so-called mystery religions."

"And for good reasons," Moreland replied. "First, there's no hard evidence that any mystery religion believed in gods dying and rising, until after the New Testament period. So if there was any borrowing, they borrowed from Christianity.

"Second, the practice of baptism came from Jewish customs, and the Jews were very much against allowing Gentile or Greek ideas to affect their worship. And third, these two sacraments can be dated back to the very earliest Christian community—too early for the influence of any other religions to creep into their understanding of what Jesus' death meant."

EXHIBIT 5: The Emergence of the Church

Moreland prefaced this final point by saying, "When a major cultural shift takes place, historians always look for events that can explain it."

"Yes, that makes sense," I said.

"OK, then let's think about the start of the Christian church. There's no question it began shortly after the death of Jesus and spread so rapidly that within a period of maybe twenty years it had even reached Caesar's palace in Rome. Not only that, but this movement triumphed over a number of competing ideologies and eventually overwhelmed the entire Roman empire.

"Now, if you were a Martian looking down on the first century, would you think Christianity or the Roman Empire would survive? You probably wouldn't put money on a ragtag group of people whose primary message was that a crucified carpenter from an obscure village had triumphed over the grave. Yet it was so successful that today we name our children Peter and Paul and our dogs Caesar and Nero!

"I like the way C. F. D. Moule, the Cambridge New Testament scholar, put it: 'If the coming into existence of the Nazarenes, a phenomenon undeniably attested by the New Testament, rips a great hole in history, a hole the size and shape of resurrection, what does the secular historian propose to stop it up with?'"[3]

While this wasn't Moreland's strongest point, since other religious movements have popped up and spread too, circumstantial evidence doesn't rely solely on the strength of one fact. Rather, it's the cumulative weight of several facts that together tip the scales toward a conclusion. And to Moreland, the conclusion is clear.

"Look," he said, "if someone wants to consider this circumstantial evidence and reach the verdict that Jesus did not rise from the dead— fair enough. But they've got to offer an alternative explanation that is plausible for all five of these facts.

"Remember, there's no doubt these facts are true; what's in question is how to explain them. And I've never seen a better explanation than the resurrection."

I mentally played back the tape of the circumstantial evidence: the willingness of the disciples to suffer and even die for what they experienced; the revolutionized lives of skeptics like James and Saul; the radical changes in social structures cherished by Jews for centuries; the sudden appearance of Communion and baptism; and the amazing emergence and growth of the church.

Given all five uncontested facts, I had to agree with Moreland that the resurrection, and only the resurrection, makes sense of them all. No other explanation comes close. And that's just the indirect evidence.

When I added the potent proof for the empty tomb of Jesus, and the convincing testimony about his post-resurrection appearances, the case seemed conclusive.

That was also the assessment of Sir Lionel Luckhoo, the brilliant and savvy attorney whose astounding 245 consecutive murder acquittals earned him a place in *The Guinness Book of World Records* as the world's most successful lawyer.[4] Knighted twice by Queen Elizabeth, this former justice and diplomat subjected the historical facts about the resurrection to his own rigorous analysis for several years before declaring, "I say unequivocally that the evidence for the resurrection of Jesus Christ is so overwhelming that it compels acceptance by proof which leaves absolutely no room for doubt."[5]

But wait. There is more.

Taking the Final Step

Our interview over, Moreland and I were bantering about football as I unplugged my tape recorder and began packing away my notes. Though I was in a bit of a hurry to catch my flight back to Chicago, he said something that prompted me to pause.

"There's one other category of evidence you haven't asked about," he remarked.

My mind reviewed our interview. "I give up," I said. "What is it?"

"It's the ongoing encounter with the resurrected Christ that happens all over the world, in every culture, to people from all kinds of backgrounds and personalities—well educated and not, rich and poor, thinkers and feelers, men and women," he said. "They all will testify that more than any single thing in their lives, Jesus Christ has changed them."

Moreland leaned forward for emphasis. "To me, this provides the final evidence—not the only evidence but the final confirming proof—that the message of Jesus can open the door to a direct encounter with the risen Christ."

"I assume you've had an encounter like that," I said. "Tell me about it."

"In 1968 I was a cynical chemistry major at the University of Missouri, when I was confronted with the fact that if I examined the claims of Jesus Christ critically but with an open mind, there was more than enough evidence for me to believe it.

"So I took a step of faith in the same direction the evidence was pointing, by receiving Jesus as my forgiver and leader, and I began to relate to him—to the resurrected Christ—in a very real and ongoing way.

"In three decades I've had hundreds of specific answers to prayers, I've had things happen that simply cannot be explained by natural explanations, and I have experienced a changed life beyond anything I could have imagined."

But, I protested, people experience life change in other religions whose tenets contradict Christianity. "Isn't it dangerous to base a decision on subjective experiences?" I asked.

"Let me make two things clear," he said. "First, I'm not saying, 'Just trust your experience.' I'm saying, 'Use your mind calmly and weigh the evidence, and then let experience be a confirming piece of evidence.' Second, if what this evidence points to is true—that is, if all these lines of evidence really do point to the resurrection of Jesus—the evidence itself begs for an experiential test."

"Define that," I said.

"The experiential test is, 'He's still alive, and I can find out by relating to him.' If you were on a jury and heard enough evidence to convince you of someone's guilt, it wouldn't make sense to stop short of the final step of convicting him. And for people to accept the evidence for the resurrection of Jesus and not take the final step of testing it experientially would be to miss where the evidence is ultimately pointing."

"So," I said, "if the evidence points strongly in this direction, it's only rational and logical to follow it into the experiential realm."

He nodded in approval. "That's precisely right," he said. "It's the final confirmation of the evidence. In fact, I'll say this: The evidence screams out for the experiential test."

Deliberations
Questions for Reflection or Group Study

1. The disciples were in the unique position of knowing for certain whether Jesus had returned from the dead, and they were willing to

suffer and even die for their conviction that he did. Can you think of anyone in history who has knowingly and willingly died for a lie? What degree of certainty would you need before you would be willing to lay down your life for a belief? How thoroughly would you investigate a matter if you were going to base your life on it?

2. What are your most cherished beliefs? What would it take for you to abandon or radically rethink those treasured opinions—especially if you truly believed you were risking the damnation of your soul if you were wrong? How does your answer relate to the historical fact that thousands of Jews suddenly abandoned five key social and religious structures shortly after the crucifixion of Jesus?

3. Other than the resurrection of Jesus, can you think of any explanation that would simultaneously account for all five categories of evidence that J. P. Moreland discussed? How do you think someone like him would respond to your hypothesis?

4. Moreland ended his interview by talking about the experiential test. What would have to happen before you would be willing to take that step yourself?

For Further Evidence
More Resources on This Topic

Groothuis, Douglas. "The Resurrection of Jesus." In *Christian Apologetics: A Comprehensive Case for the Christian Faith*, 527–563. Downers Grove, IL: InterVarsity Academic, 2011.

Licona, Michael R. "New Explanations Have Refuted Jesus' Resurrection" and "The Cross-Examination." In Lee Strobel, *The Case for the Real Jesus*, 101–155. Grand Rapids: Zondervan, 2007.

McDowell, Josh, and Sean McDowell. *Evidence for the Resurrection*. Ventura, CA: Regal, 2009.

Moreland, J. P. "The Resurrection of Jesus." In *Scaling the Secular City*, 159–183. Grand Rapids: Baker, 1987.

Mettinger, Tryggve N.D. *The Riddle of the Resurrection*. Stockholm, Sweden: Almqvist & Wiksell International, 2001.

CONCLUSION: THE VERDICT OF HISTORY

What Does the Evidence Establish—
And What Does It Mean Today?

On a November afternoon in 1981, I locked myself in my bedroom and spent hours replaying the spiritual journey I had been traveling for twenty-one months.

I never intended to write about my experience; in fact, it would be years later when I would decide to retrace and expand upon my original investigation by traveling the country to interview scholars for this book. Still, my probe from January 20, 1980, to November 8, 1981, had been thorough and exhilarating. I had studied history, sifted archaeology, asked questions, and analyzed answers with as much of an open mind as I could muster. Now I had reached critical mass. The evidence seemed clear. The one remaining issue was what I would do with it.

Pulling out a yellow legal pad, I began listing the questions I had posed as I embarked on my investigation, as well as the key facts I had uncovered. In a similar way, I can sum up the substance of what we've learned in our own examination of the evidence through the experts in this book.

• Can the Biographies of Jesus Be Trusted?

I once thought the gospels were merely religious propaganda, hopelessly tainted by overactive imaginations and evangelistic zeal. However, Craig Blomberg, one of the country's foremost authorities on the topic, built a convincing case that they reflect direct and indirect eyewitness testimony and bear the unmistakable earmarks of accuracy. So early are these biographies that they cannot be explained away as merely being a legendary invention. In fact, the fundamental beliefs in Jesus' miracles, resurrection, and deity go way back to the very dawning of the Christian movement.

• Do the Biographies of Jesus Stand Up to Scrutiny?

Blomberg argued persuasively that the gospel writers intended to preserve reliable history, were able to do so, were honest and willing to include difficult-to-explain material, and didn't allow bias to unduly color their reporting. The harmony among the gospels on essential facts, coupled with divergence on some details, lends historical credibility to the accounts. What's more, the early church couldn't have taken root and flourished right there in Jerusalem if it had been teaching facts about Jesus that his own contemporaries could have exposed as exaggerated or false. In short, the gospels were able to pass all eight evidential tests.

• Were Jesus' Biographies Reliably Preserved for Us?

World-class scholar Bruce Metzger said that compared with other ancient documents, there is an unprecedented number of New Testament manuscripts, and that they can be dated extremely close to the original writings. None of the textual variants, which tend to be minor spelling and grammatical differences, put any major Christian doctrines in doubt. The criteria used by the early church to determine which books should be considered authoritative have ensured that we possess the best records about Jesus.

• Is There Credible Evidence for Jesus outside His Biographies?

"We have better historical documentation for Jesus than for the founder of any other ancient religion," said Edwin Yamauchi. Sources from outside the Bible corroborate that many people believed Jesus performed healings and was the Messiah, that he was crucified, and that despite this shameful death, his followers, who believed he was still alive, worshiped him as God. One expert documented thirty-nine ancient sources that corroborate more than one hundred facts concerning Jesus' life, teachings, crucifixion, and resurrection. Seven secular sources and several early creeds concern the deity of Jesus, a doctrine "definitely present in the earliest church," according to scholar Gary Habermas.

• Does Archaeology Confirm or Contradict Jesus' Biographies?

Archaeologist John McRay said there's no question that archaeological findings have enhanced the New Testament's credibility. No discovery has ever disproved a biblical reference. Further, archaeology has established that Luke, who wrote about one-quarter of the New Testament, was an especially careful historian. Concluded one expert, "If Luke was so painstakingly accurate in his historical reporting [of minor details], on what logical basis may we assume he was credulous or inaccurate in his reporting of matters that were far more important, not only to him but to others as well?" Like, for instance, the resurrection of Jesus.

• Is the Jesus of History the Same as the Jesus of Faith?

Gregory Boyd said the much-publicized Jesus Seminar, which doubts Jesus said most of what's attributed to him, was made up of "an extremely small number of radical-fringe scholars who are on the far, far left wing of New Testament thinking." The Seminar ruled out the possibility of miracles at the outset, it employed questionable criteria, and some participants have touted myth-riddled documents of extremely dubious quality. Further, the idea that stories about Jesus emerged from mythology about gods dying and rising fails to withstand scrutiny. Said Boyd, "The evidence for Jesus being who the disciples said he was . . . is just light-years beyond my reasons for thinking that the left-wing scholarship of the Jesus Seminar is correct." In sum, the Jesus of faith is the same as the Jesus of history.

• Was Jesus Really Convinced That He Was the Son of God?

By going back to the very earliest traditions, which are unquestionably safe from legendary development, Ben Witherington III was able to show that Jesus had a supreme and transcendent self-understanding. Based on the evidence, Witherington said, "Did Jesus believe he was the Son of God, the anointed one of God? The answer is yes. Did he see himself as the Son of Man? The answer is yes. Did he see himself as the final Messiah? Yes, that's the way he viewed himself. Did he believe that anybody less than God could save the world? No, I don't believe he did."

• Was Jesus Crazy When He Claimed to Be the Son of God?

Well-known psychologist Gary Collins said Jesus exhibited no inappropriate emotions, was in contact with reality, was brilliant and had amazing insights into human nature, and enjoyed deep and abiding relationships. "I just don't see signs that Jesus was suffering from any known mental illness," he concluded. In addition, Jesus backed up his claim to being God through miraculous feats of healing, astounding demonstrations of power over nature, unrivaled teaching, divine understanding of people, and with his own resurrection, which was the final authentication of his identity.

• Did Jesus Fulfill the Attributes of God?

While the incarnation—God becoming man, the infinite becoming finite—stretches our imagination, prominent theologian D. A. Carson pointed out that there's lots of evidence that Jesus exhibited the characteristics of deity. Based on Philippians 2, many theologians believe Jesus voluntarily emptied himself of the independent use of these divine attributes as he pursued his mission of human redemption. Even so, the New Testament specifically confirms that Jesus ultimately possessed every qualification of deity, including omniscience, omnipresence, omnipotence, eternality, and immutability.

• Did Jesus—and Jesus Alone—Match the Identity of the Messiah?

Hundreds of years before Jesus was born, prophets foretold the coming of the Messiah, or the Anointed One, who would redeem God's people. In effect, dozens of these Old Testament prophecies created a fingerprint that only the true Messiah could fit. This gave Israel a way to rule out impostors and validate the credentials of the authentic Messiah. Against astronomical odds—one chance in a trillion, trillion, trillion, trillion, trillion, trillion, trillion, trillion, trillion, trillion, trillion, trillion—Jesus, and only Jesus throughout history, matched this prophetic fingerprint. This confirms Jesus' identity to an incredible degree of certainty.

• Was Jesus' Death a Sham and His Resurrection a Hoax?

By analyzing the medical and historical data, Dr. Alexander Metherell concluded Jesus could not have survived the gruesome rigors of crucifixion, much less the gaping wound that pierced his lung and heart. The idea that he somehow swooned on the cross and pretended to be dead lacks any evidential basis. Roman executioners were grimly efficient, knowing that they themselves would face death if any of their victims were to come down from the cross alive. Even if Jesus had somehow lived through the torture, his ghastly condition could never have inspired a worldwide movement based on the premise that he had gloriously triumphed over the grave.

• Was Jesus' Body Really Absent from His Tomb?

William Lane Craig presented striking evidence that the enduring symbol of Easter—the vacant tomb of Jesus—was a historical reality. The empty grave is reported or implied in extremely early sources—Mark's gospel and the 1 Corinthians 15 creed—which date so close to the event that they could not possibly have been products of legend. The fact that the gospels report that women discovered the empty tomb bolsters the story's authenticity. The site of Jesus' tomb was known to both Christian and Jew alike, so it could have been checked by skeptics. In fact, nobody, not even the Roman authorities or Jewish leaders, ever claimed that the tomb still contained Jesus' body. Instead they were forced to invent the absurd story that the disciples, despite having no motive or opportunity, had stolen the body—a theory that not even the most skeptical critic believes today.

• Was Jesus Seen Alive after His Death on the Cross?

The evidence for the post-resurrection appearances of Jesus didn't develop gradually over the years as mythology distorted memories of his life. Rather, said resurrection expert Gary Habermas, the resurrection was "the central proclamation of the early church from the very beginning." The ancient creed from 1 Corinthians 15 mentions individuals and groups who encountered the risen Christ, and Paul even challenged first-century doubters to talk with these witnesses personally to determine the truth of the matter for themselves. The book of Acts is littered with extremely early affirmations of Jesus' resurrection, while the gospels describe numerous encounters in detail. Concluded British theologian Michael Green, "The appearances of Jesus are as well authenticated as anything in antiquity. . . . There can be no rational doubt that they occurred."

• Are There Any Supporting Facts That Point to the Resurrection?

J. P. Moreland's circumstantial evidence added final documentation for the resurrection. First, the disciples were in a unique position to know whether the resurrection happened, and they were willing to endure suffering and deprivation proclaiming it was true. Second, apart from the resurrection, there's no good reason why skeptics like Paul and James would have been converted and would have died for their faith. Nobody knowingly and willingly dies for a lie. Third, within weeks of the crucifixion, thousands of Jews began abandoning key social practices that had critical sociological and religious importance for centuries. They believed they risked damnation if they were wrong. Fourth, the early sacraments of Communion and baptism affirmed Jesus' resurrection and deity. And fifth, the miraculous emergence of the church in the face of brutal Roman persecution "rips a great hole in history, a hole the size and shape of resurrection," as C. F. D. Moule put it.

Failing Müller's Challenge

I'll admit it: I was ambushed by the amount and quality of the evidence that Jesus is the unique Son of God. As I sat in my room that Sunday afternoon, I shook my head in amazement. I had seen defendants carted off to the death chamber on much less convincing proof! The cumulative facts and data pointed unmistakably toward a conclusion that I wasn't entirely comfortable in reaching.

Frankly, I had wanted to believe that the deification of Jesus was the result of legendary development in which well-meaning but misguided people slowly turned a wise sage into the mythological Son of God. That seemed safe and reassuring; after all, a roving apocalyptic preacher from the first century could make no demands on me. But while I went into my investigation thinking that this legendary explanation was intuitively obvious, I emerged convinced it was totally without basis.

What clinched it for me was the comment by A. N. Sherwin-White, the great classical historian from Oxford University, that William Lane Craig alluded to in our interview. Sherwin-White understood the rate at which legend accrued in the ancient world. His conclusion: Not even two full generations was enough time for legend to develop and to wipe out a solid core of historical truth.[1]

Now consider the case of Jesus. Historically speaking, the news of his empty tomb, the eyewitness accounts of his post-resurrection appearances, and the conviction that he was indeed God's unique Son emerged virtually instantaneously.

The 1 Corinthians 15 creed, affirming Jesus' death for our sins and listing his post-resurrection appearances to named eyewitnesses, was formulated within months after the crucifixion. Mark's account of the empty tomb was drawn from material that dates back to within a few years of the event itself.

The gospels, attesting to Jesus' teachings, miracles, and resurrection, were circulating within the lifetimes of Jesus' contemporaries, who would have been only too glad to set the record straight if there had been embellishment or falsehood. The most primitive Christian hymns affirm Jesus' divine nature.

Blomberg summed it up this way: "*Within the first two years after his death*, then, significant numbers of Jesus' followers seem to have formulated a doctrine of the atonement, were convinced that he had been raised from the dead in bodily form, associated Jesus with God, and believed they found support for all these convictions in the Old Testament."[2]

Concluded William Lane Craig, "The time span necessary for significant accrual of legend concerning the events of the gospels would place us in the second century AD, *just the time in fact when the legendary apocryphal gospels were born*. These are the legendary accounts sought by the critics."[3]

There was simply nowhere near enough time for mythology to thoroughly corrupt the historical record of Jesus, especially in the midst of eyewitnesses who still had personal knowledge of him. When

German theologian Julius Müller in 1844 challenged anyone to find a single example of legend developing that fast anywhere in history, the response from the scholars of his day—and to the present time—was resounding silence.[4]

On November 8, 1981, I realized that my biggest objection to Jesus also had been quieted by the evidence of history. I found myself chuckling at how the tables had been turned.

In light of the convincing facts I had learned during my investigation, in the face of this overwhelming avalanche of evidence in the case for Christ, the great irony was this: It would require much more faith for me to maintain my atheism than to trust in Jesus of Nazareth!

Implications of the Evidence

Remember the story of James Dixon in the introduction of this book? The evidence pointed powerfully toward his guilt for shooting a Chicago police sergeant. He even admitted he did it!

Yet when a more thorough investigation was conducted, suddenly a shift occurred: The scenario that fit the facts most perfectly was that the sergeant had framed Dixon, who was innocent of the shooting. Dixon was set free, and it was the officer who found himself convicted. As we conclude our investigation in the case for Christ, it's worth revisiting the two big lessons from that story.

• First, Has the Collection of Evidence Really Been Thorough?

Yes, it has been. I selected experts who could state their position and defend it with historical evidence that I could then test through cross-examination. I wasn't merely interested in their opinions; I wanted facts. I challenged them with the current theories of atheists and liberal professors. Given their background, credentials, experience, and character, these scholars were more than qualified to present reliable historical data concerning Jesus.

• Second, Which Explanation Best Fits the Totality of the Evidence?

By November 8, 1981, my legend thesis, to which I had doggedly clung for so many years, had been thoroughly dismantled. What's more, my journalistic skepticism toward the supernatural had melted in light of the breathtaking historical evidence that the resurrection of Jesus was a real, historical event. In fact, my mind could not conjure up a single explanation that fit the evidence of history nearly as well as the conclusion that Jesus was who he claimed to be: the one and only Son of God.

The atheism I had embraced for so long buckled under the weight of historical truth. It was a stunning and radical outcome, certainly not what I had anticipated when I embarked on this investigative process. But it was, in my opinion, a decision compelled by the facts.

All of which led me to the "So what?" question. If this is true, what difference does it make? There were several obvious implications.

- If Jesus is the Son of God, his teachings are more than just good ideas from a wise teacher; they are divine insights on which I can confidently build my life.
- If Jesus sets the standard for morality, I can now have an unwavering foundation for my choices and decisions, rather than basing them on the ever-shifting sands of expediency and self-centeredness.
- If Jesus did rise from the dead, he's still alive today and available for me to encounter on a personal basis.
- If Jesus conquered death, he can open the door of eternal life for me, too.
- If Jesus has divine power, he has the supernatural ability to guide me and help me and transform me as I follow him.
- If Jesus personally knows the pain of loss and suffering, he can comfort and encourage me in the midst of the turbulence that he himself warned is inevitable in a world corrupted by sin.
- If Jesus loves me as he says, he has my best interests at heart. That means I have nothing to lose and everything to gain by committing myself to him and his purposes.
- If Jesus is who he claims to be (and remember, no leader of any other major religion has even pretended to be God), as my Creator he rightfully deserves my allegiance, obedience, and worship.

I remember writing out these implications on my legal pad and then leaning back in my chair. I had reached the culmination of my nearly two-year journey. It was finally time to deal with the most pressing question of all: "Now what?"

The Formula of Faith

After a personal investigation that spanned more than six hundred days and countless hours, my own verdict in the case for Christ was clear. However, as I sat at my desk, I realized that I needed more than an intellectual decision. I wanted to take the experiential step that J. P. Moreland had described in the last interview.

Looking for a way to bring that about, I reached over to a Bible and opened it to John 1:12, a verse I had encountered during my investigation: "Yet to all who received him, to those who believed in his name, he gave the right to become children of God."

The key verbs in that verse spell out with mathematical precision what it takes to go beyond mere mental assent to Jesus' deity and enter into an ongoing relationship with him by becoming adopted into God's family: believe + receive = become.

1. Believe

As someone educated in journalism and law, I was trained to respond to the facts, wherever they lead. For me, the data demonstrated convincingly that Jesus is the Son of God who died as my substitute to pay the penalty I deserved for the wrongdoing I had committed.

And there was plenty of wrongdoing. I'll spare myself the embarrassment of going into details, but the truth is that I had been living a profane, drunken, self-absorbed, and immoral lifestyle. In my career, I had backstabbed my colleagues to gain a personal advantage and had routinely violated legal and ethical standards in pursuit of stories. In my personal life, I was sacrificing my wife and children on the altar of success. I was a liar, a cheater, and a deceiver.

My heart had shrunk to the point where it was rock hard toward anyone else. My main motivator was personal pleasure—and ironically, the more I hungrily sought after it, the more elusive and self-destructive it became.

When I read in the Bible that these sins separated me from God, who is holy and morally pure, this resonated as being true. Certainly God, whose existence I had denied for years, seemed extremely distant, and it became obvious to me that I needed the cross of Jesus to bridge that gulf. Said the apostle Peter, "For Christ also suffered once for sins, the righteous for the unrighteous, to bring you to God" (1 Peter 3:18).

All this I now believed. The evidence of history and of my own experience was too strong to ignore.

2. Receive

Every other faith system I studied during my investigation was based on the "do" plan. In other words, it was necessary for people to do something—for example, use a Tibetan prayer wheel, pay alms, go on pilgrimages, undergo reincarnations, work off karma from past misdeeds, reform their character—to try to somehow earn their way back to God. Despite their best efforts, lots of sincere people just wouldn't make it.

Christianity is unique. It's based on the "done" plan—Jesus has done for us on the cross what we cannot do for ourselves: He has paid the death penalty that we deserve for our rebellion and wrongdoing, so we can become reconciled with God.

I didn't have to struggle and strive to try to do the impossible of making myself worthy. Over and over the Bible says that Jesus offers forgiveness and eternal life as a free gift that cannot be earned (see Rom. 6:23; Eph. 2:8–9; Titus 3:5). It's called grace—*amazing* grace, unmerited favor. It's available to anyone who receives it in a sincere prayer of repentance. Even someone like me.

Yes, I had to take a step of faith, as we do in every decision we make in life. But here's the crucial distinction: I was no longer trying to swim upstream against the strong current of evidence; instead, I was choosing to go in the same direction that the torrent of facts was flowing. That was reasonable, that was rational, that was logical. What's more, in an inner and inexplicable way, it was also what I sensed God's Spirit was nudging me to do.

So on November 8, 1981, I talked with God in a heartfelt and unedited prayer, admitting and turning from my wrongdoing, and receiving the gift of forgiveness and eternal life through Jesus. I told him that with his help I wanted to follow him and his ways from here on out.

There were no lightning bolts, no audible replies, no tingly sensations. I know that some people feel a rush of emotion at such a moment; as for me, however, there was something else that was equally exhilarating: There was the rush of reason.

3. Become

After taking that step, I knew from John 1:12 that I had crossed the threshold into a new experience. I had become something different: a child of God, forever adopted into his family through the historical, risen Jesus. Said the apostle Paul, "Therefore, if anyone is in Christ, the new creation has come: The old has gone, the new is here!" (2 Cor. 5:17).

Sure enough, over time, as I endeavored to follow Jesus' teachings and open myself to his transforming power, my priorities, my values, and my character were (and continue to be) gradually changed. Increasingly I want Jesus' motives and perspective to be my own. To paraphrase Martin Luther King Jr., I may not yet be the man I should be or the man, with Christ's help, I someday will be—but thank God I'm not the man I used to be!

Maybe that sounds mystical to you; I don't know. Not so long ago it would have to me. But it's very real to me now and to those around me. In fact, so radical was the difference in my life that a few months after I became a follower of Jesus, our five-year-old daughter Alison went up to my wife and said, "Mommy, I want God to do for me what he's done for Daddy."

Here was a little girl who had only known a father who was profane, angry, verbally harsh, and all too often absent. And even though she had never interviewed a scholar, never analyzed the data, never investigated historical evidence, she had seen up close the influence that Jesus can have on one person's life. In effect, she was saying, "If this is what God does to a human being, that's what I want for me."

Looking back all these years later, I can see with clarity that the day I personally made a decision in the case for Christ was nothing less than the pivotal event of my entire life.

Reaching Your Own Verdict

Now to you. At the outset I encouraged you to approach the evidence in this book as a fair and impartial juror as much as possible, drawing your conclusions based on the weight of the evidence. In the end the verdict is yours and yours alone. Nobody else can cast the ballot for you.

Perhaps after reading expert after expert, listening to argument after argument, seeing the answers to question after question, and testing the evidence with your logic and common sense, you've found, as I have, that the case for Christ is conclusive.

The belief part of John 1:12 is firmly in place; all that's left is to receive Jesus' grace, and then you'll become his son or daughter, engaged in a spiritual adventure that can flourish for the rest of your life and into eternity. For you, the time for the experiential step has arrived, and I can't encourage you more strongly to take that step with enthusiasm.

On the other hand, maybe questions still linger for you. Perhaps I didn't address the objection that's uppermost in your mind. Fair enough. No single book can deal with every nuance. However, I trust that the amount of information reported in these pages will at least have convinced you that it's reasonable—in fact, imperative—to continue your investigation.

Pinpoint where you think the evidence needs to be bolstered and then seek out additional answers from well-respected experts. If you believe you've come up with a scenario that better accounts for the facts, be willing to subject it to tough-minded scrutiny. Use the suggested resources in this book to delve deeper. Study the Bible yourself (one suggestion: *The Journey*, a special edition of the Bible that's designed for people who don't yet believe it's the word of God).[5]

Resolve that you'll reach a verdict when you've gathered a sufficient amount of information, knowing that you'll never have full resolution of every single issue. You may even want to whisper a prayer to the God you're not yet sure exists, asking him to guide you to the truth about him. And through it all, you'll have my sincere encouragement as you continue in your spiritual quest.

At the same time, I do feel a strong obligation to urge you to make this a front-burner issue in your life. Don't approach it casually or flippantly, because there's a lot riding on your conclusion. As Michael Murphy aptly put it, "We ourselves—and not merely the truth claims—are at stake in the investigation."[6] In other words, if my conclusion in the case for Christ is correct, your future and eternity hinge on how you respond to Christ. As Jesus declared, "If you do not believe that I am he, you will indeed die in your sins" (John 8:24).

Those are sober words, offered out of authentic and loving concern. I cite them to underline the magnitude of this matter and with the hope that they will spur you to actively and thoroughly examine the case for Christ.

In the end, however, remember that some options just aren't viable. The accumulated evidence has already closed them off. Observed C. S. Lewis, the brilliant and once skeptical Cambridge University professor who was eventually won over by evidence for Jesus,

> I am trying here to prevent anyone saying the really foolish thing that people often say about Him: "I'm ready to accept Jesus as a great moral teacher, but I don't accept His claim to be God." That is the one thing we must not say. A man who was merely a man and said the sort of things Jesus said would not be a great moral teacher. He would either be a lunatic . . . or else he would be the Devil of Hell. You must make your choice. Either this man was, and is, the Son of God: or else a madman or something worse. You can shut Him up for a fool, you can spit at Him and kill Him as a demon; or you can fall at His feet and call Him Lord and God. But let us not come with any patronizing nonsense about His being a great human teacher. He has not left that open to us. He did not intend to.[7]

An Interview with Lee Strobel

As the twentieth anniversary of *The Case for Christ* approached, best-selling author Mark Mittelberg turned the tables on Lee Strobel by interviewing him about the legacy of the book, challenges by critics, and how his own life has changed. Mittelberg, whose own books include *The Questions Christians Hope No One Will Ask* and *Confident Faith*, has been a close ministry associate of Strobel since 1987.

Q. How surprised have you been by the impact of The Case for Christ since it came out in 1998? I'm sure you never anticipated it would sell nearly ten million copies in its various formats or be translated into twenty languages.

A. I've been astounded, really. Since I grew up as a Chicago Cubs fan, I like to think of an analogy involving Wrigley Field. Often, a batter hits a pop-up, and it's caught by the center fielder. But sometimes, if the wind is blowing just right, the breeze lifts the ball over the wall. The batter didn't hit the ball any harder, but circumstances turned it into a home run. And that's how I feel about *The Case for Christ*. I made contact with the ball—in other words, I researched and wrote the book in the best way I knew how—but God has lifted and taken it far, far beyond what my meager efforts could ever have achieved.

Q. I know you've got some great stories about people who have been influenced by the book. Are there a few that stand out in your mind?

A. It has been humbling and encouraging. Through the years I've received so many emails, Tweets, letters, and phone calls from people who have come to faith in Jesus after reading the book. Some have ended up going to seminary and into the ministry. A few have become influential defenders of the faith because this was the first book to pique their interest in Christian apologetics.

I remember getting a letter shortly after the book came out from an atheist who had gone into a bookstore to buy an astronomy magazine. He settled onto a bench to look at it and realized he had sat on something—it was a copy of *The Case for Christ*. He thumbed through it, said to himself, "I don't believe this stuff," and tossed it aside. But he said there was like an inner voice that told him he should read it—so he bought the book, read it, and came to faith in Christ! In fact, I got a letter from him the other day; he's still following Jesus.

Recently a Christian told me that he had ordered *The Case for Christ* from an online bookseller. When it was delivered to his house, his father—who was a spiritual skeptic—answered the doorbell. He thought the package was for him, so he opened it. He saw the book and was just about to set it aside, but he became intrigued by its title. He read it cover-to-cover and ended up coming to faith in Christ.

In Colorado there was an atheist computer engineer who read the book in order to discredit it. He checked all the footnotes, read all the references for himself, and ultimately concluded the case for Christianity was compelling. He put his trust in Jesus and then went to a large church the following Sunday. At the point in the service when the pastor encouraged everyone to greet one another, he turned around and extended his hand—*to me*. I had recently moved to Colorado and was visiting the church. I just happened to take the seat directly behind him. When he told me his story, we were astounded by the "coincidence." Since then Doug and I have become close friends.

I could go on and on. Whenever I do a speaking engagement, people tell me story after story about how God has used the book in their lives, or their dad's life, or a friend's life. It's very inspiring. I like to think that even when I'm sleeping at night, somebody in China, India, or Indonesia is reading the book and considering the case for Christianity.

Q. *Then there was Evel Knievel . . .*

A. Yes, the daredevil motorcycle jumper and cultural icon who lived a wild and narcissistic life. He was on the beach one day and out of the blue he felt God saying to him, "Robert, I've saved you more times than you'll ever know. Now I need you to come to me through my son, Jesus." He was stunned. He called the only Christians he knew and asked them about Jesus. They recommended *The Case for Christ*. He read it and said that God used it to cement his new faith in Jesus.

God radically changed his values, character, and morality. When he was baptized, he told his story, and hundreds of people responded by receiving Christ and being baptized on the spot. We became friends; he would call and ask me historical and theological questions. He died a couple of years later—and his tombstone, by his request, is etched with the words: *Believe in Jesus.*

Q. *The book has been so well received by a wide range of readers—men, women, those who are religious as well as skeptics, and folks from different races and cultures. How have young people responded?*

A. This has been especially surprising. When I was interviewing one of the scholars for the book—

Q. *Which one?*

A. Well, I don't want to say. But during a break in our conversation, while I was putting a new tape in my recorder, he said, "I'm afraid nobody's going to read your book." I was startled. I asked, "Why not?" He said, "We live in a postmodern culture. Nobody's interested in historical evidence for Christianity anymore, especially young people." I remember getting depressed and going home to lament to Leslie, "Nobody's going to read my book."

Q. *So what happened?*

A. We were stunned when the book came out because the biggest response we received was from sixteen- to twenty-four-year-olds. This was the group that reported the most people who had received Christ after reading the book. It turns out they are very interested in evidence for the faith. In fact, that's what prompted me to team up with Jane Vogel to write the Student Edition of the book.

Q. *Our friend, Cliffe Knechtle, says, "A person coming to faith is like a chain with many links. There's a beginning link, a middle link, and a final link." What do you say to readers for whom this book is just the beginning of their spiritual journey or maybe one more step along a long path?*

A. I know what it's like to be in the process of spiritually seeking. It's exhilarating, it's exciting, it's challenging, it's frustrating, it's confusing at times—and ultimately, it's worth it. My advice is to persevere, to weed out bias and prejudice as much as possible, to follow the evidence wherever it leads, and to keep asking questions. Oh, and to ask God—even if you're not sure he exists—to guide you to the truth. Then once the evidence is in, courageously reach a verdict.

Q. *Are there aspects of The Case for Christ that have gotten stronger since the book has come out?*

A. One trend is that scholars are taking the New Testament a lot more seriously these days. Mark D. Roberts, who earned his doctorate in New Testament at Harvard, observed that "some of the brightest and most influential New Testament scholars have argued that the New Testament Gospels are reliable sources of historical information about Jesus." And he added: "If you look squarely at the facts as they are widely understood, and if you do not color them with pejorative bias or atheistic presuppositions, then you'll find that it's reasonable to trust the Gospels."[1]

One of the most highly respected New Testament scholars is Craig **A.** Evans, who has written or edited fifty books and lectured at Cambridge, Oxford, and Yale. He told me: "I would say the Gospels are essentially reliable, and there are lots and lots of other scholars who agree. There's every reason to conclude that the Gospels have fairly and accurately reported the essential elements of Jesus' teachings, life, death, and resurrection. They're early enough, they're rooted into the right streams that go back to Jesus and the original people, there's continuity, there's proximity, there's verification of certain distinct points with archaeology and other documents, and then there's the inner logic."[2]

There have also been strides in research on the resurrection. A few years ago, Michael Licona wrote a landmark 718-page book called *The Resurrection of Jesus: A New Historiographical Approach*, while N. T. Wright authored an ambitious work called *The Resurrection of the Son of God*. As scholarship has increased in these areas, the strength of the case for Christianity has grown along with it.

Q. *Certainly the field of Christian apologetics, or the defense of the faith, has changed since the time when your book came out.*

A. Yes, enormously. When I wrote *The Case for Christ*, there weren't many popular books available on the evidence for faith. Today, there is a proliferation of excellent books, academic programs, websites, blogs, videos, and curricula. Plus, there's more and more preaching on the topic at churches.

Q. *Do you think your book helped to spark any of that?*

A. I think it's largely due to changes in the culture that are creating an increasing demand for the answers found in Christian apologetics. In spite of the growing body of evidence that supports Christianity, there are more and more people who doubt. In 2014, I commissioned a national poll and found that while 82 percent of Baby Boomers (ages 50–68) are certain God exists, just 62 percent of Millennials (ages 18–30) said the same thing.[3] Researcher David Kinnaman discovered that three of the six reasons young people give for leaving the church are related to intellectual questions and concerns.[4] So there's a big need for apologetics, and I'm glad to see more and more materials being produced to meet that demand.

Q. *Because of its high profile, The Case for Christ has attracted a lot of attention, including from some critics.*

A. I've actually been encouraged by the reception the book has received from most skeptics because their objections seem so unconvincing to me. One critic called the scholars I interviewed "alleged experts," as if Bruce Metzger, William Lane Craig, D. A. Carson, Ben Witherington III, Craig Blomberg, Edwin Yamauchi, J. P Moreland and the others—with doctorates from Cambridge, Princeton, Brandeis, and elsewhere, and with hundreds of scholarly publications—are somehow underqualified. Other reviewers have been more thoughtful, but I'm always relieved when I read the critiques because they are usually pretty easily answered.

Q. *Some critics claim you weren't really an atheist when you wrote the book.*

A. Well, they're right! I never claimed to be. It's true that I was an atheist for much of my life, until my wife Leslie's conversion to Christianity prompted me to use my journalism and legal training to investigate whether there's any credibility to Christianity or any other world religion. I did that for a year and nine months.

Q. What happened next?

A. On November 8, 1981, alone in my bedroom, I summarized the evidence for and against Christianity on a yellow legal pad. Based on the avalanche of evidence that pointed so powerfully toward the truth of Christianity, I concluded that it would take more faith for me to maintain my atheism than to become a Christian. That's when I prayed to receive Jesus as my forgiver and leader. It wasn't until the late 1990s that I wrote *The Case for Christ*. As I said in the introduction, the book retraces and expands upon my original investigation.

Q. Why did you feel a need to do that?

A. Because when I did my personal investigation, I was never intending to write anything about it. I didn't keep very good notes; in fact, to this day I can't find that yellow legal pad! I did read books, both for and against Christianity; I asked experts questions; I thoroughly explored ancient history and archaeology; but I was doing all of this out of my own curiosity. Years later, when I decided to write *The Case for Christ*, I wanted to approach the issue more systematically and conduct fully documented interviews with world-class scholars in order to get the most current and cutting-edge evidence that was available. That way, I could lay out the facts in the most logical and accessible format.

Q. If you never planned to write a book when you were doing your personal investigation, what prompted you to eventually create one?

A. After I came to faith in Christ in 1981, I stayed in journalism for a while but ultimately left to join the staff of Willow Creek Community Church, where you and I first met. There, I was mentored in theology, ordained, and became a teaching pastor. One day I was assigned to do a three-week sermon series, and I decided to call it "The Case for Christ." I set up the platform to look like a courtroom and I called experts to the witness stand by showing videos of interviews I had conducted with them.

A few months later, I was taking a walk with Leslie and she suggested I turn that series into a book. I shrugged off the idea at first, saying it was based on videos. But then I stopped in my tracks—I can take you back to the very spot on the sidewalk—and said, "Wait a minute! That might work." That's when I decided to propose the book to Zondervan. I thought they'd reject the idea because at the time books on apologetics rarely did well, but they surprised me by giving the project a green light.

Q. *Did they say why they approved it?*

A. They said it was because they could see my obvious passion for the project. And I think they believed that the book would have a unique perspective because of my background as both an atheist and a journalist.

Q. *Was it difficult to get interviews with the scholars?*

A. That was really surprising—it wasn't difficult at all. Every scholar I called immediately agreed to be interviewed, even though most of them had no idea who I was. These people spend their lives living in the minutia of academic research, and frankly, they're often thrilled when someone carefully reads their books and wants to talk with them about what they've written. In the end, it took me five months—using up weekend, evenings, and vacation time—to put *The Case for Christ* together.

Q. *That's pretty fast!*

A. Looking back, that's one way I can detect God's hand on the project. I don't see how it's possible to have done it that quickly.

Q. *Did you face any challenges during the writing of the book?*

A. Yes, a very scary one. Originally, my idea was to format the book like this Q&A, unadorned by any descriptive material. But my editor, John Sloan, urged me to write the book as a narrative, taking the reader with me as I interviewed the scholars. He wanted me to describe the setting, talk about my emotions, and paint a picture of how this adventure unfolded.

Q. *Great idea! Were you excited about it?*

A. Definitely not. I had already written the first chapter as a straight Q&A and felt the need to keep my momentum. But Sloan took a stab at rewriting part of it as a narrative. I showed both versions to Leslie and asked, "Which is better?" She said, "Well, his." I knew in my heart she was right, but I doubted whether I had the skill as a writer to pull it off. I'm grateful that Sloan coached me through the experience.

Q. You didn't interview any skeptics for the book. Some have criticized you for that.

A. I think they misunderstand my approach. I was standing in the shoes of the skeptic. As the subtitle says, this was "a journalist's *personal* investigation of the evidence for Jesus." I was asking the questions I had when I was an atheist. Obviously, as you can tell from the footnotes and many of my questions, I had digested the writings of skeptical scholars. Then I confronted Christian experts with what I considered to be the skeptics' most potent objections—which also were the ones I personally wrestled with—to see if they could offer cogent and convincing answers. Then I reported their answers left it to readers to reach their own verdict.

Q. Let me press you by focusing on a common objection to your book. For your chapter titled "The Rebuttal Evidence," you interviewed a critic of the Jesus Seminar, and yet you didn't question anyone from the Jesus Seminar itself. Some people have called that unfair.

A. There's no secret about what the Jesus Seminar believed. They clearly set out their methodology in their writings. As you know, the Seminar was founded by the late Robert Funk, a liberal New Testament scholar, and it became famous for claiming that Jesus never said 82 percent of what the Gospels report him as saying. The Seminar was made up of left-wing scholars and laypeople who claimed they were doing an unbiased investigation of Jesus, and yet nobody criticizes them for not giving conservative scholars space in their books to refute their assertions.

Q. You interviewed Jesus Seminar critic Gregory Boyd. He said the Seminar embraced naturalism, the belief that every event has a natural cause, and ruled out even the possibility of the supernatural at the outset. Yet critics point out that Funk once said, "Nothing is impossible, unless we exclude logical impossibilities, such as square circles."[5] Also, Jesus Seminar cochairman John Dominic Crossan said, "I leave absolutely open what God could do."[6]

A. Let me give you the rest of the story. First of all, Funk was straightforward about his foundational beliefs. He said: "The God of the metaphysical age is dead. There is not a personal god out there external to human beings and the material world." He added: "The notion that God interferes with the order of nature from time to time in order to aid or punish is no longer credible. . . . Miracles are conceivable only as the inexplicable; otherwise they contradict the regularity of the order of the physical universe." Further, Funk said: "We should give Jesus a demotion. It is no longer credible to think of Jesus as divine."[7]

As for Crossan, he did deny in a debate with William Lane Craig that he was a naturalist.[8] But he conceded he has "a theological presupposition" that God doesn't directly intervene in affairs.[9] He said, "The supernatural *always* (at least till this is disproved for me) operates through the screen of the natural."[10] And yet, as Craig pointed out, "that *is* naturalism"—a belief that God acts in the world only mediately through natural causes.[11] In fact, despite Craig's prodding, Crossan refused to affirm that God really exists outside of our imagination.[12]

Crossan's presupposition about the supernatural has huge implications. "Very simply," said Craig, "it rules out in advance the historicity of events like the resurrection."[13]

Let's be clear: the introduction to the Jesus Seminar's book *The Five Gospels* says in "this scientific age . . . the Christ of creed and dogma . . . can no longer command the assent of those who have seen the heavens through Galileo's telescope."[14] The Seminar's first "pillar of scholarly wisdom" is the distinction between the historical Jesus and the Christ of faith—in other words, citing German scholar D. F. Strauss, between the natural Jesus and the supernatural Jesus.[15] "The Jesus of the gospels," said the Jesus Seminar, "is an imaginative theological construct."[16]

William Lane Craig was blunt in an academic article he wrote after his debate with Crossan. He said: "The Jesus Seminar is remarkably candid about its presupposition of naturalism. . . . If you begin by presupposing naturalism, then of course what you wind up with is a purely natural Jesus! This reconstructed, naturalistic Jesus is not based on evidence, but on definition. What is amazing is that the Jesus Seminar makes no attempt to defend this naturalism; it is just presupposed. But this presupposition is wholly unjustified. . . . Reject this presupposition and the whole construction collapses."[17]

Scholar Mark Roberts was a colleague of seven of the Jesus Seminar participants at Harvard. He wrote: "Though some of the fellows are fine biblical scholars, the Seminar itself was not a truly academic exercise. It was, in fact, a carefully contrived effort to erode classic Christian faith. . . . Funk was quite clear about his anti-Christian agenda. . . . It was obvious from the beginning that Funk's agenda for the Jesus Seminar was not consistent with classical Christianity."[18]

Undoubtedly, there were some differences between the beliefs of various members of the Seminar. I know at least one who goes so far as to say that there's insufficient evidence Jesus ever lived, which is absurd in my opinion.[19] But as a group, the Seminar made its positions very clearly known, and consequently it should expect to be open to critique, just as everyone's writings are.

Q. *There are a few people who have critiqued your book by saying you were too easily persuaded by the people you interviewed. Evidently you didn't ask some of the follow-up questions they wish you had.*

A. Everyone approaches the topic of Jesus with their own set of questions or objections. One book can't deal with every possible issue. Anyone can say, "You could have gone deeper on this or that topic," but the mass-market paperback of *The Case for Christ* was already four hundred pages. So I determined to stay focused on the subjects that most concerned me. Hopefully, they are the same topics that are on the minds of most readers, but others may have some different issues. That's okay.

For those who want more information, I have now updated the recommended reading list at the end of each chapter. These resources can be a great next step. Also, my follow-up book *The Case for the Real Jesus*, which is currently being reissued under the title *In Defense of Jesus*, delves further into such issues as the resurrection, mythology, the reliability of the New Testament text, fulfilled prophecies, and claims about alternative gospels.

Q. *When it comes to Christianity, do you think some people erect walls of resistance that they don't generally erect in other areas of their lives?*

A. Most of the spiritual seekers I meet are sincere and authentically interested in finding answers, which is great. But then there are some who seem to intentionally ratchet up their skepticism. Sometimes when a person asks me a particularly pointed question, I want to say, "First, prove to me who you are. And don't try to show me a driver's license—we know those can be forged. Don't try to show me a birth certificate. How would I know if it's genuine? Don't have a friend or spouse attest to your identity, because we all know that people can lie."

You see, it's very easy to fold our arms in defiance and raise the bar of our skepticism unreasonably high. But that's not how we live our lives in other areas. When we use our common sense and evaluate evidence for Christianity as we would for anything else, I think it's very persuasive.

Q. *You must be excited about the news that The Case for Christ has now been translated into Arabic.*

A. Yes, my hope is that it will reach a larger Muslim audience than ever before. After all, the book offers strong evidence in support of several key points denied by Islam—that Jesus is the unique Son of God, that he was killed by crucifixion, and that he was resurrected from the dead. Perhaps it will encourage Muslims to investigate where history really does point.

Q. *I've seen in my own friend Fayz how The Case for Christ can help Muslims find the real Jesus. Do you have more books planned?*

A. As you know, there are several books already in the series. *The Case for a Creator* looks at scientific evidence that points toward a Creator who happens to look a lot like the God of the Bible. *The Case for Faith*, which opens with an interview with an outspoken spiritual skeptic, explores the eight biggest objections to Christianity. I've mentioned *The Case for the Real Jesus*, which deals with many of the current objections to the claims of Christ. That's currently being reprinted as *In Defense of Jesus*. And *The Case for Grace* offers the experiential evidence by telling the stories of lives so radically changed that God seems the best explanation. I've also produced *The Case for Christ Study Bible* and gift books called *The Case for Hope* and *The Case for Christianity Answer Book*. I'm working on several other projects right now, but I don't want to say anything about them quite yet.

Q. *How has your life changed since The Case for Christ came out?*

A. You and I wrote a book together called *The Unexpected Adventure*, and that's a pretty good description of what life has been like for me. I've had the pleasure of hosting a national network television show called *Faith Under Fire*, during which I moderated debates between Christians, atheists, Muslims, Hindus, Baha'is, and others, on a variety of religious and social topics. I've spoken at conferences, seminars, and churches around the world. And today I'm a Professor of Christian Thought at Houston Baptist University.

Q. *In your talks, you're painfully candid about the way your life as an atheist negatively affected your children when they were young. You admit to living an immoral, drunken, and narcissistic lifestyle.*

A. I don't want to suggest that all spiritual skeptics live that way. Most certainly don't. But in my opinion, if there were no God or ultimate accountability, then the most logical way to live my life was as a hedonist, someone who just pursued pleasure. And that's what I did—to the detriment of my family and myself.

Q. *How have your kids been impacted by the difference in your life since you became a follower of Jesus?*

A. They saw the changes God brought about in my character, values, and morality, and I'm grateful that today they're both devoted followers of Jesus. Alison has written several novels with Christian themes, and she and her husband, Dan, who has a graduate degree in apologetics, have authored two children's books about God.

Kyle received his doctorate in theology from the University of Aberdeen and is now a professor at the Talbot School of Theology at Biola University. He has written both popular and academic books, and his scholarly work has been published in the *Harvard Theological Review* and elsewhere. Plus, I've been blessed with three wonderful granddaughters and one grandson, Oliver Lee Strobel.

Q. *I noticed you mentioned his full name.*

A. Yeah, I had to get in that middle name. Very proud of that.

Q. *You said in The Case for Christ that after your investigation was over, it would have taken more faith for you to maintain your atheism than to become a Christian. Do you ever wrestle with doubts?*

A. Sure, there are difficult times when I might question aspects of my faith, but they're only temporary. I always go back to the evidence of science—cosmology, physics, biochemistry, genetics, and human consciousness point powerfully toward the existence of a Creator. And I go back to history—Jesus claimed to be divine and then backed up that assertion by returning from the dead. Still, there's more to my faith than that.

Q. *What do you mean?*

A. William Lane Craig crystalized the issue for me. He told me, "Ultimately, the way a Christian really knows that Christianity is true is through the self-authenticating witness of God's Spirit. The Holy Spirit whispers to our spirit that we belong to God. That's one of his roles. Other evidence, though still valid, is basically confirmatory."

He illustrated the point this way: "Let's say you're going to the office to see if your boss is in. You see his car in the parking lot. You ask the secretary if he's in, and she says, 'Yes, I just spoke with him.' You see the light from under his office door. You listen and hear his voice on the telephone. On the basis of all this evidence, you have good grounds for concluding that your boss is in his office.

"But you could do something quite different. You could go to the door and knock on it and meet the boss face-to-face. At that point, the evidence of the car in the parking lot, the secretary's testimony, the light under the door, the voice on the telephone—all of that would still be valid, but it would take a secondary role, because now you've met the boss face-to-face.

"And in the same way, when we've met God, so to speak, face-to-face, all of the arguments and evidence for his existence—though still perfectly valid—take a secondary role. They now become confirmatory of what God himself has shown us in a supernatural way through the witness of the Holy Spirit in our hearts."[20]

So I'm grateful for the evidence described in *The Case for Christ*, because it was pivotal in knocking down the barriers between Jesus and me. But if you ask me today how I know for sure that Jesus is alive and is the Son of God, I'd say: "Because I know him personally. Because he is now my friend."

That's something we can all experience when we come to him in repentance and faith. And let me be totally transparent: that's my hope for everyone who reads *The Case for Christ*.

List of Citations

Archer—Gleason L. Archer, *The Encyclopedia of Bible Difficulties* (Grand Rapids: Zondervan, 1982).

Anderson—J. N. D. Anderson, *The Evidence for the Resurrection* (Downers Grove, IL: InterVarsity Press, 1966).

Ankerberg—John Ankerberg and John Weldon, *The Facts on the Mormon Church* (Eugene, OR: Harvest House, 1991).

Ankerberg—John Ankerberg and John Weldon, *Knowing the Truth about the Resurrection* (Eugene, OR: Harvest House, 1996).

Ankerberg—John Ankerberg and John Weldon, *Ready with an Answer* (Eugene, OR: Harvest House, 1997).

Armstrong—Karen Armstrong, *A History of God* (New York: Ballantine/ Epiphany, 1993).

Baigent—Michael Baigent, Richard Leigh, and Henry Lincoln, *Holy Blood, Holy Grail* (New York: Delacorte, 1982).

Barnett—Paul Barnett, *Is the New Testament History?* (Ann Arbor, MI: Vine, 1986).

Barnett—Paul Barnett, *Jesus and the Logic of History* (Grand Rapids: Eerdmans, 1997).

Black—Henry Campbell Black, *Black's Law Dictionary*, 5th ed. (St. Paul, MN: West, 1979).

Blomberg—Craig Blomberg, *The Historical Reliability of the Gospels* (Downers Grove, IL: InterVarsity Press, 1987).

Boyd—Gregory A. Boyd, *Cynic Sage or Son of God? Recovering the Real Jesus in an Age of Revisionist Replies* (Wheaton, IL: BridgePoint, 1995).

Boyd—Gregory A. Boyd, *Jesus under Siege* (Wheaton, IL: Victor, 1995).

Boyd—Robert Boyd, *Tells, Tombs, and Treasure* (Grand Rapids: Baker, 1969).

Braaten—Carl Braaten, *History and Hermeneutics*, vol. 2 of *New Directions in Theology Today*, ed. William Hordern (Philadelphia: Westminster Press, 1966).

British Medical Journal—"A Case of Congenital Ichthyosiform Erythrodermia of Brocq Treated by Hypnosis," *British Medical Journal* 2 (1952).

Brown—R. E. Brown, "Did Jesus Know He Was God?" *Biblical Theology Bulletin* 15 (1985).

Bruce—F. F. Bruce, *The New Testament Documents: Are They Reliable?* (Grand Rapids: Eerdmans, 1960).

Bruce—F. F. Bruce, *The Books and the Parchments* (Old Tappan, NJ: Revell, 1963).

Bruce—F. F. Bruce, *Jesus and Christian Origins outside the New Testament* (Grand Rapids: Eerdmans, 1974).

Bruce—F. F. Bruce, *The Canon of Scripture* (Downers Grove, IL: InterVarsity Press, 1988).

Chicago Tribune—"Bomb Victim's Body Not in Grave," *Chicago Tribune* (January 14, 1998).

Clifford—Ross Clifford, *The Case for the Empty Tomb* (Claremont, CA: Albatross, 1991).

Collins—Gary R. Collins, *Can You Trust Psychology?* (Downers Grove, IL: InterVarsity Press, 1988).

Collins—Gary R. Collins, *Christian Counseling: A Comprehensive Guide* (Dallas: Word, 1988).

Collins—Gary R. Collins, *The Soul Search* (Nashville: Thomas Nelson, 1998).

Craig—William Lane Craig, *Knowing the Truth about the Resurrection* (Ann Arbor, MI: Servant, 1988).

Craig—William Lane Craig, *Reasonable Faith* (Westchester, IL: Crossway, 1994).

Craig—William Lane Craig, *The Son Rises: Historical Evidence for the Resurrection of Jesus* (Chicago: Moody Press, 1981).

Craig—William Lane Craig and Frank Zindler, *Atheism vs. Christianity: Where Does the Evidence Point?* (Grand Rapids: Zondervan, 1993). Videocassette.

Crossan—John Dominic Crossan, *The Historical Jesus* (San Francisco: HarperSanFrancisco, 1991).

Donato—Marla Donato, "That Guilty Look," *Chicago Tribune* (April 1, 1994).

Drane—John Drane, *Introducing the New Testament* (San Francisco: Harper & Row, 1986).

Dunn—James D. G. Dunn, *Jesus and the Spirit* (London: SCM Press, 1975).

Dunn—James Dunn, *The Living Word* (Philadelphia: Fortress, 1988).

Edwards—William D. Edwards et al., "On the Physical Death of Jesus Christ," *Journal of the American Medical Association* (March 21, 1986), 1455–63.

Evans—Colin Evans, *The Casebook of Forensic Detection* (New York: John Wiley & Sons, 1996).

Finegan—Jack Finegan, *The Archaeology of the New Testament* (Princeton: Princeton University Press, 1992).

Foreman—Dale Foreman, *Crucify Him* (Grand Rapids: Zondervan, 1990).

France—R. T. France, *The Evidence for Jesus* (Downers Grove, IL: InterVarsity Press, 1986).

Fruchtenbaum—Arnold Fruchtenbaum, *Jesus Was a Jew* (Tustin, CA: Ariel Ministries, 1981).

Frydland—Rachmiel Frydland, *What the Rabbis Know about the Messiah* (Cincinnati: Messianic, 1993).

Geisler—Norman Geisler and Thomas Howe, *When Critics Ask* (Wheaton, IL: Victor, 1992).

Geisler—Norman L. Geisler and William E. Nix, *A General Introduction to the Bible* (1968; reprint, Chicago: Moody Press, 1980).

Geivett—R. Douglas Geivett and Gary R. Habermas, eds., *In Defense of Miracles* (Downers Grove, IL: InterVarsity Press, 1997).

Grant—Michael Grant, *Jesus: An Historian's Review of the Gospels* (New York: Charles Scribner's Sons, 1977).

Green—Michael Green, *Christ Is Risen: So What?* (Kent, England: Sovereign World, 1995).

Green—Michael Green, *The Empty Cross of Jesus* (Downers Grove, IL: InterVarsity Press, 1984).

Greenleaf—Simon Greenleaf, *The Testimony of the Evangelists* (Grand Rapids: Baker, 1984).

Gregory—Leland H. Gregory III, "Top Ten Government Bloopers," *George* (November 1997).

Gruenler—Royce Gordon Gruenler, *New Approaches to Jesus and the Gospels* (Grand Rapids: Baker, 1982).

Habermas—Gary Habermas, *The Historical Jesus* (Joplin, MO: College Press, 1996).

Habermas—Gary Habermas, *The Verdict of History* (Nashville: Thomas Nelson, 1988).

Habermas—Gary Habermas and Antony Flew, *Did Jesus Rise from the Dead? The Resurrection Debate* (San Francisco: Harper & Row, 1987), xiv.

Habermas—Gary Habermas and J. P. Moreland, *Beyond Death: Exploring the Evidence for Immortality* (Westchester, IL: Crossway, 1998).

Habermas—Gary Habermas and J. P. Moreland, *Immortality: The Other Side of Death* (Nashville: Thomas Nelson, 1992).

Harris—Murray J. Harris, *Jesus As God* (Grand Rapids: Baker, 1993).

Harris—Murray J. Harris, *Three Crucial Questions about Jesus* (Grand Rapids: Baker, 1994).

Hengel—M. Hengel, *Crucifixion in the Ancient World* (Philadelphia: Fortress, 1977).

Ignatius—Ignatius, *Trallians* 9.

Irenaeus—Irenaeus, *Adversus Haereses* 3.3.4.

Johnson—Denny Johnson, "Police Add Electronic 'Sketch Artist' to Their Bag of Tricks," *Chicago Tribune* (June 22, 1997).

Johnson—Luke Timothy Johnson, *The Real Jesus* (San Francisco: HarperSanFrancisco, 1996).

Josephus—Josephus, *The Antiquities* 20.200.

Kaiser—Walter C. Kaiser Jr., *The Messiah in the Old Testament* (Grand Rapids: Zondervan, 1995).

Kenyon—Frederic Kenyon, *Handbook to the Textual Criticism of the New Testament* (New York: Macmillan, 1912).

Kenyon—Frederic Kenyon, *The Bible and Archaeology* (New York: Harper, 1940).

Lake—Kirsopp Lake, *The Historical Evidence for the Resurrection of Jesus Christ* (London: Williams & Norgate, 1907).

Lawrence—D. H. Lawrence, *Love among the Haystacks and Other Stories* (New York: Penguin, 1960).

Lewis—C. S. Lewis, *Mere Christianity* (New York: Macmillan-Collier, 1960).

Lewis—C. S. Lewis, *The Screwtape Letters* (London: Collins-Fontana, 1942).

Maier—Paul L. Maier, *Pontius Pilate* (Wheaton, IL: Tyndale House, 1968).

Maier—P. Maier, "Sejanus, Pilate, and the Date of the Crucifixion," *Church History* 37 (1968).

Marshall—I. Howard Marshall, *I Believe in the Historical Jesus* (Grand Rapids: Eerdmans, 1977).

Martin—Michael Martin, *The Case against Christianity* (Philadelphia: Temple University Press, 1991).

Martin—W. J. Martin, *The Deity of Christ* (Chicago: Moody Press, 1964).

McDowell—Josh McDowell, *Evidence That Demands a Verdict* (1972; reprint, San Bernardino, CA: Here's Life, 1986).

McDowell—Josh McDowell, *More Than a Carpenter* (Wheaton, IL: Living Books, 1977).

McDowell—Josh McDowell, *The Resurrection Factor* (San Bernardino, CA: Here's Life, 1981).

McDowell—Josh McDowell and Bart Larson, *Jesus: A Biblical Defense of His Deity* (San Bernardino, CA: Here's Life, 1983).

McDowell—Josh McDowell and Bill Wilson, *He Walked among Us* (Nashville: Thomas Nelson, 1994).

McFarlan—Donald McFarlan, ed., *The Guinness Book of World Records* (New York: Bantam, 1991).

McGinniss—Joe McGinniss, *Fatal Vision* (New York: New American Library, 1989).

McRay—John McRay, *Archaeology and the New Testament* (Grand Rapids: Baker, 1991).

Metzger—Bruce M. Metzger, *The Canon of the New Testament* (Oxford: Clarendon Press, 1988).

Metzger—Bruce M. Metzger, *The Text of the New Testament* (Oxford: Oxford University Press, 1992).

Miller—Kevin D. Miller, "The War of the Scrolls," *Christianity Today* (October 6, 1997).

Montgomery—John Warwick Montgomery, ed., *Christianity for the Tough-Minded* (Minneapolis: Bethany House, 1973).

Moreland—J. P. Moreland, *Scaling the Secular City* (Grand Rapids: Baker, 1987).

Morison—Frank Morison, *Who Moved the Stone?* (Grand Rapids: Zondervan, 1987).

Moule—C. F. D. Moule, *The Phenomenon of the New Testament* (London: SCM Press, 1967).

Müller—Julius Müller, *The Theory of Myths, in Its Application to the Gospel History, Examined and Confuted* (London: John Chapman, 1844).

Neill—Stephen Neill, *The Interpretation of the New Testament 1861–1961* (London: O.U.P., 1964).

O'Collins—Gerald O'Collins, *The Easter Jesus* (London: Darton, Longman & Todd, 1973).

Patzia—Arthur G. Patzia, *The Making of the New Testament* (Downers Grove, IL: InterVarsity Press, 1995).

Peck—M. Scott Peck, *People of the Lie* (New York: Touchstone, 1997).

Pelikan—Jaroslav Pelikan, *The Christian Tradition: A History of the Development of Doctrine*, vol. 1, *The Emergence of the Catholic Tradition (100–600)* (Chicago: University of Chicago Press, 1971).

Phlegon—Phlegon, *Olympiades he Chronika* 13, ed. Otto Keller, *Rerum Naturalium Scriptores Graeci Minores*, I (Leipzig: Teurber, 1877).

Possley—Maurice Possley, "Mob Hit Man Aleman Gets One Hundred to Three Hundred Years," *Chicago Tribune* (November 26, 1997).

Proctor—William Proctor, *The Resurrection Report* (Nashville: Broadman & Holman, 1998).

Rosen—Marjorie Rosen, "Getting Inside the Mind of a Serial Killer," *Biography* (October 1997).

Rosen—Moishe Rosen, *Y'shua, the Jewish Way to Say Jesus* (Chicago: Moody Press, 1982).

Rosen—Ruth Rosen, ed., *Jewish Doctors Meet the Great Physician* (San Francisco: Purple Pomegranate, 1997).

Schaff—Philip Schaff, *The Person of Christ* (New York: American Tract Society, 1918).

Schonfield—Hugh Schonfield, *The Passover Plot* (New York: Bantam, 1965).

Sherwin-White—A. N. Sherwin-White, *Roman Society and Roman Law in the New Testament* (Oxford: Clarendon Press, 1963).

Smith—Morton Smith, "Biblical Arguments for Slavery," *Free Inquiry* (Spring 1987), 30.

Sowell—Thomas Sowell, *Race and Culture* (New York: Basic, 1995).

Stoner—Peter W. Stoner, *Science Speaks* (Chicago: Moody Press, 1969).

Stott—John Stott, *Basic Christianity* (Grand Rapids: Eerdmans, 1986).

Strobel—Lee Strobel, "His 'I Shot Him' Stuns Courtroom," *Chicago Tribune* (June 20, 1975).

Strobel—Lee Strobel, "Pal's Confession Fails; Defendant Ruled Guilty," *Chicago Tribune* (June 21, 1975).

Strobel—Lee Strobel, "Jury in Makeshift Courtroom Hears Dying Boy Tell of Attack," *Chicago Tribune* (February 24, 1976).

Strobel—Lee Strobel, "'Textbook' Thumbprint Aids Conviction in Coed's Killing," *Chicago Tribune* (June 29, 1976).

Strobel—Lee Strobel, "Four Years in Jail—and Innocent," *Chicago Tribune* (August 22, 1976).

Strobel—Lee Strobel, "Youth's Testimony Convicts Killers, but Death Stays Near," *Chicago Tribune* (October 25, 1976).

Strobel—Lee Strobel, "Did Justice Close Her Eyes?" *Chicago Tribune* (August 21, 1977).

Strobel—Lee Patrick Strobel, *Reckless Homicide: Ford's Pinto Trial* (South Bend, IN: And Books, 1980).

Strobel—Lee Strobel, *God's Outrageous Claims* (Grand Rapids: Zondervan, 1997).

Telchin—Stan Telchin, *Betrayed!* (Grand Rapids: Chosen, 1982).

Templeton—Charles Templeton, *Act of God* (New York: Bantam, 1979).

Templeton—Charles Templeton, *Farewell to God* (Toronto: McClelland & Stewart, 1996).

Thompson—J. A. Thompson, *The Bible and Archaeology* (Grand Rapids: Eerdmans, 1975).

Warfield—Benjamin B. Warfield, *Introduction to Textual Criticism of the New Testament* (London: Hodder & Stoughton, 1907).

Webster's—*Webster's Encyclopedic Unabridged Dictionary of the English Language* (New York: Gramercy, 1989).

Wilcox—M. Wilcox, "Jesus in the Light of His Jewish Environment," *Aufstieg und Niedergang der römischen Welt* 2, no. 25.1 (1982).

Wilkins—Michael J. Wilkins and J. P. Moreland, eds., *Jesus under Fire* (Grand Rapids: Zondervan, 1995).

Wilson—Ian Wilson, *Jesus: The Evidence* (1984; reprint, San Francisco: HarperSanFrancisco, 1988).

Witherington—Ben Witherington III, *The Christology of Jesus* (Minneapolis: Fortress, 1990).

Yamauchi—Edwin Yamauchi, "Josephus and the Scriptures," *Fides et Historia* 13 (1980).

Yamauchi—Edwin Yamauchi, *The Stones and the Scriptures* (New York: J. B. Lippincott, 1972).

Zindler—Frank Zindler, "Where Jesus Never Walked," *American Atheist* (Winter 1996–1997).

Zodhiates—Spiros Zodhiates, *Was Christ God?* (Grand Rapids: Eerdmans, 1966).

Zondervan—*The Journey Bible* (Grand Rapids: Zondervan, 1996).

Notes

INTRODUCTION

1. Lee Strobel, "Four Years in Jail—and Innocent," *Chicago Tribune* (August 22, 1976) and "Did Justice Close Her Eyes?" *Chicago Tribune* (August 21, 1977).

CHAPTER 1: The Eyewitness Evidence

1. Lee Strobel, "Youth's Testimony Convicts Killers, but Death Stays Near," *Chicago Tribune* (October 25, 1976).
2. Irenaeus, *Adversus Haereses* 3.3.4.
3. Arthur G. Patzia, *The Making of the New Testament* (Downers Grove, IL: InterVarsity Press, 1995), 164.
4. Ibid., 49.
5. Karen Armstrong, *A History of God* (New York: Ballantine/Epiphany, 1993), 82.
6. William Lane Craig, *The Son Rises: Historical Evidence for the Resurrection of Jesus* (Chicago: Moody Press, 1981), 140.
7. Armstrong, *A History of God*, 79.
8. 1 Corinthians 15:3–7.

CHAPTER 2: Testing the Eyewitness Evidence

1. Lee Strobel, "Jury in Makeshift Courtroom Hears Dying Boy Tell of Attack," *Chicago Tribune* (February 24, 1976).
2. Luke 1:1–4.
3. Seven ancient sources report the willingness of the disciples to suffer for their conviction that Jesus rose from the dead: Acts, Clement of Rome, Polycarp, Ignatius, Dionysius of Corinth (quote found in Eusebius), Tertullian, and Origen. If the martyrdoms of Paul and Jesus' half-brother James are included, there are eleven sources. See the interview with resurrection scholar Michael Licona in: *The Case for the Real Jesus*, by Lee Strobel (Grand Rapids: Zondervan, 2007), 118.
4. Simon Greenleaf, *The Testimony of the Evangelists* (Grand Rapids: Baker, 1984), vii.
5. Cited in Craig Blomberg, "Where Do We Start Studying Jesus?" in

Michael J. Wilkins and J. P. Moreland, eds., *Jesus under Fire* (Grand Rapids: Zondervan, 1995), 34.

6. See Gleason L. Archer, *The Encyclopedia of Bible Difficulties* (Grand Rapids: Zondervan, 1982) and Norman Geisler and Thomas Howe, *When Critics Ask* (Wheaton, IL: Victor, 1992).

CHAPTER 3: The Documentary Evidence

1. See Lee Patrick Strobel, *Reckless Homicide: Ford's Pinto Trial* (South Bend, IN: And Books, 1980), 75–92, and Lee Strobel, *God's Outrageous Claims* (Grand Rapids: Zondervan, 1997), 43–58. Ford was ultimately acquitted of criminal charges after the judge withheld key documents from the jury, though the automaker was successfully sued in civil cases. Allegations about the Pinto were first reported in *Mother Jones* magazine.

2. Bruce M. Metzger died in 2007.

3. According to Daniel B. Wallace of the Center for the Study of New Testament Manuscripts, the official total of New Testament Greek manuscripts as of mid-2015 was 5,843. Included were 129 Papyri, 323 Majuscules, 2,928 Minuscules, and 2,463 Lectionaries. However, because of various factors in counting, Wallace said he believed the totals were closer to 5,600.

4. F. F. Bruce, *The Books and the Parchments* (Old Tappan, NJ: Revell, 1963), 178, cited in Josh McDowell, *Evidence That Demands a Verdict* (1972; reprint, San Bernardino, CA: Here's Life, 1986), 42.

5. Frederic Kenyon, *Handbook to the Textual Criticism of the New Testament* (New York: Macmillan, 1912), 5, cited in Ross Clifford, *The Case for the Empty Tomb* (Claremont, CA: Albatross, 1991), 33.

6. Frederic Kenyon, *The Bible and Archaeology* (New York: Harper, 1940), 288.

7. For more on variants between New Testament manuscripts, estimated to number between 200,000 and 400,000, see: Lee Strobel, *The Case for the Real Jesus* (Grand Rapids: Zondervan, 2007), 65–100. In an interview, Daniel B. Wallace, one of the world's foremost authorities on textual criticism, explained how variants are counted: "If there's any manuscript or church father who has a different word in one place, that counts as a textual variant.... If a single fourteenth-century manuscript misspells a word, that counts as a variant." He added: "Only one percent of variants are both meaningful, which means they affect the meaning of the text to some degree, and viable, which means they go back to the original text." Most of those are insignificant issues. He emphasized: "No cardinal or essential doctrine of altered by any textual variant that has plausibility of going back to the original."

8. Patzia, *The Making of the New Testament*, 158.

9. Subsequent analysis by scholars puts the dating of Thomas at no earlier

than AD 175 and probably closer to 200. See interview with New Testament scholar Craig A. Evans in *The Case for the Real Jesus*, by Lee Strobel (Grand Rapids: Zondervan, 2007), 35–43.

10. Benjamin B. Warfield, *Introduction to Textual Criticism of the New Testament* (London: Hodder & Stoughton, 1907), 12–13.

11. Geisler and Nix, *A General Introduction to the Bible*, 195. They note that some include Philemon, 1 Peter, and 1 John among the disputed books, but "it is probably better to refer to these as omitted rather than disputed books."

12. Ibid., 207.

13. Ibid., 199. This does not include the Apocrypha, which were accepted by particular churches for a particular period of time and today are considered valuable though not canonical. Examples: Shepherd of Hermas, Epistle to the Corinthians, Epistle of Pseudo-Barnabas, Didache, Apocalypse of Peter, The Acts of Paul and Thecla, and Ancient Homily or the Second Epistle of Clement.

14. Ibid.

CHAPTER 4: The Corroborating Evidence

1. *Webster's Encyclopedic Unabridged Dictionary of the English Language* (New York: Gramercy, 1989), 328.

2. Maurice Possley, "Mob Hit Man Aleman Gets One Hundred to Three Hundred Years," *Chicago Tribune* (November 26, 1997).

3. Charles Templeton, *Act of God* (New York: Bantam, 1979), 152.

4. Josephus, *The Antiquities* 20.200. See also Edwin Yamauchi, "Josephus and the Scriptures," *Fides et Historia* 13 (1980), 42–63.

5. Josephus, *The Antiquities* 18.63–64.

6. Michael Martin, *The Case against Christianity* (Philadelphia: Temple University Press, 1991), 49.

7. Tacitus, *Annals* 15.44.

8. Pliny the Younger, *Letters* 10.96.

9. Gary Habermas, *The Historical Jesus* (Joplin, MO: College Press, 1996), 196–97.

10. Paul L. Maier, *Pontius Pilate* (Wheaton, IL: Tyndale House, 1968), 366, citing a fragment from Phlegon, *Olympiades he Chronika* 13, ed. Otto Keller, *Rerum Naturalium Scriptores Graeci Minores*, 1 (Leipzig: Teurber, 1877), 101. Translation by Maier.

11. See P. Maier, "Sejanus, Pilate, and the Date of the Crucifixion," *Church History* 37 (1968), 1–11.

12. M. Wilcox, "Jesus in the Light of His Jewish Environment," *Aufstieg und Niedergang der römischen Welt* 2, no. 25.1 (1982), 133.

13. Luke Timothy Johnson, *The Real Jesus* (San Francisco: HarperSanFrancisco, 1996), 120.

14. Ignatius, *Trallians* 9.
15. *The Verdict of History* was later retitled: *The Historical Jesus: Ancient Evidence for the Life of Christ*, by Gary Habermas (Joplin, MO: College Press, 1996).
16. See Gary Habermas, *The Verdict of History* (Nashville: Thomas Nelson, 1988).
17. Ibid, 169.

CHAPTER 5: The Scientific Evidence

1. For the full story, see Joe McGinniss, *Fatal Vision* (New York: New American Library, 1989). For a description of the scientific evidence, see Colin Evans, *The Casebook of Forensic Detection* (New York: John Wiley & Sons, 1996), 277–80.
2. Luke 18:35, Mark 10:46.
3. Norman Geisler and Thomas Howe, *When Critics Ask* (Wheaton, IL: Victor, 1992), 385.
4. John Ankerberg and John Weldon, *Ready with an Answer* (Eugene, OR: Harvest House, 1997), 272.
5. Michael Martin, *The Case against Christianity* (Philadelphia: Temple University Press, 1991), 69, emphasis added.
6. John McRay, *Archaeology and the New Testament* (Grand Rapids: Baker, 1991), 155, emphasis added.
7. See: Darrell L. Bock, *Luke 1:1-9:50: Baker Exegetical Commentary on the New Testament* (Grand Rapids: Baker, 1994), 905.
8. William Mitchell Ramsay, *The Bearing of Recent Discovery on the Trustworthiness of the New Testament* (London: Forgotten Books, 2012, reprint of 1909 edition), 277.
9. For examples, see: Harold W. Hoehner, *Chronological Aspects of the Life of Christ* (Grand Rapids: Zondervan, 1977), 16.
10. Ibid., 22, 23.
11. Darrell L. Bock, *Luke 1:1-9:50: Baker Exegetical Commentary on the New Testament* (Grand Rapids: Baker Academic, 1994), 906.
12. Norman Geisler and Thomas Howe, *When Critics Ask* (Wheaton, IL: Victor, 1992), 386.
13. Harold W. Hoehner, *Chronological Aspects of the Life of Christ*, 22. See also: A. J. B. Higgins, "Sidelights on Christian Beginnings in the Greco-Roman World," *The Evangelical Quarterly* 41 (October, 1969), 200–201.
14. Darrell L. Bock, *Luke 1:1–9:50: Baker Exegetical Commentary on the New Testament*, 909.
15. Josephus also mentions the AD 6 census in *Antiquities of the Jews*.
16. Harold W. Hoehner, *Chronological Aspects of the Life of Christ*, 19.
17. Ibid.

18. Darrell L. Bock, *Luke 1:1–9:50: Baker Exegetical Commentary on the New Testament*, 909. For a thorough discussion of issues related to the census, see 903–909, and Harold W. Hoehner, *Chronological Aspects of the Life of Christ*, 11–23.

19. Frank Zindler, "Where Jesus Never Walked," *American Atheist* (Winter 1996–1997), 34.

20. Ibid.

21. See: Eric M. Meyers and James F. Strange, *Archaeology, the Rabbis, and Early Christianity* (Nashville: Abington, 1981) and article on "Nazareth" in *The Anchor Bible Dictionary* (New York: Doubleday, 1992).

22. Jack Finegan, *The Archaeology of the New Testament* (Princeton, NJ: Princeton University Press, 1992), 46.

23. See: Ken Dark, "Has Jesus' Nazareth House Been Found?" *Biblical Archaeology Review* 41.2 (March/April 2015).

24. See: Ken Dark, "Early Roman-Period Nazareth and the Sisters of Nazareth Convent," *The Antiquaries Journal* 92 (2012)

25. See: Y. Alexandre, "Mary's Well, Nazareth: The Late Hellenistic to the Ottoman Periods" *Israel Antiquities Authority Report* 49 (2012).

26. Wilkins and Moreland, *Jesus under Fire*, 209.

27. Ibid., 211.

28. Kevin D. Miller, "The War of the Scrolls," *Christianity Today* (October 6, 1997), 44, emphasis added.

29. Joseph Smith, *History of the Church*, 8 vols. (Salt Lake City: Deseret, 1978), 4:461, cited in Donald S. Tingle, *Mormonism* (Downers Grove, IL: InterVarsity Press, 1981), 17.

30. John Ankerberg and John Weldon, *The Facts on the Mormon Church* (Eugene, OR: Harvest House, 1991), 30, emphasis in original.

31. Clifford Wilson, *Rocks, Relics and Biblical Reliability* (Grand Rapids: Zondervan; Richardson, TX: Probe, 1977), 120, cited in Ankerberg and Weldon, *Ready with an Answer*, 272.

CHAPTER 6: The Rebuttal Evidence

1. Henry Campbell Black, *Black's Law Dictionary*, 5th ed. (St. Paul: West, 1979), 1139.

2. Lee Strobel, "His 'I Shot Him' Stuns Courtroom," *Chicago Tribune* (June 20, 1975) and "Pal's Confession Fails; Defendant Ruled Guilty," *Chicago Tribune* (June 21, 1975).

3. Gregory A. Boyd, *Jesus under Siege* (Wheaton, IL: Victor, 1995), 88.

4. Boyd later became well-known as a proponent of "open theism," which says that while God is omniscient, he does not know what we will freely decide to do in the future. I do not embrace this theology.

5. For more on this issue, see the interview with me in the back of this book.

6. See: "Challenge #4: Christianity's Beliefs About Jesus Were Copied From Pagan Religions," in: Lee Strobel, *The Case for the Real Jesus* (Grand Rapids: Zondervan, 2007), 157-187.

7. John Dominic Crossan, *The Historical Jesus* (San Francisco: HarperSanFrancisco, 1991), 329.

8. See: 1 Corinthians 15:17.

9. Johnson, *The Real Jesus*, 3, 5, 8.

10. Ibid, 26.

11. Ibid.

CHAPTER 7: The Identity Evidence

1. Marjorie Rosen, "Getting Inside the Mind of a Serial Killer," *Biography* (October 1997), 62–65.

2. Ibid., 64.

3. See: Luke 11:20.

4. R. E. Brown, "Did Jesus Know He Was God?" *Biblical Theology Bulletin* 15 (1985), 78, cited in Ben Witherington III, *The Christology of Jesus* (Minneapolis: Fortress, 1990), 277.

5. Jaroslav Pelikan, *The Christian Tradition: A History of the Development of Doctrine*, vol. 1, *The Emergence of the Catholic Tradition (100–600)* (Chicago: University of Chicago Press, 1971), 173, cited in William Lane Craig, *Reasonable Faith* (Westchester, IL: Crossway, 1994), 243.

6. See John 10:30.

7. Craig, *Reasonable Faith*, 252.

8. Ibid., 244.

9. Royce Gordon Gruenler, *New Approaches to Jesus and the Gospels* (Grand Rapids: Baker, 1982), 74.

10. James D. G. Dunn, *Jesus and the Spirit* (London: SCM Press, 1975), 60, cited in Craig, *Reasonable Faith*, 252, emphasis added.

CHAPTER 8: The Psychological Evidence

1. Leland H. Gregory III, "Top Ten Government Bloopers," *George* (November 1997), 78.

2. Charles Templeton, *Farewell to God* (Toronto: McClelland & Stewart, 1996), 112.

3. Wilson, *Jesus: The Evidence*, 141.

4. Ibid., 109, emphasis in original.

5. "A Case of Congenital Ichthyosiform Erythrodermia of Brocq Treated by Hypnosis," *British Medical Journal* 2 (1952), 996, cited in Wilson, *Jesus: The Evidence*, 103.

6. M. Scott Peck, *People of the Lie* (New York: Touchstone, 1997).

7. Wilson, *Jesus: The Evidence*, 107.

8. C. S. Lewis, *The Screwtape Letters* (London: Collins-Fontana, 1942), 9.
9. Philip Schaff, *The Person of Christ* (New York: American Tract Society, 1918), 97, cited in McDowell, *Evidence That Demands a Verdict*, 107, emphasis added.

CHAPTER 9: The Profile Evidence

1. Marla Donato, "That Guilty Look," *Chicago Tribune* (April 1, 1994).
2. Denny Johnson, "Police Add Electronic 'Sketch Artist' to Their Bag of Tricks," *Chicago Tribune* (June 22, 1997).
3. See John 8:46.
4. Templeton, *Farewell to God*, 230.
5. Morton Smith, "Biblical Arguments for Slavery," *Free Inquiry* (Spring 1987), 30.
6. Thomas Sowell, *Race and Culture* (New York: Basic, 1995).
7. Josh McDowell and Bart Larson, *Jesus: A Biblical Defense of His Deity* (San Bernardino, CA: Here's Life, 1983), 62–64.

CHAPTER 10: The Fingerprint Evidence

1. Evans, *The Casebook of Forensic Detection*, 98–100.
2. Lee Strobel, "'Textbook' Thumbprint Aids Conviction in Coed's Killing," *Chicago Tribune* (June 29, 1976).
3. See Darrell L. Bock, Darrell and Mitch Glaser, eds. *The Gospel According to Isaiah 53* (Grand Rapids: Kregel, 2012).
4. For basic details on fulfilled prophecies, see McDowell, *Evidence That Demands a Verdict*, 141–77.
5. Peter W. Stoner, *Science Speaks* (Chicago: Moody Press, 1969), 109.
6. For a discussion of the Daniel prophecy, see Robert C. Newman, "Fulfilled Prophecy As Miracle," in R. Douglas Geivett and Gary R. Habermas, eds., *In Defense of Miracles* (Downers Grove, IL: InterVarsity Press, 1997), 214–25.
7. Stan Telchin, *Betrayed!* (Grand Rapids: Chosen, 1982).
8. Ruth Rosen, ed., *Jewish Doctors Meet the Great Physician* (San Francisco: Purple Pomegranate, 1997), 9–23.
9. Ibid., 34–35.

CHAPTER 11: The Medical Evidence

1. Surah IV: 156–57.
2. Wilson, *Jesus: The Evidence*, 140.
3. Craig, *Reasonable Faith*, 234.
4. D. H. Lawrence, *Love among the Haystacks and Other Stories* (New York: Penguin, 1960), 125.
5. Hugh Schonfield, *The Passover Plot* (New York: Bantam, 1965), 165.

6. Habermas, *The Verdict of History*, 56.

7. Michael Baigent, Richard Leigh, and Henry Lincoln, *Holy Blood, Holy Grail* (New York: Delacorte, 1982), 372.

8. Johnson, *The Real Jesus*, 30.

9. An article in the *Journal of Medicine* analyzed 76 cases of *hematidrosis* and concluded that the most common causes were acute fear and intense mental contemplation. See: J. E. Holoubek and A. E. Holoubek, "Blood, Seat and Fear: 'A Classification of Hematidrosis," *Journal of Medicine* 1996, 27 (3-4): 115-33.

10. J. W. Hewitt, "The Use of Nails in the Crucifixion," *Harvard Theological Review* 25 (1932), 29–45, cited in Josh McDowell, *The Resurrection Factor* (San Bernardino, CA: Here's Life, 1981), 45.

11. William D. Edwards et al., "On the Physical Death of Jesus Christ," *Journal of the American Medical Association* (March 21, 1986), 1455–63.

CHAPTER 12: The Evidence of the Missing Body

1. Gerald O'Collins, *The Easter Jesus* (London: Darton, Longman & Todd, 1973), 134, cited in Craig, *The Son Rises*, 136.

2. For a tape of the debate, see William Lane Craig and Frank Zindler, *Atheism vs. Christianity: Where Does the Evidence Point?* (Grand Rapids, MI: Zondervan, 1993), videocassette.

3. Templeton, *Farewell to God*, 120.

4. Martin, *The Case against Christianity*, 78–79.

5. Ibid., 81.

6. Michael Grant, *Jesus: An Historian's Review of the Gospels* (New York: Charles Scribner's Sons, 1977), 176.

7. Researcher Glenn Miller's study of the rabbinical literature supports this. He pointed out: "Rabbi Eleazar ben Azariah, tenth in the descent from Ezra, was very specific: 'A day and a night are an *Onah* ["a portion of time"] and the portion of an *Onah* is as the whole of it" (J. Talmud, Shabbath 9.3 and b. Talmud, Pesahim 4a).

8. Kirsopp Lake, *The Historical Evidence for the Resurrection of Jesus Christ* (London: Williams & Norgate, 1907), 247–79, cited in William Lane Craig, *Knowing the Truth about the Resurrection* (Ann Arbor, MI.: Servant, 1988), 35–36.

9. For the scientific evidence for the existence of God, see: Lee Strobel, *The Case for a Creator* (Grand Rapids: Zondervan, 2005).

10. J. N. D. Anderson, *The Evidence for the Resurrection* (Downers Grove, IL: InterVarsity Press, 1966), 20.

CHAPTER 13: The Evidence of Appearances

1. "Bomb Victim's Body Not in Grave," *Chicago Tribune* (January 14, 1998).
2. Martin, *The Case against Christianity*, 87.
3. Gary Habermas and Antony Flew, *Did Jesus Rise from the Dead? The Resurrection Debate* (San Francisco: Harper & Row, 1987), xiv.
4. Ibid., xv. Flew renounced his atheism in 2004 after he became convinced there is a Creator. See: Antony Flew and Roy Abraham Varghese, *There Is a God: How the World's Most Notorious Atheist Changed His Mind* (New York: HarperOne, 2008). He died in 2010.
5. See: Gary Habermas, "The Resurrection of Jesus Time Line." In *Contending With Christianity's Critics*, edited by Paul Copan and William Lane Craig, 113-125 (Nashville, Tenn.: B&H Academic, 2009).
6. James D.G. Dunn, *Jesus Remembered*, volume 1 of *Christianity in the Making* (Grand Rapids: Eerdmans, 2003), 825 (emphasis in original).
7. Pinchas Lapide, *The Resurrection of Jesus: A Jewish Perspective* (Minneapolis: Augsburg, 1983), 99.
8. Richard Bauckham, *Jesus and the Eyewitnesses* (Grand Rapids: Eerdmans, 2006), 308.
9. Martin, *The Case against Christianity*, 90.
10. Craig, *The Son Rises*, 125.
11. John Drane, *Introducing the New Testament* (San Francisco: Harper & Row, 1986), 99.
12. Michael Green, *Christ Is Risen: So What?* (Kent, England: Sovereign World, 1995), 34.
13. Also cited in Gary Habermas and J. P. Moreland, *Immortality: The Other Side of Death* (Nashville: Thomas Nelson, 1992), 60.
14. Martin, *The Case against Christianity*, 75.
15. Carl Braaten, *History and Hermeneutics*, vol. 2 of *New Directions in Theology Today*, ed. William Hordern (Philadelphia: Westminster Press, 1966), 78, cited in Habermas and Flew, *Did Jesus Rise from the Dead?* 24.
16. Michael Green, *The Empty Cross of Jesus* (Downers Grove, IL: InterVarsity Press, 1984), 97, cited in Ankerberg and Weldon, *Knowing the Truth about the Resurrection*, 22, emphasis in original.

CHAPTER 14: The Circumstantial Evidence

1. Black, *Black's Law Dictionary*, 221.
2. See Josh McDowell, *More Than a Carpenter* (Wheaton, IL: Living Books, 1977), 60–71.
3. C. F. D. Moule, *The Phenomenon of the New Testament* (London: SCM Press, 1967), 3.

4. Donald McFarlan, ed., *The Guinness Book of World Records* (New York: Bantam, 1991), 547.

5. Clifford, *The Case for the Empty Tomb*, 112.

CONCLUSION: The Verdict of History

1. A. N. Sherwin-White, *Roman Society and Roman Law in the New Testament* (Oxford: Clarendon Press, 1963), 188–91.

2. Blomberg, "Where Do We Start Studying Jesus?" in Wilkins and Moreland, *Jesus under Fire*, 43, emphasis added.

3. Craig, *The Son Rises*, 102, emphasis added.

4. Julius Müller, *The Theory of Myths, in Its Application to the Gospel History, Examined and Confuted* (London: John Chapman, 1844), 26, cited in Craig, *The Son Rises*, 101.

5. *The Journey Bible* (Grand Rapids: Zondervan, 1996).

6. Michael Murphy, "The Two-Sided Game of Christian Faith," in John Warwick Montgomery, ed., *Christianity for the Tough-Minded* (Minneapolis: Bethany House, 1973), 125, cited in Ankerberg and Weldon, *Knowing the Truth about the Resurrection*, 44.

7. C. S. Lewis, *Mere Christianity* (New York: Macmillan-Collier, 1960), 55–56.

AN INTERVIEW WITH LEE STROBEL

1. Mark D. Roberts, *Can We Trust the Gospels?* (Wheaton, IL: Crossway, 2007), 20.

2. Lee Strobel, *The Case for the Real Jesus: A Journalist Investigates Current Attacks in the Identity of Christ* (Grand Rapids, MI: Zondervan, 2007), 58.

3. The poll by the Barna Group included 1,001 telephone interviews conducted among a representative, nationwide sample of adults ages eighteen and older. The interviews were conducted from August 25 through September 10, 2014. The sampling error is plus or minus 3.1 percentage points at the 95 percent confidence level. The cooperation rate was 78 percent.

4. See: David Kinnaman, *You Lost Me: Why Young Christians are Leaving Church . . . and Rethinking Faith* (Grand Rapids, MI: Baker, 2011).

5. Robert Funk, *Honest to Jesus* (San Francisco: HarperCollins, 1996), 60.

6. John Dominic Crossan, *Who Is Jesus?* (New York: HarperCollins, 1996), 96.

7. Robert W. Funk, "The Coming Radical Reformation: Twenty-One Theses." *The Fourth R*, Volume 11–4 (July–August 1998).

8. William Lane Craig and John Dominic Crossan, *Will the Real Jesus Please Stand Up?*, (Grand Rapids, MI: Baker, 1999), 45.

9. Ibid., 61. Also, in a radio dialogue in March 1995 on *The Milt Rosenberg Show* on WGN in Chicago, Crossan said: "God does not act directly . . .

physically, in the world in the same sense in which the miracles taken literally would seem."

10. William Lane Craig and John Dominic Crossan, *Will the Real Jesus Please Stand Up?*, 45.

11. Ibid., 169.

12. Ibid., 49–51. Also, Craig asked at one point: "What about the statement that God exists? Is that a statement of faith or fact?" Crossan replied: "It is a statement of faith for all those who make it." See p. 49.

13. Ibid., 169. Craig added: "Thus his antisupernaturalism determines his skepticism concerning the historicity of the New Testament witness to the resurrection of Jesus." See p. 170.

14. Robert W. Funk, Roy W. Hoover, and The Jesus Seminar, *The Five Gospels* (San Francisco: HarperSanFrancisco, 1997), 2.

15. Strauss is not only cited in support of the Jesus Seminar's first pillar, but *The Five Gospels* is dedicated to him, Galileo Galilei, and Thomas Jefferson, "who took scissors and paste to the gospels."

16. Robert W. Funk, Roy W. Hoover, and the Jesus Seminar, *The Five Gospels* (San Francisco: HarperSanFrancisco, 1997), 4.

17. William Lane Craig, "Rediscovering the Historical Jesus: The Presuppositions and Presumptions of the Jesus Seminar." *Faith and Mission* 15 (1998): 3–15.

18. Mark D. Roberts, "Unmasking the Jesus Seminar: A Critique of Its Methods and Conclusions," *Patheos*, http://www.patheos.com/blogs/markdroberts/series/unmasking-the-jesus-seminar/.

19. Even agnostic scholar Bart Ehrman said, "The claim that Jesus was simply made up falters on every ground. . . . Whether we like it or not, Jesus certainly existed." See Bart D. Ehrman, "Did Jesus Exist?" *HuffPost Religion*, http://www.huffingtonpost.com/bart-d-ehrman/did-jesus-exist_b_1349544.html.

20. Craig credits apologist and speaker Peter Grant for this illustration. See Lee Strobel, *The Case for Faith: A Journalist Investigates the Toughest Objections to Christianity* (Grand Rapids, MI: Zondervan, 1998), 84–85.

Index

Meet Lee Strobel

Lee Strobel, who holds a Master of Studies in Law degree from Yale Law School and a journalism degree from the University of Missouri, is the bestselling author of more than twenty books. He is the former legal editor of the *Chicago Tribune*, receiving Illinois' highest honors for both investigative reporting and public service journalism from United Press International.

Lee's journey from atheism to faith has been documented in *The Case for Christ, The Case for Faith, The Case for a Creator, The Case for the Real Jesus*, and *The Case for Grace*. He currently serves as Professor of Christian Thought at Houston Baptist University and as Teaching Pastor at Woodlands Church, one of America's largest congregations.

Lee also wrote *The Case for Hope, The Case for Christianity Answer Book, God's Outrageous Claims, Reckless Homicide, The Unexpected Adventure* (with Mark Mittelberg), *Inside the Mind of Unchurched Harry and Mary, What Jesus Would Say*, and his first novel, *The Ambition*. He is general editor of *The Case for Christ Study Bible*, which contains hundreds of notes and articles.

Lee formerly taught First Amendment Law at Roosevelt University and hosted the national TV program *Faith under Fire*, which featured debates between atheists, Christians, Muslims, Hindus, and others on a variety of social and spiritual topics. He also has been a teaching pastor at two of the country's biggest and most influential churches: Willow Creek Community Church and Saddleback Church. In 2007, Lee was honored by Southern Evangelical Seminary with the conferring of a Doctor of Divinity degree.

He has been interviewed on such TV networks as ABC, Fox, Discovery, PBS, and CNN, and his articles have appeared in a variety of periodicals, including the online editions of the *Wall Street Journal* and *Newsweek*.

Lee and Leslie, who have been married for forty-three years, co-authored *Surviving a Spiritual Mismatch in Marriage*. Their daughter Alison is a novelist and co-author (with her husband Daniel) of two books for children. With a doctorate in theology, their son Kyle is a professor of spiritual theology at the Talbot School of Theology at Biola University. He has written several academic and popular-level books, as well as scholarly articles in the *Harvard Theological Review* and elsewhere.

Lee's website is www.LeeStrobel.com. His Twitter account is @LeeStrobel.